Praise for *Last Man Out*

"A nail-biting account of how the men struggle to keep hold of their spirits as they starve and wait, sharing dreams of sunlight and family ... In a series of devastating, finely drawn portraits, Greene deeply examines the lives of her characters ... the sturdy reticence of men too strong to admit they may be doomed. Bottom Line: A tragic triumph."
—*People*

"[Greene] writes about the futile explorations and attempts to escape, the incremental loss of light as one by one the battery-powered lamps were exhausted until the men waited in impenetrable blackness, the acceptance of death by some, the rejection by others, the thirsts so great that men drank urine, the emergence of unexpected strengths and finally the delirious joy of salvation."
—*The New York Times Book Review*

"*Last Man Out*, by a natural-born storyteller from the American South, is as good a book about a Canadian disaster as you're ever likely to find. ... By combining interviews with her own vivid prose and high sensitivity to human anguish, Greene has created a book that is ... deep, moving and timeless."
—*The Toronto Globe & Mail*

"With every book, Greene further refines her art of rich, literary nonfiction. And she continues to find these perfect stories—stories that stand on their own but also serve to show something much bigger, much darker, below the surface."
—*The Atlanta Journal-Constitution*

"[A] most vivid account of horror and heroism, of exemplary human behavior under the most adverse circumstances and of the buffoonery of those who tried to exploit those admirable survivors." —*Chicago Tribune*

"Greene, focusing on two groups of survivors, captures for us some of the agony of their waiting, raging with thirst in utter darkness, for rescue or, what seems increasingly likely, death.... Then, when she tells the stories of each survivor's recovery, the narrative opens up, like the petals of a flower."

—*The Denver Post*

"This is a superb study of the human condition in extremis." —*BookPage*

"Through interviews with survivors, the autobiography of the local doctor, and, most fascinatingly, a study of survival strategies conducted after the disaster, the award-winning Greene recreates the extraordinary efforts undertaken by those trapped and those on top to keep themselves from flying apart under the circumstances.... She captures the gloom in all its manifestations.... A strikingly told story." —*Kirkus Reviews*

Last
Man Out

The Story of
the Springhill
Mine Disaster

MELISSA FAY GREENE

A HARVEST BOOK
HARCOURT, INC.
Orlando   Austin   New York   San Diego   Toronto   London

www.HarcourtBooks.com

Library of Congress Cataloging-in-Publication Data
Greene, Melissa Fay.
Last man out: the story of the Springhill Mine Disaster/Melissa Fay Greene—1st ed.
p.   cm.
ISBN 0-15-100559-1
ISBN 0-15-602957-X (pbk.)
1. Springhill Mine Disaster, Springhill, N.S., 1958.   I. Title.
TN806.C2G74 2003
363.11'9622334'0971611—dc21   2002155849

Text set in Granjon
Designed by Linda Lockowitz

Printed in the United States of America

First Harvest edition 2004
K J I H G F E D C B A

To our kids:
Molly, Seth, Lee,
Lily, Jesse, and Helen

Contents

Part I

Part II

Part I

1

The Thunder of Baritones

In the town of Springhill, Nova Scotia, in 1958, coal-mining men dropped through the crust of the earth to a few of the deepest roads on the planet. All day and all night they chiseled toward the earth's core, carving an architecture like the downward-coiling tunnels of a child's plastic ant farm. In helmets, coveralls, and pit boots, they shuffled along pebbly paths a vertical mile underground, to the sound of infernal dripping. At that distance above ground, planes crossed the clouds.

The darkness was like that of deep space. With his head-lamp turned off, a man couldn't see his fingers in front of his eyes. Pit ponies once labored in these mines in permanent midnight, tugging the coal cars back and forth on subterranean avenues, and all went blind. In that era of oil lamps, miners risked their lives for the hiss of flame, never knowing when an invisible cloud of gas might ignite. By 1958, the ponies had been displaced by an underground rail system, and the gas lanterns had been swapped for battery-powered headlamps. The black tunnels gleamed briefly as the men tramped along, looking like cumbersome fireflies; drapes of pure darkness swung down behind them the moment they passed by.

"The No. 2 mine is like an underground city, eh?" said an

impish fellow named Gorley Kempt. "It's a maze of streets and alleys down there. And all the work is done in darkness."

"When I am all the way down," observed a miner they called Pep, "you know that's the farthest away from home I ever been?"

At the end of each shift, the men toppled into the trolley of coal cars for a ride up the dark twelve-foot-wide funnel known as the Back Slope. The 13,000-foot commute was steep, like the sheer nauseating ascent of a roller coaster toward its greatest peak. At a stopping place at the top of the Back Slope, the workers disembarked, walked through a tunnel to the Main Slope, and seated themselves in a second trolley. Fifty filthy men unwound together, gossiping and grousing, wheezing and napping, while the hoist at the pithead cranked them up through the chute.

When Maurice Ruddick was among them, he led songs for the hour. He was forty-six years old and rather vain of his trim build, pencil-thin mustache, and pomaded, middle-parted hair, though all were buried under the grit of the day's work. He blew the coal dust from his throat with a few warm-up notes, then launched a popular radio song, a song from a Hollywood musical, or an off-color blues or jazz ditty. He nudged his comrades to practice a song they'd mangled the day before. Some snoozed and some ignored him, but many threw in their voices from out of their coal-blackened faces. "Dem Bones," they laughingly sang, and "Don't Be Cruel" and "Bye Bye Love," combining their voices in harmonies and arrangements of Ruddick's invention.

Light-eyed, olive-skinned Ruddick represented the third generation of a Negro Nova Scotia coal-mining family. "Both Mother and Father had colored blood in them," is how Ruddick put it. He was neither particularly liked nor disliked by his fellows as a result; it was, in a way, just one more peculiar thing about Ruddick, who was a bit of an odd duck. You could run into Ruddick off shift strolling down Main Street in a pastel-colored shirt unbuttoned to the chest and a felt fedora tilted back on his head, with a cigar in a cigar holder clenched in a grin or grimace as he greeted you. On this windy northern peninsula, in this utilitarian town, Ruddick offered a bright bit of elegance, a dash of the Hollywood look.

In the coal car riding up out of the pit, Maurice Ruddick, with muscles burning from hard labor, moving stiffly in his crusty outerwear and helmet, turned around to see whom he had to work with before trying to assemble a bit of harmony. He whacked the side of the trolley with his lunch pail for percussion as the other men howled along, their mouths moist red Os in the blackness.

The company men who worked on the surface could hear the miners coming from a long way off, the thunder of their baritones echoing up through the caverns.

When the miners ducked, squinting, out of the aluminum sheds that covered the pitheads of the Cumberland Railway and Coal Company's No. 2 and No. 4 mines, coal dust coated their faces and the cracks in their necks and hands. From under the shade of soot-covered helmets glowed the whites of their eyes and the red of their gums.

What the world wanted lay deeply hidden, had to be exhumed. When the men brought it up, they were the pride of the Canadian government. It was soft coal, the finest in Canada. Black it was, too—so black it looked like the miners had chipped and pried apart chunks of the subterranean darkness in which they grappled. Of such pure, primeval blackness was this rock, of the earth's first order of blackness, that it had become one of the names of the color black: *coal* black. The stuff had last seen the light of day in the Paleozoic Era, three hundred million years ago, when it fanned its fingers in the sunlight as ferns.

At the redbrick lamp cabin, each miner returned his head-lamp and battery for recharging when he was finished for the day, and received in exchange, like a hat-check token, a brass tag with his identification number. His battery was engraved with the same number. A plywood board full of hooks, like the board on which keys are hung in a parking garage, displayed the brass tags of the men currently on shift, wearing their head-lamps. In a time of mishap or disaster, the board glittered with tags for too long, describing, at a glance, the number of men still underground. If the worst came to pass, the identity of a man killed in the pit could be confirmed by the identification number on his battery.

In the washhouse, the miners shucked off their stiff cover-alls like football players unbuckling their protective gear in a locker room and suddenly they seemed to diminish in size by half. Odd little wormy creatures they looked then, with their sun-deprived, coal-speckled bodies and blackened, earthy heads and hands. Vigorous scrub downs in the shower only dulled the charcoal black of the men's skin to blue, but their wives were tol-erant. The women knew that nothing in this town, least of all their husbands, would ever truly be clean.

Like sailors and their ships, the miners called the No. 2 mine "she." "She's taking on water in the sinking," they'd say of the mine's deepest level, or "She's a bit warm this evening." Most of them loved the mine, the work, the fellowship. "Why, I am just as comfortable in the mine," said old-timer Bill James, "as sitting in my chair at home."

"I really do enjoy the mine," said Cecil Colwell, who had worked it since 1930. "I haven't got a bone in my body that has not been broken."

But unhappily, and with increasing frequency, in the late summer and fall of 1958, they heard themselves saying, "She's restless today."

Springhill was a hilly, shady, comfortable town sitting atop a vault of coal, an "underground palace of coal," it used to be said. "The mines consist of entire mountains of coal," enthused a letter writer in 1765, "and are sufficient to supply all the British plantations in North America for ten centuries."

"There was a time when men got coal out of their backyards," according to a local historian. "Shallow pits were found everywhere.... There have been instances when a homeowner would step out of his door only to find a big gaping hole where his driveway had been." A couple of churches and schools, a dusty baseball field, and a few pubs and shops on Main Street all brightened and faded under the moving shadows of the bottom-heavy clouds of a maritime peninsula. Pine and birch trees lined the streets. Sugar maples were festooned with buckets, which clattered as sap drained out of the trees every spring, and men in the sugarhouses fired up the stoves.

History was measured like time in a whaling village: There were years of good haul and high prices for coal, which meant new shoes for the children; new winter coats for the women; and record players, hunting rifles, magazine subscriptions, or re-treaded car tires for the men. And there were years of catastrophe, when tents were erected to shelter the bodies pending identification; undertakers from nearby towns drove in to assist; and newly widowed mothers wailed at the bedsides of their sleeping children, mourning, anew, their own fatherless childhoods.

There was a growling of discontent, which the men were keeping amongst themselves that fall, two years after the 1956 Explosion in the No. 4 mine had killed thirty-nine of their buddies. It was part of an unwritten miners' code not to show weakness or admit fear. But a sense of alarm was rising over engineer-designed renovations in the No. 2 mine.

Under the rearrangement, the mine was shaped like an italicized letter *E*. The backbone of the *E* was the Back Slope, the two-and-a-half-mile tunnel poking at a thirty-three-degree angle into the earth, up and down which the men rode in the coal cars, or trolley.

The arms of the *E* were the three working tunnels, called levels. Three different teams of men extracted coal simultaneously at three different distances from the earth's surface. There were work sites at the 13,000 level (13,000 feet of trolley track from the pithead), the 13,400 level (13,400 feet of rail), and the 13,800 level. The workers knocked coal from the coal face at each level and shoveled it into troughlike pans. The coal jiggled inside the engine-driven pans toward a conveyor belt, dropped onto the conveyor belt, rolled to a loading machine, was tipped into the coal cars of the trolley, and was hauled by the ton to the surface.

The miners were unhappy with their 1958 levels. For efficiency's sake, they'd been asked to set up the walls in parallel lines rather than in a staggered arrangement. The old-timers feared the three-pronged attack was thinning out the deep rock surrounding and cushioning the workers.

"The old-timers know, they know it's coming," said Doug Jewkes in the washhouse. In the showers, the men could let their guard down, along with their coveralls. A young man with a long face and some blackened teeth, Doug Jewkes looked somewhat off kilter. He had been pegged as an awfully chatty fellow among men who would as soon grunt as give an intelligible response to anything, so he wasn't keenly attended to. "But the company pays no heed a'tall. Joey Tabor told me it's coming. Did you hear he quit? Said, 'I ain't working in that place.' He knows it's coming. All the old-timers know. But what can we do? Either work or be out of a job."

The men lowered buckets, in which their street clothes were stored, from the ceiling of the washhouse. "Well, none of us are too proud of the way we've set the walls up, lining them up straight," Harold Brine would say.

"I have never liked No. 2 like I did No. 4, and it's worse now," Frank Hunter always said.

"Since the Explosion, there is always some little thing to keep your nerves on edge," Joe Holloway would agree.

"Oh, we have always been scared of her," said Percy McCormick, who had worked in No. 2 for twenty-two years. He was one of the old-timers admired by the rookies for his uncanny instinct and the finesse with which he could pry off a chunk of rock and provoke a cascade of glistening coal. Like all the old-timers, he hinted at secret exits, and he knew survival tricks like ducking his face close to a rivulet of water on the floor—if gas was loose in the mine—to capture rising molecules of oxygen. "We all know what she can do," he said. "She bumps and, sooner or later, someone gets it. You just got to hope that she'll bump between shifts. She has, many a time, bumped between shifts and no one got caught."

"If I had the education some fellows has got, I'd be gone," said Doug Jewkes.

"So go already, Jewkes," someone would snap. They were all fed up with him.

"What the devil's the use of me going?" he'd protest. "What could I get?"

"The engineers must know more about it than us," Joe Holloway would say. "So we had better keep still about it."

"If there's a big one," an old guy muttered almost inaudibly low, with his gaunt blue backside turned toward the group, "she'll take all three levels when she goes."

2

A World without Sun

"Miners," sniffed a Springhill mine manager to a royal commission in 1888, "are queer people; you do not know them."

"Can nothing be done with these strange men?" a Springhill superintendent once complained to the shareholders.

"Miners are, when at their work, shut out from the light of day, from the sun-light, from the freedom of surface life," wrote the *Halifax Herald* in 1920. "Ever groping in semi-darkness, guided in their getting about by artificial light, they become canny, suspicious of hidden danger, ever on the defensive, and it is but natural that in a measure it stamps itself upon their demeanor, above, as well as below ground."

Owners and stockholders sneered at the bleak Nova Scotia villages blinking through the coal dust and at the miners striding to and fro in shades of brown as they hiked toward the pit-head and in black when they returned from it. As industry was transformed by "scientific management," university-educated engineers nailed up new regulations at the mines and stockholders gleefully anticipated greater profits, each group congratulating the other on its intellectual superiority to coal miners. In folklore, miners are portrayed as gnomes, elves, dwarves, and midgets.

The townsfolk saw them differently: the miners of Nova

Scotia were known to be dedicated, strong, and canny. One by one, starting as teenagers, they had been initiated into the laws of the landscape without sun, a world under intense geologic pressure. Only the miners knew how to rob the earth of its riches and escape with their lives.

Not only was the skilled craft of mining relayed by fathers to sons for generations, but the mines themselves were handed down. Springhill's No. 2 slope, the deepest coal mine in the world, was carved out in the 1870s, in an era when coal was called "black gold." In the 1950s, the colliers groped through the same labyrinths their forebears had prowled eight decades earlier.

The unwritten Miners' Code was bequeathed to each new generation along with the mines. Solidarity was the cornerstone; the workers struck the mines together, refused to be bought off separately, and never gave up on a man lost in the pit until he was brought up, dead or alive. The first coal miners' union in North America was founded in Springhill in 1879. The miners dominated Canadian labor history from 1880 to 1930 and inspired the United Mine Workers of America. "They were giants," writes Canadian historian Ian McKay of the mining men of Nova Scotia. "When they marched, the region shook."

Their solidarity frustrated the owners and engineers, whose new regulations and blueprints wilted in the wind at the pithead. While the miners rode wisecracking into the depths, the experts hesitated at the mine entrance, ignorant and afraid of the dark.

When the off-shift miners emerged from the washhouse and swung chatting and laughing up Main Street, the townspeople felt they knew things. Surely they had seen, heard, smelled, and even tasted things beyond common knowledge.

What the miners occasionally *smelled*—or, worse, did not smell—were the poisonous gases exhaled by the decomposition of ancient ferns. The gases named firedamp, afterdamp, and blackdamp were stranglers. The miners' picks occasionally hooked into closed pockets of them, releasing pernicious seepage, and carelessness with fire or dynamite could result in cataclysmic gas explosions like the Great Springhill Explosion of 1891.

On the east slope at 12:43 P.M. on February 21 of that year, underground workers were stunned by a loud roar. There was a sudden storm of wind and flame. Eyewitnesses later described the force of the wind, "which swept like a tornado through the dark passages, hurling timbers and clouds of dust and flying missiles before it." Balls of fire barreled through the tunnels, followed by "a solid body of fierce flame that filled the passages, and literally roasted everything in its path." Men not instantly burned to death raced away from the flames; near the tunnel to the east slope, rescuers later found twenty dead sprawled facedown. "Most . . . were in the attitude of making violent efforts to escape," the rescuers reported, "before invisible gas overtook them." One hundred twenty-five men and boys died, as did seventeen blind, husky little pit ponies.

The miners alone knew the secrets of the underworld upon which the industrial revolution and the economy of the British Empire depended, but even that knowledge together with their Miners' Code and their solidarity was not always enough to keep them alive. They knew that, too.

A dozen of the men—though rolling cheerily along with the rest after work and stepping into darkened pubs on the route home to rinse away the grit in their teeth—carried private burdens of horrible things seen and endured. A line of beer mugs stood along the wet bar of an alehouse, imprinted with the black half-moons of the miners' lips; the kisses they would bestow on their wives' and children's faces also would leave such prints: of moons, in eclipse. One of the men smacking his lips upon the froth with his buddies was Hughie Guthro. He was a rubbery-limbed, rubbery-faced, smiling, accommodating, kindhearted man. He had a round, gleaming head with a high creased fore-head. He and Margie had two children, Jerry, five, and Linda, seven. "He never complains about anything," Margie told her friends. "If I want to get mad at him about something, he goes and sits in a chair in the front room and doesn't open his mouth. He won't fight back."

Hughie enjoyed a gentle, rather pointless kind of humor. "Dot!" he called teasing to their neighbor across the road. "The door blew out at the post office!"

"Oh my goodness, oh my, what happened?" Dot would cry.

And humble, round-shouldered countrywoman Margie, with a head covered with busy tight brown curls, would cup her hand over her bad teeth and laugh. "Hughie, stop tormenting her! Dot! You *know* what he's like."

Hughie was quiet, though he'd listen attentively if one of his pals spoke an opinion on something. He'd weigh it first, and then agree—"Yup, that's it, eh?"—if there was sense in it. If there was no sense in it, Hughie would duck his round head and dunk his lips in his brew again and say nothing.

"To tell you the truth, I'm never scared in a coal mine," Hughie had said a few years earlier. "Lot of people are, but I like the work. You know what you have to do, you go down, and you do it."

But Hughie Guthro had been caught by the twentieth century's worst disaster in Springhill: the 1956 Explosion. Now he found that the trouble with beer was that if he sipped enough of it to loosen the knot he kept on his stack of memories, the awful images would start to stir and swirl about. It was why, without a word to anybody, he sometimes shoved off from the bar, grabbed his cap from the hat rack, and trudged home alone, his sad round head yo-yoing above his chest. If the children clamored about his legs when he stepped into his yard, he set them aside—"Not now, eh?"—and closed himself into the bathroom, where he'd stand and look out the half-open window onto his weedy back lot and try to go blank again.

On Thursday, November 1, 1956, a section of the coal train had broken loose on the Back Slope and rolled backward into the depths. The steel boxes, carrying tons of raw coal, whirled faster and faster until they launched into the air and scraped an electric cable strung along the roof of the tunnel. Sparks ignited the standing haze of coal dust. A roaring fireball bellowed all the way up out of the mouth of the mine. It swallowed everyone in its path and shot men sky-high. The fiery sphere billowed up into the air and turned inside out like a mushroom cloud. Half the town saw it, the other half heard it, and all came running.

Margie Guthro was standing among the scratchy weeds of her backyard, taking clothes off the line. She looked up and saw men in the distance somersaulting high in the air. "It's Hughie's shift!" Hurrying to the pit, Margie learned instantly that her two uncles, surface workers, had both been caught and burned to death.

The emergency whistle was screaming. All the buildings that covered the No. 4 mine portal were burning. The wives of some of the men trapped in the burning buildings had always

corrected anyone who referred to their husbands as "miners"—
as if, if a wife could emphasize, "No, dear, my Leonard is a *surface worker,*" she could keep her man out of danger. But, this
time, surface workers were killed.

"Our generation has never had anything like this," said
miner Bill James, standing near Margie in the red heat of the
disaster. "Mine officials, either."

After the fires were quenched, volunteer rescue workers
called draegermen, specially trained in the use of gas masks,
began groping their way down the Main Slope from the pithead.
They moved heavily, clumsily, as if in diving suits on the ocean
floor. Several staggered and slowly toppled forward as the afterdamp penetrated their gas masks. From the portal on the surface,
other miners watched the draegermen fall, but dared not descend. Two finally were dragged to the surface by their fellow
draegermen, but they were dead already.

Meanwhile, miners on the deepest levels hadn't heard the
explosion. They knocked off work and walked right into the gas
on the Back Slope. They choked, dropped to their knees, and
died. The carbon monoxide standing in the depths was invisible
and odorless, but the experienced men could taste it. Those who
tasted it waited behind it for help to come.

Hughie Guthro, who'd heard nothing, tasted the gas in the
air—it had a metallic tang to it, as if he'd bitten down on a
paper clip—and he went no farther. "Stay calm," he told a large
crew of men who had gathered. "This is like in a war or anything. Try not to panic. It's the panic that'll kill you." His neighbor Alec was among the group.

"No sir," said Alec, "I walked in that level and I'm going
back out that level." He could see the way clear to escape.

"I know it is hard to stay put," Hughie said. "You need that willpower. Use your head and try to think out what to do."

But Alec couldn't stand it. Inexperienced and young, he shook free of Hughie's thick hand on his shoulder and ran up the slope, betting that he could outrun the gas. Margie Guthro would see Alec again before Hughie would, when rescuers brought up his body.

Hughie slithered, with the others, across the floor under the standing gas, crawling like soldiers under fire, keeping their heads down. The overman, Conrad Embree, was telling the fellows to get themselves to one of the compressed-air hoses. The miners' power tools were driven by compressed air coursing through air hoses that resembled those at gas stations for filling tires. Embree unsnarled one of the air hoses and punctured holes like snakebites in its flank, then put his mouth to it and sucked in the half-decent air. The others did the same.

Con Embree then crawled away from the air hose long enough to build a stopping, a barrier made of debris and cloth, to divert the inflow of gases. On the outside of it, he wrote, FOR GOD'S SAKE COME AS FAST AS YOU CAN — 47 MEN ALIVE HERE.

At the surface, black smoke and poisonous gas billowed out of the mine, showing the authorities that the depths were on fire. On Friday morning, General Manager Harold Gordon was obliged to seal the entrance to the mine to reduce the oxygen feeding the fire. Only after the fire was extinguished would it be possible to descend in search of survivors.

"But the hand is fluctuating on the compressed-air machine," protested an engineer on the surface. "I think there's men alive below, using that air."

"No," a manager said. "In all probability, the fluctuation is caused by falling stones. In all probability, there is no life left in the mine."

"They're closing No. 4, sealing her up with a big seal of cement!" cried Margie Guthro. "They can't! Not until they get them out of there! There are a hundred and eighty-eight men down there!"

She felt quite baffled and unable to absorb this challenge to everything she thought she knew about the Miners' Code, including never abandoning trapped men. A sweet and obedient woman, she tried to accommodate herself to the new rules. "We have no front step on our bungalow!" she cried to her brother. "Buddy, you'd better build me a step, because with no funeral home, and I figure they're all done for, they'll be bringing Hughie's body to the house."

Deep in the pit, below the fires, Kenny Melanson yelled, "There's water running down the mine!" He was a gangly kid, nineteen years old, still living with his parents. "We're being sealed off."

"Yup, we're being sealed off," agreed Hughie Guthro. " If they turn off that air compressor, we'll be dead in ten minutes."

Conrad Embree wrote in his book, "I am writing no more in this book," and he passed it around with a pencil to the other fellows. Some wrote out their wills, some wrote farewells to their wives.

"Dear Marilyn," wrote Charles Michielson, "Make sure you look after the kids. I guess this is the way it has to be. Tell Nan and the rest of the family it couldn't be helped. Love, Sonny." Then he added, "Please see this note gets to my wife. Sonny."

"I'm too scared to write," Kenny said. He lay down, crossed

his hands under his head, and said, "If I could just see a piece of blue sky again.'"

"Lord," a man prayed aloud, "let me see the light one more time and you will never catch me in a coal mine again."

When the fire and smoke diminished, the seal over the mine was pulled away and rescue crews, who'd driven in from across the province, tried again to descend.

"Nobody could have stood that blast," said a draegerman from the town of Stellerton. "There's no one alive."

"That's where you're wrong," said Cecil Colwell, a hometown volunteer. "There's a different breed of men in Springhill to what there is in Stellerton, Westport, *or* Cape Breton."

Saturday night, two and a half days after the explosion, a team of draegermen reached the stopping erected by Embree, and the trapped men were saved. They fell into the arms of their rescuers and cried. An oxygen tank was set up and everyone got a good whiff. The Main and Back Slopes were still thick with gas. It was Monday morning before the survivors could be brought out.

Kenny Melanson ducked into the daylight, squinted in search of his parents, and heard a manager boom out, "Kenny Melanson!" The emerging survivors were so encrusted with coal dust, they were unrecognizable to the waiting crowd. Just behind Kenny, as another survivor appeared, the manager announced the man's name, then intoned, "Last man out!"

"So that's how folks are told their loved ones are dead," Kenny thought as he pushed into his mother's arms. "They didn't come out and that's it. If he's not out by the time they call 'Last man out,' he's not coming. That's how you find out."

Joe McDonald, a gentle man devoted to his wife and two

sons, had worked in the coal mines for eighteen years prior to being trapped in the Explosion. From the day he got home, he slept with a night-light. "When I wake up in the night," he told his wife, "I want to see *light*."

"Lord, Hughie," said Margie when she saw her husband emerge. They hugged in the country way, thudding their chests together and looking off in two different directions. "The mine is still unstable, so they're leaving all the bodies down there," she told him. "They can't even take the bodies out. They're shutting everything down."

It was February of the following year before management judged it safe for rescue crews to descend into No. 4 with aluminum coffins. The No. 4 mine was closed, throwing four hundred men out of work; the rest moved over to No. 2.

After 1956, Hughie Guthro was changed, leery of relaxing with a pint like he used to. "If he has a beer, Hughie will start to cry about the Explosion," Margie whispered to her friends. "He'll say, 'There's things you wouldn't want to know.' Three friends on our street was killed. One night after a beer, Hughie told me he seen his friend down there and went to see if he was hurt, but touching him was like touching a bowl of jelly. From the compression."

In 1957, Hughie Guthro and his best pal, Joe Holloway, got lost in the woods together during a hunting trip. When a sheriff's deputy came to the house to tell Margie that Hughie was missing, she said, "He can't miss a thing, can he?"

Hughie returned safely, sheepishly, from his hunting trip gone astray, but Margie's friends said to her, "Margie, tie a ball of yarn around that man, would you? You keep hold of one end and that way you'll always know where he's at."

For the two years since the Explosion, Hughie's fingers shook when he tried to button his shirt in the morning. "You always figure," he told Margie, just one time but she never forgot it, "are we going to get it tonight?"

"Holy mackerel," Margie thought, standing at her kitchen window to watch Hughie trudge down the road toward the pit, "what's not going to happen to him?"

What the miners *heard,* once or twice a month, was the distant cannon boom of shifting rock, sometimes accompanied by a brief earthquake-like flutter of the ground and walls around them. It was known in the trade as a bump, and the Springhill coalfield was infamous for them. A small bump was welcome, because it loosened the coal. But for a heart-stopping instant— above and below ground—a big bump was a Mayday sound, an SOS that the rock roof and rock floor might crash together, that the coal seam might shoot out and crush men on the wall. High above, on the sidewalks in town, when the population sensed a bigger bump, the wheeling of baby strollers and grocery carts squeaked to a halt. Everyone froze. Commerce ceased. Hearing no further cascade of sound, the women and shopkeepers and retired miners made brief eye contact, said little, emitted small coughs of forced laughter, and pushed on.

Underground, the old-timers reminded the novices, "If you *hear* a bump, you're all right, eh?"

But the adage was only half comforting. The unspoken half was, "You won't even hear the bump that kills you."

The black underground chambers grew familiar to the men, like their rooms at home. But the bumps gave warning that underground tunnels and rooms were unnatural; despite their familiarity, they were home to no living thing. Manmade pockets and tunnels and rooms of air between the core of the earth and the crust would not be tolerated indefinitely.

"If you really thought about No. 2," snarled Ted Michniak, "you wouldn't work in it, would you?"

"They're going to kill us," skinny Gorley Kempt said to his wife, Margie, who was smart and feisty and five years younger than he. He relaxed on the kitchen couch after supper, watching her tidy up. "I know I got no education and here come these fellows with their piece of paper framed on their walls—'Oh no, this is the right thing,' they say. But the old men say they're not doing it right, making the walls one right above the other. They say it's weakening the floors and ceilings. They're going to kill us all."

In fact, the Nova Scotia Mines Minister, E. A. Manson, considered the Springhill mines more dangerous than average. Two experts from the Federal Department of Technical Surveys collaborated with two experts from the Nova Scotia Research Foundation in the last couple of months to determine the cause of the frequent bumps. Their report had not yet been completed.

Gorley's complaint and the miners' fears made sense to Margie. Any housewife knew that if you tested the doneness of an angel food cake with all the prongs of your fork, instead of with the single needle of a cake tester, the cake would exhale and collapse.

3

Home of the Long Tides

From narrow provinces
Of fish and bread and tea,
Home of the long tides
Where the bay leaves the sea
Twice a day and takes
The herrings long rides...

Elizabeth Bishop, *The Moose*

Depending on the season and on whether they worked the day shift or night shift, the miners turned gratefully to the pleasures and aggravations of child rearing, carpentry, fishing, hunting, ice-skating, softball, beer drinking, church suppers, and house parties. They strolled or limped from the washhouse as the closest of buddies. They were friendly with the surface workers and the front-office workers, but the unspoken fraternity of the deep didn't apply. "Everybody's pals," said Herb Pepperdine. "Lots of fun. Jokes and call one another names and have a nickname. One fellow we call Blister Snout, and there's Gravy Eye, and Bunny. Leon Melanson used to work as a butcher, so we call him T-Bone. They call me Pep. We all meet up in the washhouse after work and holler at one another. We're all good friends.

Why, even if you have an argument, after you hit the surface it's all over. You walk home together."

"Miners is awful close-knit people," Hughie Guthro thought. "When you're doing something, you have more help than you need. If you're building a house and going to run a wall, you come out in the morning and your whole shift is there."

"People stand around all the time like a flock of birds," Garnet Clarke observed. "Fourteen people in somebody's yard talking about the mines. 'Got to go, I'm afternoon shift,' you'll say. Everybody in town has somebody in the mine."

Miners found all sorts of ways to spend their leisure time together. Bingo, pool, and darts were played in the social halls of the Rotarians, the Knights of Pythias, the Holy Name Society, the Knights of Columbus, the Odd Fellows, and the Order of Buffaloes. Four churches—Catholic, Baptist, Anglican, and Presbyterian—divided the devout among them, and there was even one Jewish family, the Saffrons, Polish emigrants who had left Lodz in 1905. They owned the furniture store. The three Saffron children attended the public schools, mostly without incident. The youngest, Artie, now in his seventies, a whimsical and literary man with wild white hair, does recall being chased home once by a group of boys yelling that he'd killed Jesus. He burst into his house crying. "You march right back out there, young man, " his mother scolded, "and tell them that you, Artie Saffron, had nothing to do with it."

Card parties, dance parties, and supper parties rotated through the front rooms of the tall wood houses and the company row houses near the pithead on King Street and Queen Street. "No calling up ahead of time," sighed Margie Kempt, propping open her screen door as uninvited guests stomped their feet on her porch. "Come on in. I've got something baked."

"I've always got something baked," she muttered to herself, "because I always got to have something for Gorley's lunch pail."

Friends played bridge and poker by the heat of coal-burning stoves. "Down the street they have parties with a fiddle player," said Ruth Tabor. "And there are beautiful men singers." Shy Ruth was a good cook, thus a target for many visitors. "I always have a pie made when my husband comes home," she said innocently, not connecting her flair with the frequency of after-work visitors. She assumed her husband's work buddies were just very polite and hated to pass by the house without stepping in to tell her hello. "Butterscotch, lemon, coconut... I try to have something different every day." The Tabors had three daughters and a son. Raymond coached his son's Little League team, and he called his youngest daughter Suzie Bubblegum.

Day-shift men, who came up for air at 4 P.M., enjoyed the lines of maroon in the sky at dusk as much as a full-blast noonday sun. Whether that light was fraying to gray or blanketed by rising dust from the lit-up baseball field of a Springhill Fencebusters game, those streaks in the western sky were *light*.

Blacktop roads ran uphill from Main Street. In patched-together houses, children multiplied. They required diapers, sweaters, and milk; porridge, shoes, and pencils. In the Ruddicks' house lived Maurice, Norma, and their children: Colleen, Sylvia, Valerie, Alder, Ellen, Dean, Chuckie, Revere, Leah, Jesse, Iris, and newborn Katrina. The Ruddicks had been married thirteen years and recently had welcomed their twelfth child. "When we first married we cooked the turkey," Norma would recite to her church friends. She was a small light-skinned black woman balancing a tall copper hairdo. "And the wishbone of the turkey, a lot of people wishes on it, eh? And he said, 'Come on, it's dry, let's wish on the wishbone.' So I went to work and he went to work and he took the biggest half, which he would get his wish. And it must have been three or four weeks after, I said to him, 'What did you wish on the wishbone?' He said, 'I wished we'd have twelve children.' And I said, 'You wished *what?*'"

After work Maurice Ruddick soaked in his tub at home for an hour before arranging himself in front of the steamed-up bathroom mirror, assembling aftershave and hair lotions on the lip of the sink. He lubricated his wavy hair and parted it sharply down the middle, then delicately combed his thin mustache into straight lines. Head on, and in profile, he looked a lot like Errol Flynn. A bow tie, plaid jacket, and plaid pants hung on a hook behind the door. He cinched the stylishly baggy pants around his trim waist and laced up his brown pointed-toe shoes. Outside the privacy of his bathroom and closet, he was rarely without a toddler or baby in his arms. Still, he maintained a thin, invisible zone of self-preservation: the crisp, clean outfit on the modish middle-aged father even as he held in his hands—just ever so slightly away from his ironed shirt—a squirming, half-unbuttoned child with a bit of dinner clinging to its cheeks.

Maurice's plaid jacket and pants, to the mortification of his oldest daughters, often were not made from the same plaid. This was revealed when he finally opened the door of the steamy bathroom. "Floral shirt coming," the oldest girls would warn each other, clowning at the bottom of the stairs. "He thinks everyone is thinking, 'Not many folks can dress like this,'" whispered Sylvia. And Colleen whispered back: "Folks are really thinking, 'Who would *want* to dress like that?'" But Maurice marched down the stairs and through the bevy of teasing daughters, who parted as if he had pushed through a rack of draped satin scarves. He let himself out the front door and ignored the outburst of laughter behind it.

No matter his fine taste, Ruddick's care for the cut and flare of his wardrobe expressed itself in the purchase of, at most, one, maybe two, articles of clothing a year, and the careful preservation—over many, many years—of each item. With all those mouths to feed, he couldn't afford more.

At home in the evenings, Maurice retreated to a basement corner with a battered sofa, rug, and hanging lightbulb, and cooked up a melody with an old guitar and a kazoo, or by playing hambone with his hands, chest, and lap, or by making rhythm sounds with his mouth. He was an original, a musical eccentric, a one-man band. His many children were growing up to the sound of Daddy buzzing and honking and slapping away downstairs. "Off by himself? With that guitar? That man will go crazy," his wife, Norma, told her church friends. At night Maurice pulled a kitchen chair to a back bedroom and sat beside the crib, smacking on the dinged-up guitar and crooning to the baby. He liked to sing all his children to sleep, but lately a few of the oldest, the preteen girls, laughingly protested, "We're trying to *sleep,* Dad."

On Sundays he herded all but the babies downstairs and made them rehearse songs in harmony. Maureen, at age three, pounded a child's ukulele. Maurice took four or five of them at a time and drove around to other towns, billing the ensemble as "The Singing Miner and the Minerettes." The boys wore navy blue slacks and white shirts, the girls navy blue skirts and polka-dot tops. Rural audiences clapped approvingly for the well-groomed, respectful "colored" children in the matching home-made outfits and for their crooning father, stroking his acoustic guitar and directing the children hither and yon with the raise of his eyebrows. They sang in Baptist churches on Sundays and at Wednesday supper clubs midweek. They sang "Going to the Chapel" at a lobster festival. At a Lion's Club meeting in Sackville, Ellen performed the limbo.

Ruddick was susceptible to dreams of the American type. He was determined to win wider celebrity than the local church's pie supper offered. Though he and his family hadn't yet been invited to appear on a regional television variety show, he figured it was just a matter of time, and then how their lives would change! The tilt of his hat, the even grin, the cigar, the star turns performed on the stages of drafty school auditoriums, all seemed part of the same well-practiced machinery, powered by self-promotion and the desire to be singled out for admiration. Whether his ambition was fed by, or frustrated by, long drives on freezing nights along muddy provincial roads with Iris, Treena, Leah, and Jesse crumpled together asleep in the backseat of the station wagon, and the financial need to report for work at the pithead early the next morning, he himself barely knew.

In later years Maurice's children, some of whom became professional or amateur musicians, would say of him, "He only knew a few chords on a four-string guitar. But he was just full of talent. He was way, way ahead of his time. The music was so good, almost on the verge of jazz. He was inventing his own form of scat, then turning right around and doing a spiritual or a barbershop. He had a Mills Brothers, an Ink Spots, sound. And he never even owned a record player."

Though Maurice saw himself as a black man, "Maurice is not *very* black," was the type of thing folks said about him.

"They're just as good as white people," a miner's wife said, "and they really aren't that dark anyway. *Mulatto,* they call it."

There were too few black children in Nova Scotia for segregation of schools, but neighborhoods, restaurants, hotels, buses, beauty parlors, and movie theaters were segregated in big cities across the country. Black customers were not permitted to try on clothes in stores. Marian Anderson was turned away from white hotels in the late 1950s. Factory jobs were not offered to black workers until the manpower shortage of the Second World War.

"I work with plenty of colored people. They're same as us," is how Herb Pepperdine thought about it. "A fellow couldn't get a better buddy than some of those fellows. Couldn't get better guys to have for a buddy. Maurice is a jolly fellow down at work. He don't mind you calling him nigger. Nobody means anything by it. The only thing I don't agree with: whites and blacks getting married. Black should marry a black and a white should marry a white, eh? There's a lot of it goes on. Big celebrities marry colored people."

Underground, Ruddick worked as hard as the next man. Besides, all the miners had dreams of escape, large or small. Whether they saved money in order to build on an extra bedroom, or to buy new shocks for the car, or to chip in with a brother-in-law on a fishing cabin, or to pay for a daughter's wedding, all day underground they talked about and planned for events in the open air.

For the Kempts, the escape was to a summer cottage at the Minas Basin, an inlet of the Bay of Fundy, which has the highest tides in the world. The bright water evacuates its own harbor twice a day and dashes out to sea, then dashes back in. At the ebb tide, the floor of the ocean is exposed to the sun, and shorebirds forage for mud shrimp. When the water rushes back in, the birds scatter, tourists and shell collectors jog for land, and rowboats bob up off the corrugated mud floor.

Gorley urged his best friends to buy cottages near the village of Five Islands. They could fix them up, or not—mattresses thrown onto the wood-planked floor would do fine. They roasted wieners over the coals of a campfire and they set out lines for flounder, as easy to gather in as letters from a mailbox. "Well, we've had flounder for breakfast, dinner, and supper every day this week," Margie would announce on a summer morning. "We got company coming tonight. Hey, what say we fry up some flounder?" On another day she called to him, "Gorley! Good news! We're out of flounder! We're having baloney for supper tonight. I can't wait!"

Gorley Kempt, thirty-nine years old, a scamp whom everyone loved, had pretty much stuck Margie with the chores of house and children. He'd head to a pal's house after work, crowd around a kitchen, and call out useless advice to someone trying to fix a stopped-up drain. It never occurred to him to peer under Margie's mediocre appliances, much less recruit his buddies to help fix anything. Margie gave him heck for being a drinker and a ne'er-do-well around the house while being such an amiable fellow around town. He'd come in late for dinner, whistling, with a satisfied half smile on his face and then was startled when Margie threw harsh words, if not something made of cast iron, at him. "I was too young to marry him at sixteen," Margie would think, plopping a bowl of beef stew in front of Gorley. "But everybody was doing it. Marrying a miner— well, we hadn't much choice but to marry a miner. Young, strong, fine-looking fellows they were, and the best pay package in town."

Even barefoot and in a swimsuit, she was a tough little nut to crack, darkly tanned, windblown, and freckled. Her best friend was Margaret, who had ten children. Margaret cut their hair, sewed their jeans, and gave the girls do-it-yourself home permanents. Margie admired her. There was no electricity on the inlet, so the families made do with gas lanterns, iceboxes, campfires.

On Saturday nights the Kempts played cards with Margaret and her husband, Alfred, and four other couples. They put in twenty-five cents apiece and nibbled on sandwiches or sweets. They played on kitchen tables by the light of Coleman lanterns, as the bleating of loons and hoot owls blew through the unscreened windows. They could hear the tide thrashing closer.

Margie loved Alfred, thought he was such a great fellow, even when drinking. "Most men drinking really irritate me, but Alfred isn't alive unless he had a couple of drinks in him. He is a riot. I think the world of him."

Alfred would say to Gorley, "Now when things get tough, will you lend me Margie? I never saw anybody could get as much out of a can of beans as Margie."

"All I know is, what is shared is shared around," said Margie.

Gorley turned up the volume on every gathering he was part of. He himself was not loud, but, like a leprechaun, he spread merriment around him. "Margie, get me something to eat, because the tide's coming in!" Gorley would holler through the smoke of cigarettes, kerosene lanterns, and fried fish. An hour later it was, "Margie, get me something to eat, because the tide's going out!"

4

The Bump

Thursday, October 23, 1958, was an Indian summer day so bright and full of promise, it seemed as if the holiday spices waiting at the end of December had whisked back in time to sweep about with the autumn leaves. Nuts and leaves and dust spun down the street in small whirlwinds the colors of peppermint, cinnamon, cloves, and oranges. "What a beautiful day," said Margie Kempt, "a gorgeous day. People are going out in their shirtsleeves." Under a sharp blue sky, the trees up and down the hilly roads were aglow.

Caleb Rushton slept in that morning, in a front-room armchair into which he'd stiffly, achingly lowered himself after midnight. He was thirty-five, a clean-shaven, churchgoing, rosy-cheeked young man with a large sensitive nose pinched by wire spectacles. He and his wife, Pat, lived in a nice farmhouse on the rim of a green valley outside town. Caleb was a steady and intelligent man who might have found his destiny elsewhere, perhaps in the study of history or economics, if he hadn't come of age in a coal-mining town. He was a direct descendant of the eighteenth-century United Empire Loyalists, who received grants of land in Nova Scotia in 1785 from the English Crown. "I'm entitled to write 'UE' after my signature," he joshingly told Pat in their courting days—he had an almost Irish lilt to his voice—"but I don't want people to think I'm that old."

Unlike most of his workmates, Caleb saw to it that the walls of his farmhouse were lined with books. He borrowed books from Dr. Burden, read them, and returned them in perfect condition. In the small hours of the morning of October 23, he let himself in quietly after work so as not to wake up Pat and their son, and he sat down to read near the warm, charred logs in the fireplace, a shawl across his legs. He pored over the rattling pages with a curious, avuncular air, his gray eyes growing melancholy, until the exhaustion of the day overtook him.

Pat, in a bathrobe, heading his way with a hot cup of tea and a cookie, discovered him asleep. She untangled his spectacles from his ears and folded them and his book onto the side table, turned off the lamp, and tiptoed out.

On that bright fall day, Norma Ruddick, still wan from childbirth and weary from her messy nights with a newborn, slipped an apron over her damp-chested flannel nightgown, pushed up the sleeves of her gown, and lowered some kettles and pans to a couple of toddlers underfoot so they could get down to some banging. "Whoops!" she said, and tiptoed down the back hall to shut the bedroom door so that Maurice, whose shift had ended at midnight the night before, could sleep. Norma baked ten loaves of white bread every day, as well as cooking a big stew or a pot of boiled scallops for dinner. "They never go to bed hungry, thank God. Maurice sees to that," she would say. "On the weekends, he has a treat for them. One week he'll have hot dogs and ice cream and pop for them; the next week it will be hamburg."

Maurice's and Norma's forebears had lived in Nova Scotia as long as Caleb Rushton's. In the late 1700s, English Loyalists, who'd chosen the losing side in the American Revolution, were given land in Nova Scotia by the British crown. They moved north and took their slaves with them. Ruddick had been born into a coal-mining family in the town of Joggins, twenty-eight miles from Springhill. His mother had lost two infant girls before Maurice's birth; consequently, Mrs. Ruddick had treated Maurice as delicate and had coddled him throughout his childhood. But when he was twelve, his mother died of tuberculosis after nursing a friend through it. He toughened up under his father's administration, became an amateur boxer as a teenager, and had kept himself in fighting trim ever since. He finished eleventh grade before entering the mines.

Aware of the perception of "colored" people, Maurice Ruddick was the model comrade on the job: ready with a strong shoulder to assist a man, he was also generous with cake, coffee, chewing gum, cold chicken. Most often he contented himself with luncheons of brown bread and honey and cheese. But he'd go hungry himself before he'd hide his own lunch from someone who'd forgotten his. He offered that reliable smile, that willing hand. He never leveled any reproaches or corrections at anybody; he kept it light. In return, the other miners shared stories with him (knowing he'd laugh a warm, chesty chuckle, but more than was warranted) and they sang along on his trolley songfests.

"Let him sleep," Norma thought that morning. "I know Maurice is coming and going trying to wonder where the next thing is coming from."

On the morning of October 23, Elaine Turnbull got up first, as always, to start the washing. After four children, she still had a light-hearted, girlish manner; she was shy, with unconventional looks: ringlets of short hair, dark eyebrows, a prominent nose, and an overbite. She was both shy and winning, and had captured a conventionally handsome and popular man. "Maybe Bill can sleep in till I finish," she thought. "He doesn't like the washer going and clothes everywhere, but it's such a nice morning, I want to get them out on the clothesline." In the late morning, Bill came downstairs and had lunch with Elaine and the children: John, seven; Arthur, five; Kathy, two; and Clair, five months old. The young couple had chosen to have their children close together, and right away, so they could raise them and then have time to be alone together again.

At noon, Elaine brought in the clothes and put them in the sunporch, because there was to be a funeral nearby. She stood folding the clothes and watching the cars park and the mourners gather. It was for a two-year-old child. "How do people survive such a tragedy?" she wondered.

"Honey, can you fill my lunch can?" called Bill. "I'm heading down early so I can talk to some of the boys before going down."

"I'm always amazed at how much I can get into the lunch can," thought Elaine. "Six slices of bread made into sandwiches and three sweets. He has a good appetite! But, then, he works very hard."

"Keep the fire on," he said teasingly when he left.

"I know! I will!" she cried.

"I am the worst one for letting it go too low," Elaine would say of herself, "and then I add coal and smother it and it goes out. We burned wood at my home when I was growing up and I've never made friends with coal."

When she and Billy took a walk, they still linked arms or held hands. "That pretty much sums up our life," she would think. "We are very much a couple. Of course, he's everybody's friend. He's such an extrovert! He knows he is a bit of a ham; he likes to clown it up, and he makes me laugh! He is more cute than handsome. Dark brown eyes and dark curly hair and a wide grin. But he doesn't like me to call him cute."

"See you," she called through the porch as he crossed the small yard.

Bev Reynolds's four-year-old son was just getting over the chicken pox, but it was such a mild and lovely afternoon that she phoned Dr. Burden for permission to let Danny play outside. Danny had a cart and a tricycle and was engrossed in trying to tie them together. His dad, Wes, stepped outside, bent over, and finished the job—"There you go, young sir," and he then allowed Danny to pedal behind him and Gorley Kempt all the way to the end of the pavement as they headed for the mines. "You go back now," Wes Reynolds bade his son, and the child turned around and pedaled back.

Percy Rector and Leon Melanson, best friends, brothers-in-law, and former housemates, strolled down a hilly road toward town. Realizing they were a little early to clock in at the pit, they stepped into Miners' Hall for a game of darts and a couple of bottles of pop. Their wives—sisters—counted themselves the luckiest women in town. Leon was handsome, blond, suave on the dance floor, with blue eyes as light as glass marbles; when he'd worked for a while as a butcher, he'd been pegged by his pals forever after as T-Bone. Percy was a big bear of a man, with a deep laugh and a big heart. When he volunteered to grocery-shop, he sometimes bought groceries for Leon's household, too, pushing open the screen door with his foot, arms full, hollering in jest to his sister-in-law, "Honey, I'm home!" After darts, the two pals walked down Main Street to the mine.

When the sun went down in the late afternoon, the glittering leaves flickered off as if strings of electric lights were being unplugged one strand at a time, from the lowest rungs to the highest. A last pinpoint of sunlight glittered at the top of the highest tree, and then it, too, went dark, and the town wordlessly swung east toward a new source of light, a burnt-orange three-quarters moon. "We'll listen to the baseball play-offs in a little while!" thought Margie Kempt. Up and down the street, children were called in from play, and baths were poured for them from stove-heated kettles.

Later that evening, the miners' wives wiped dry the cookpots and sealed up the leftovers, the day-shift miners threw food scraps to dogs in the yard, and entire families seated themselves in front of their televisions. The Springhill High School band was performing on the Don Messer variety show at seven-thirty.

Elaine Turnbull bathed all her children and put them to bed. She set up the ironing board in the living room so she could watch the program while tending to her chores.

At eight o'clock, adults all over town angled the rabbit-eared antennas of their television sets in the hopes of intercepting *I Love Lucy* without too much static from a Hollywood so distant and exotic, it might as well have been Hong Kong. Meanwhile, their husbands and brothers and sons, fathers and step-fathers and fathers-in-law, grandfathers and uncles and cousins and friends were underground, chopping and shoveling, shouting and sweating, causing the lights on the surface to dim for a moment, as they rummaged around in the common basement that was the coal mine yawning open under Springhill.

THURSDAY, OCTOBER 23, 8:06 P.M.

At 8:06, a deep, powerful BOOM! sounded, shaking every building and street in town. Everyone in Springhill lurched at the same instant. The wetly combed children sitting cross-legged on the floor in their pajamas jumped like the hiccups and looked to their parents. Damp-aproned mothers bending to empty out the tin bathtubs froze, and the stocking-footed day-shift miners already snoring on the couches woke up mad, yelling "What the—?"

Margie Guthro's telephone jumped up off its table, the table teetered then righted itself, the phone landed back on the table, and the receiver dropped back on the hook, as if black magic had sprinkled flying dust on it all for a moment. "Oh my God, what's going on?" she cried.

In an overheated meeting room in City Hall, the mayor and city councilmen ceased circumlocuting and grabbed the sides of their chairs to keep from falling.

In houses all over town, windows and mirrors shivered, flatware and cutlery jingled in kitchen drawers. On closet floors, shoes inched forward.

The mayor's wife, Grace Gilroy, felt her house begin to shake and heard her dishes rattle, and she ran out to the street. "It's an earthquake!" she thought.

Jim Nodwell, office and payroll manager for the mine, was taking a walk to enjoy the spring evening. The bump lifted him off the road. "I'm hopping," he thought. "Did a car hit a telephone pole?"

Lloyd Henwood was in his car, nearing home, and felt nothing. A neighbor flagged him down and yelled, "Did you feel that?"

"No," said Lloyd, "that was just me coming over the bridge with the car."

"My Jesus, Lloyd, that was not you!" cried the neighbor.

Percy McCormick had dropped by to visit Margie Kempt; he was sitting in a chair in the kitchen watching her scrape out the soot from her stove. At the first bang, he said, "My God above," and Margie said, "It happened." Percy jumped up to go. "If you hear anything, come back and tell me," she said, and he yelled, "I'll get back to you!" as he dashed out the door.

Norma Ruddick and her family were watching Don Messer's Jubilee. A singer had just performed a song with the words, "Further along, you'll know all about it / Further along, you'll understand why..." when the television went dead Norma thought the aerial had blown off the roof.

Before folks could catch their breath and ease the responsive pounding of their hearts, another *bang!* sounded as a rock floor rose and slammed into the one above it, echoing through all the caverns that underlay the town. Then the townspeople knew it was a bump, a big one. The No. 2 mine, underneath Springhill, was in convulsion.

Bobby Jewkes, a miner, was strolling down Mechanic Street. "What in Jesus is that?" he yelled.

Mrs. Megeney ran out her front door and yelled, "What on earth?"

"I don't know!" said Bobby. "I think some kids put a bomb under Jim Legere's house!"

He jogged back to his house and called to his wife, "Did you feel that?"

"It knocked me off the couch," she cried.

"Lord God," he said, "it's a bump; it's the whole three walls must have went."

He ran out again and headed to the pit, thinking of his two brothers underground, panting as he ran. "Billy and Doug, they're gone."

Floyd Gilroy, age forty-two, the father of ten children, was part of a team nicknamed the Wrecking Crew, volunteers who tried to be the first on the scene in a time of disaster. He had just sat down on his chesterfield to watch some television when he was jolted up and out of it. Naturally, he figured it was the kids. He hung over the banister to yell up the stairs for them to stop whatever it was they were doing, but encountered his nine-year-old daughter already peering down the stairs. "Daddy, I don't know what happened but something threw me right off the toilet."

"It's a bump," said Floyd's wife.

"Yeah, and a damn good 'un, too," he said. " I'm going."

Then there was another *bang!* John Totten and his wife were coming into the front room from their garage when he was thrown into her, knocking her down. "There's a big bump," he said. "If it's in the wall, every man's gone."

"Daddy's down there!" she cried. "My father!"

With the first crash, Elaine Turnbull had jumped up and yelled reprovingly up the stairs, "Boys!" They liked to prop their blackboard against their beds and use it as a slide. But when the house shook with a second shock, she ran up the stairs two at a time and met her older boys in the hall, looking frightened. "What was that?" asked John.

She flew back downstairs just as the kitchen door opened

and her next-door neighbor barged in. "What *was* that?" asked Elaine.

"*That,*" said Helen Campbell, "was a bump."

"Oh my God, oh my God, Billy." Elaine felt instantly, thickly nauseated. She moved in slow motion across the rocking, jolting terrain of the kitchen linoleum to the phone to call Bill's mother. She dialed shakily and got a wrong number. She'd reached the lamp cabin. "What's going on out there?" she pleaded, and a man said, "Please hang up, lady, I can't tell you anything." Then her mother-in-law burst in with her rosary beads spinning through her hands. Elaine opened her mouth to pray, too, but in her panic she forgot the words.

Mrs. Arnold Burden was sitting and reading a magazine in her immaculate living room, where the windowsills fluttered with African violets and miniature white poodles napped on the Oriental rug, when the teacups and saucers began vibrating on their shelves. The lightbulbs buzzed like trapped bees. The poodles bounced up, barking. In town, Dr. Burden had just finished examining a patient in his second-story office, when he felt three distinct shock waves and was transported momentarily back to the ground in Europe, where he had been under aerial attack during the Second World War. "It's like a fighter bomber has just dropped a stick of bombs, exploding fractions of a second apart," he thought. "It's a major mine disaster."

The subterranean roars shook the town of Amherst, fifteen miles away; rolled seventeen seconds later into a seismograph in Halifax, seventy-five miles away, registering as a small earthquake; and thudded against ships in the North Atlantic. Then the town fell horribly silent, the silence worse, in its way, than the preceding clamor.

8:12 P.M.

Women in bathrobes and house slippers, wearing turbans of damp bath towels, and men with belts unloosed or suspenders hanging, flew out their front doors, their suddenly wailing children stumbling behind them. Entire families slipped and skidded across the wet leaves of their yards and into the roads, heading toward the pithead a few blocks south of town.

Sadie Allen ran pell-mell down Main Street with her four children sprinting behind her. "Something is terribly wrong," she thought as she ran among other women. "We all know it. Nobody needs to tell us. We can just tell."

"Your father's in the mine," said Pat Rushton to her son in their farmhouse on a hill. She picked up the keys to the truck and wordlessly handed the little boy his jacket.

In town, people began running faster and faster in panic, as if their haste now could undo something that had happened while they'd been caught catnapping, soaking in a tub, or spooning up a dish of ice cream in front of the TV, as if they were somehow at fault for not remaining vigilant every minute their loved ones were underground. In neighborhoods close to the mine, few took time to start their cars; they simply stumbled across the leaf-plastered front yards and trotted into place in the moving panorama. "Please dear God, please dear God, Jesus God and Mary," huffed Ruth Tabor, unaccustomed to running.

"You stay here by me!" mothers shrieked at their children, the children's lives suddenly seeming vulnerable, too.

In other neighborhoods, cars were backing out of all the driveways at once. The Ruddicks did not own a telephone. When Norma looked outside to see if her TV antenna actually had fallen off the roof into the yard, she saw that cars were bumper-to-bumper in her small quiet street. "Oh my God, Maurice," she said. She closed her robe, wrapped up her nursing new-born, and moved gingerly through the house. Her feet were still swollen, so she shoved them into a pair of Maurice's sneakers. Her three older girls took sweaters and ran out the door.

In ten minutes, the neighborhoods were empty. A deep sky sparkled above the leafy streets. In the cool of the evening, the front doors of many houses stood wide open. Unseen television audiences hee-hawed with laughter into empty living rooms, the raucous sound booming out open windows onto the black yards and empty streets.

8:22 P.M.

At the pithead, eddies of people, made frantic by confusion and helplessness, collided with one another outside the aluminum shed that sheltered the mine entrance. The possibility of an invisible wall of poisonous gas blocked their stampede through the door and down the open slope. Wives and parents and children held themselves back, despite the impulse to run into the darkness calling out names. Mine officials fought their way through the mob to get to the on-site plywood office.

The No. 2 mine was worked nonstop by men on day shift (7 A.M. to 3 P.M.), afternoon shift (3 P.M. to 11 P.M.), and night shift (11 P.M. to 7 A.M.). At that moment, 174 miners of the afternoon shift were underground.

When the bumps ceased, Cecil Colwell, who had rescued men in '56, got up and headed for his front door, half-hopping into his boots as he ran. "I have to go," he told his wife. "Them men that's trapped down there, they're expecting somebody to come for them."

"There's probably nobody alive," she cried.

"No, that's not right," Cecil said.

If the first principle of the Miners' Code told a man to rescue men trapped in a disaster, the second principle told him always to believe in the possibility that men were still alive.

Margie Guthro, who was getting trained by life to expect the worst, stood among the rest at the pithead and closed her eyes in pain. She had always told her husband, "Hughie, if we didn't have bad luck, we wouldn't have any kind of luck."

5

"What Am I Doing Here? What Am I Doing Here?"

THURSDAY, OCTOBER 23, 8:06 P.M.

At seven o'clock, on October 23, 1958, a small bump had fluttered through No. 2. The men froze, looked at each other for a long moment, shrugged, spat, and went back to work. No one was injured.

But at 8:06 P.M. the mine seized up, and coal came crashing up through nearly all the open spaces in the underground maze. The disaster of No. 2 came not as a cave-in. Instead, the rock floor heaved upwards. From an oceanic depth, a ball of fiery gas threw off its stone layers, like a feverish child in the night angrily kicking off the covers. The deepest stone floor rose faster than an elevator. It smashed into the floor above it, and the two, stacked together, hurtled up into the third, like granite dominos falling upward. The stone-and-lumber pillars, or "packs," built by the miners to support the roofs over their heads, were clapped to smithereens in an instant by a force from below.

When the bedrock underneath the mine arched its back, miners were thrown off balance. They briefly had a giddy sensation, as if they were lurching through a carnival fun house. But they knew it was a bump. Two-ton machines somersaulted through the air.

Men found themselves riding toward the ceilings upon the surging floors. They closed their eyes and held their breath against impact and instant death. In a few odd sections, the floor shot up and then stopped just shy of the roof. It was the only reason anyone survived.

Where the 12,600 level met the wall, the bump hoisted a few of the guys and twirled them in the air like batons above a marching band, then rammed them into holes and kicked dust in their faces. An invisible hand spun Maurice Ruddick around and screwed him into the floor. The bang sounded like a cannon to Currie Smith. As he flew through the air, he had the thought that he himself was the cannonball.

Herb Pepperdine felt himself picked up from behind as if by a bully, and punched hard on the ear, and then shaken hard, like an angry woman might handle a bad pup, and then he was hurled into the waste. When he tried to crawl out of it, a twister of coal dust blocked his path.

The bump did not surge on and on like an ocean wave. The mine was finite. The bump pulsed powerfully through it, clapping the floors together, and then it stopped. The roar died down, like the sound of a symphony audience that has given three standing ovations of shouted bravos and vigorous applause and then quickly sits down at first sign of an encore.

Dozens of miners were dead. Those knocked unconscious did not awaken immediately. They slept for many hours. For the men of No. 2's afternoon shift, it was as if they'd been hit by a third of the plagues of Egypt at once: blood, rock falling like hail, darkness, and death of the firstborn.

Higher in the mine, Leon Melanson, T-Bone, with the sunlit blue eyes and the smooth moves on the dance floor, had been putting up timber, building a pack, with his buddy, Eddie Bobbie. Eddie asked, "Are you using your measuring sticks?"

"No," said Leon. And Eddie put his hand out for the sticks.

Then it seemed to Leon that he was dreaming; he was drowning in a black sea of tar. It was utterly dark and he couldn't move his arms or feel his legs. All the air was being pushed deliberately out of his chest. He fought to wake up, strained like a dinosaur trying to free itself from a tar pit, but the only body part he could move was his eyelids. That he could blink was the only difference between him and a petrified man. After immeasurable time, he made out that he was buried in coal to the neck, and the ceiling was close overhead. Pretty sure now that he was awake and not dreaming, Leon called for his partner, to whom he'd handed the measuring sticks a second earlier. Was it a second earlier? "Eddie?" he asked, but his voice was swallowed and whirled away in the blue-black darkness and the storm of coal dust. "Eddie? Eddie!"

He sat as still as a statue of Buddha, enclosed in coal, his eyes opening and closing in the midnight air. "Eddie?" he asked now and again, forlornly. "Eddie, is that you?"

9:45 P.M.

Where the 12,600 level met the wall, six stunned survivors began to wake up. They sensed, rather than saw, the roiling mixture of coal dust and gas blowing through the chambers. They tried to duck under the gales of free gas, knowing that the mine could explode as it had in '56 and release a fireball above ground that consumed every man in its orbit. They heard coal particles skittering along the rock face, like thousands of matches scraping along flint, eager to ignite.

Garnet Clarke jumped up and took off in fright but was stopped at every turn by a new wall of coal. He was in a black maze of dead ends. With shaking hands, he rearranged his headlamp and turned it back on, but it was like a car's high beam in dense fog, illuminating the haze from within. Blind in the bright hailstorm of rock, Garnet heard a man screaming and he moved toward the sound.

The boom had blown out Frank Hunter's eardrums. When he reached up to feel his head, he pulled away hands sticky with blood. From far away, it seemed, he, too, could hear a man screaming. He put on his helmet to go in search of him, but the helmet was full of coal dust, which poured over and clung to the streaming blood on his face and neck.

Doug Jewkes had been working beside Les Bouchard at the coal face. The bump had kicked Jewkes backward seven feet and buried him to the chest. When he awoke, he looked over to Les but saw only a fresh hillock of coal, like a new grave.

In the dark, Maurice Ruddick, trying to unscrew himself from his hole of coal, freed his hands and patted the ground nearby until he found his helmet. Working with only a cone of meager yellow light, he detached himself from the floor like a city worker hoisting himself out of a manhole. He, too, heard horrible shrieks close at hand, so he began crawling through the wild haze to investigate.

Black-faced in the swirling coal dust, hollering for help, five men crawled toward each other, squinting and grunting. All around them was a windy and ramshackle blackness. The coal lay in heaps, burying all indication that men had tried to civilize the place. The timbered walls, the pillars, the tools, everything man-made had been swallowed. It was surreal, like discovering, after a night of thick snowfall, that one's yard and fence and mailbox and car have been blanketed, and are recognizable only by location and fattened silhouette. So the men crunched on hands and knees over new-fallen black rock that hid everything they knew, including untold numbers of their pals.

"It is you, Garnie?" someone rasped, though it was hard to hear over the screams of a man nearby.

"That's me."

"Maurice? You all right?"

"I'm all right. Frank, you alive? Frank? Frank!"

"I'm alive."

"That you, Pep?"

"I'm here."

"Man, that thing just went bang and come up the wall and everything went flying!" said Currie Smith.

"I heard that *whoo!* and next I know, I'm buried to my waist," said Maurice Ruddick.

Maurice Ruddick, Herb "Pep" Pepperdine, Currie Smith, Garnet Clarke, and Frank Hunter blotted the coal and blood from their faces with their dusty sleeves and found themselves on a sloping floor about forty feet square, with barely enough headroom to stand up. Suddenly Doug Jewkes showed up, shouting like a crazy man. He had gotten out, dug for his buddy Les Bouchard, and touched Les's dead arm. Now he was being burned by leaking battery acid soaking through his pant leg onto his thigh. He yanked, squealing, at his coveralls, like a man with a hornet inside his pants. "Damn, damn, damn, damn," he cried, jitterbugging, till he got his boots off, pulled the wet pants off, and fell onto the coal to cool the scorched skin.

But someone else nearby was screaming: ungodly, tongue-protruding shrieks, a man's red throat turning inside out in blares of agony, with scarcely a catch in the sound for air to be bellowed back in. The miners waved to clear the swirling air and hobbled toward the screeching.

The six survivors found a seventh. It was a terrible thing to see.

Big, good-natured Percy Rector was caught by one arm in a standing slouch. When the bump had thrown everything and everyone up in the air, the pack—crisscrossed, stacked lumber, the pillar that had once held up the roof—bounced apart and then came together with Rector's elbow area flattened between two beams the size of railroad ties. The weight of a mile of rock stood upon the pack compressing his arm.

Percy half stood, half hung, with tears pouring from his red eyes and inhuman sounds coming from his open red mouth, his face a coal-black wet mask of affliction.

The men hustled around him. "Oh my God, oh my God," they said. "Oh Jesus, oh Jesus." Those with working headlamps eyed every side of the structure, scarcely able to believe what they saw. "Oh, Jesus, his arm is all the way in there," said Frank Hunter. "Boys, look, his hand is sticking out on the other side."

"What am I doing here? What am I doing here?" Currie Smith thought wildly to himself. "I'm not going to be able to stand this. When anybody talks about blood, whenever I see blood, I generally faint."

Rector's upper arm was flattened as if he had no arm there at all, but rather an armless shirtsleeve like an amputee's. If you slammed the fat of your hand in the hinge of a car door, with lightning speed you would get to the handle and wrench the door open. Percy's speed and desperation were no less. Open-mouthed, panting, wailing, wild-eyed, Percy looked from one to another of the men. He was savage for them to free him. With his free arm and shoulder, he went almost double-jointed trying to grasp the lumber trapping him.

"Get me out!" he wailed. "Get me out! Get me out! Get me out!"

He was a fox with his paw in a trap; he would gnaw off his arm if he could get his teeth on it. The others had only their bare hands with which to try to spring him. An upheaval from the core of the earth had flung up these timbers and bounced them down again; how could the few bare-handed survivors have the strength to undo it? They'd have as much luck putting their shoulders against the brick post office in town and trying to shove it a few meters.

Rooting around in the debris, a couple of men uncovered a piece of a rusty saw. While Percy dangled, in spasms of agony, they angled the blade against a piece of the pack wood to see if they might cut him loose. But in a terrifying instant, the pack groaned and shifted, the cave trembled, and pebbles pelted their helmets. Percy's pack was the pillar holding up the rock ceiling! It was as if they huddled in a tent with one post, with only a canopy between them and a million tons of dirt and rock. Too much fiddling and they might, like Samson, bring down the roof.

"Please," Percy sobbed. "Please. Help me. *Please!*" His big free arm swung out like the oar of a rowboat.

Maurice Ruddick brought water and, wiping Percy's face with his fingers, calmed him long enough to take a sip. Percy gagged down the water, choking and wailing between swallows, as the uninjured men sat nearby with lowered heads.

6

When a Miner Says It's Bad, Look Out

THURSDAY, OCTOBER 23, 8:26 P.M.

"Move back! Move back! They're coming out!" called onlookers at the pithead twenty minutes after the bump. Those in front tried to shove the others back, while those in the rear pushed forward to have a look. As folks jostled and shouldered in a sort of reverse tug-of-war, a dozen miners emerged. Dazed men materialized at the door of the shed, some limping, some holding their arms, some bleeding from their noses, some helping others to walk. They were unrecognizable, striped black and red. "Are you all right?" someone called, and though he kept walking, one miner said, "It looks like a pile of spaghetti down there."

The crowd hushed, in awe.

"When a *miner* says it's bad, look out," Dr. Arnold Burden thought.

John Totten's brother stumbled out of the shed and John ran to him. "What happened?"

The miner had to get away from the crowd, find a building, and sit down with his back against the wall before he could catch his breath and talk. "I was running a double-down haulage on the low side of the level, at thirteen-four, and it knocked me down, give me a big bat on the side of the face, knocked my teeth out, and feels like it busted my eardrums. The level is all in."

"Well, there will be no chance at all on the wall, then," said John. He helped his brother to the car and headed for the hospital.

8:40 P.M.

Arnold Burden, one of the town's two doctors, a World War II veteran, and a summer mine worker during his student years, threaded his way through the mob into the mine manager's office. It was chaos there, too. "The telephones are out from the 7800 level on down!" the shift foreman was shouting. Burden volunteered to enter the mine to look for survivors.

Arnold Burden had been a know-it-all pipsqueak of a kid, in possession of polysyllabic words and straight-A report cards. His father was a machinist and his grandfather a mine manager. On the street as a child, Arnold let fly with sneers instead of putting up his fists; but, if a bully turned out to be too obtuse to appreciate clever barbs, the boy tried to stand his ground, bolstering his courage with thoughts of literary and military heroes. He never did bulk up; he arrived at adulthood pale, thin, and short, a nasal-voiced elf in a business suit, living in a town of men built like fullbacks. But there was that brainpower, of which he was rightfully proud. Unlike his peers, he had gone to college, then on to medical school, served in World War II as a medic, and returned to Springhill to practice. Now the miners' sons—miners themselves—squeezed into the armchairs in the carpeted waiting room of Dr. Burden's office. At home, Mrs. Burden, wearing a pearl necklace, tended to the African violets. The dining-room table gleamed with lemon wax.

At the pithead in the early moments of tumult, Burden was like a benchwarmer in a losing game, jogging in place and urging, "Put me in, Coach."

The manager called over Burden's head to Wrecking Crew member Floyd Gilroy: "Floyd, get changed and get down there." But like a coach who sees that the game is going straight to hell and realizes that he can use all the help he can get, the mine manager looked Burden up and down and said one word: "Go."

The doctor ran to the washhouse, changed into an outsize miner's outfit—the coveralls and boots so big on him, he might have been a child playing dress-up—and climbed into the "rake," the trolley, along with a mine official and ten draegermen, the trained volunteer rescuers in gas masks. Doc Burden traveled bare-faced because he had not been trained in the use of a mask. He rode down into the stirred-up darkness beside silent creatures in gas masks who looked as smoothly indestructible as giant cockroaches.

And yet their courage was almost as great as his. In the Explosion of 1956, draegermen in gas masks had tumbled forward into poisonous clouds of gas and died.

9:00 P.M.

A forty-nine-year-old miner named Lloyd who had come under fire in World War II and had done bare-faced rescue work in '56, reached three times for his coveralls but could not take them from the hook in the washhouse. "I've lost my nerve," he thought. "I just can't. I can't make it. That's all there is to it." Instead, he tried to offer himself as a volunteer on the surface, to help out in any way he could. But there were plenty of volunteers on the surface, and he could see he was in the way. "I feel terrible. I know that I broke. I completely broke and I can't go down. If I go down there and go all to pieces, I'll have to have two men to bring me up, where those two men could continue on and do something valuable."

Floyd Gilroy, the father of ten whose daughter had been bounced off the toilet, was among the first to enter No. 2. He rode down at 9 P.M., fifty-five minutes after the bump. He got the hang of the situation rapidly and was asked to orient the fresh rescue workers as they reported for duty underground.

"You got to dig them out," he told a group of bare-faced miners. "Maybe strike a boot-toe first, maybe strike a cap first. You might strike his fingers first. Some of them are in fairly decent shape and other ones are not." He stayed underground till 5 A.M., then went home to sleep for a few hours. He told his wife, "My buddy took so sick he had to go home. I think maybe my stomach is just a little stronger than his, could take a little more. The smell was starting to turn; we had that spray stuff which did help a lot but didn't kill it all. We had rubber gloves on, but even so we had to handle every body. I just took sick and went to throw up and went back to work. Some fellows just to look at them would turn sick, and some fellows couldn't eat." He slept a few hours and then returned to the pit.

9:30 P.M.

An off-shift miner named Arthur anxiously hung around the pithead in the dusky hours after the disaster. High-wattage spotlights kept the oceans of night away. It was a dusty, stirred-up, tawdry dusk, like a carnival night. Cigarette smoke made the clear night hazy. The site flared an even brighter gray when television newsmen drove in from the towns of Amherst and Moncton, and brighter still when journalists arrived from the cities of Halifax and Toronto with their camera lights up on stilts. Arthur's clenched hands twisted in and out of his jacket pockets; his thin neck stretched for news. He was thirty-one, had been in the mines for seventeen years, and hated the work.

A father of four, he'd been underground that May when a minor bump had rippled through No. 2 and buried him in a fall of coal. His comrades had discovered his stuck fingers wiggling at the top of the heap, and when they freed him, Arthur was wild to get out, in claustrophobic panic. He looked frantically at his rescuers, then took off running for the slope.

He'd laid out from work for four months and enrolled in bookkeeping and typing courses. But money was tight and he had returned to his regular shift in No. 2 in September. A smaller bump had rattled the mine just a few days earlier and Arthur had sprinted down the wall. When the small bump—a hiccup, really—died down, he halted, turned, and came back silently; sick with fear, head down, he barely registered his buddies laughing at him.

Now he paced for news at the pithead. He had an idea where his father had been working and he buttonholed everyone emerging from the shed.

"We can't find out nothing!" he exploded after another stunned survivor limped by him. "They don't know nothing!"

Two hours after the cave-in, Arthur spotted a man he knew. "Carmen! Carmen Fraser! Is that Carmen? Where's my father?"

"He's coming up."

"Is he all right?"

"Yeah, he's all right."

Arthur, jittery, wanted more news. "What about Bill Millard?" he called.

"He's all right," a man said, and Arthur ran off to tell Millard's wife the good news. He returned to the pit, found his father, and drove him home, then went to his own house.

But there was no thought of going to bed, not for anyone that night. With his wife, Arthur watched scenes from the pithead on the local TV news, but he was desperately afraid he was going to be called in for rescue work. He was planning not to volunteer and was hoping to be overlooked. "Nerves," he told his wife, pacing before a window. "My stomach couldn't stand it."

"They'll have plenty of volunteers. They won't need me," he said a while later.

And later still, "I wouldn't last down there if it was me. I'm not the type that could stand the pressure of being trapped down there alive. I'd go crazy, that's all. Or I would wander off into the waste and be killed."

He got into bed wide awake, his mouth dry. It put him in mind of the first time he had stayed up all night as a kid, sitting in the dark at the top of the stairs, because there was a dead man in the house. A man who boarded with Arthur's family had died, and seeing the open casket on the dining-room table had so upset the child, he was afraid of the dark for many years.

The miners who emerged without grave injury in the first few hours after the disaster were swept home in the arms of their crying families, or they jubilantly, haggardly burst, surrounded by pals, into a dimly lit house already tilted half into mourning. Then all the lamps came on, and the wife ran upstairs crying and got dressed and roused the children as the downstairs filled up with company, and bottles of beer were flipped open, and children flew downstairs in nightgowns and bare feet to hug their filthy pa, and folks gathered around the kitchen table to hear the terrible tale told by a man in a black mask.

7

A Dark Chaos

THURSDAY, OCTOBER 23, 8:06 P.M.

Harold Brine was a handsome guy of twenty-five who wore his shiny black hair back-combed like Elvis Presley. His thick black eyebrows and jutting rough-shaved jaw made him look cut out for manly work, if not for movie acting. To the teenage girls in town, he was a dreamboat, but married. His wife hated the mines and professed not to know why he worked there. "The wife is always growling about the mines, chewing the rag about the mines. She is dissatisfied in Springhill," he'd say to his buddies. "But I'm never afraid in the mine," he thought to himself. "Never, ever afraid."

His workplace was one level deeper than that of Maurice Ruddick and Percy Rector and the rest who landed in the Group of Seven. On Thursday night, Harold Brine rode the coal car down to Eldred Lowther's loading site at the 13,000 level and cracked, "Are you going to stand there looking at that stuff, Lowther, or are you going to load it?"

Lowther was jumpy. "Did you feel that bump a while ago?" he asked Brine nervously, but as Lowther pronounced *bump,* as if the word were an incantation, Harold Brine flew away. "Oh man, I said 'bump' and he flew," thought Lowther. "I seen him going. I seen his feet, that's it." Then Lowther took off after him.

"The roof has come in on us! No, it's we are going up to the roof! I'm like a bullet shot out of a gun. I am killed."

Throughout the underground, miners were skidding along on the seats of their pants through the dark, as if sledding along an icy hill, until they crashed into the coal face, crushing their hands and wrists in front of them trying to stop.

The bump roared at Hughie Guthro then took him and threw him underneath the conveyor pans full of coal. Hughie went in feet first and was buried up to his neck in coal under the conveyor belt. Larry Leadbetter felt a little shiver under his feet before the upheaval. Levi Milley heard a *whoosh,* which flipped him upside down. Ted Michniak felt everything on the move and himself moving with it. Joe McDonald was working at the coal face when the coal face stepped toward him.

Deep underground, darkness and silence ruled for an unknown length of time. The narrow layers of air swarmed with coal dust as if the flying particles and specks of coal were the only things in the universe, like the black, charged, stirred-up matter that must have been around in the eons before the Creation. In the swirling blackness, the men's faces stung as if in a sandstorm. Some unconscious, some dying, they were zinged and pelted where they lay by a thousand small meteorites of coal.

Gorley Kempt woke up to find himself squeezed up against the roof in air heavy with gas. Pressed tight, he squirmed, trying to find a way to duck his head beneath it. He surveyed the cave with a feeling of vertigo; it looked like gravity had given out. The massive machinery, compressors, rail tracks, and coal cars, had come unglued from the ground and had been shoved against the ceiling by the broken floors. The equipment hung in bizarre silhouettes seeming to sway slightly and a little menacingly.

Upside down and practically inside-out, Gorley had lost which way was up, the way they say a drowning man can't find his way to the surface.

Not far away, Hughie Guthro woke up in his wormhole of coal, arms squeezed by his sides. All around him the bump had taken the floor and slammed it into the ceiling—"Everywhere the same, the floor went up, except right here, where it looks like I've got about four feet of head space. Why here?" he wondered. "Why didn't my section go up?"

"Everything is right to the roof," Leadbetter saw, when he woke up in eight inches of breathing space. "The rails, and the unit I was operating, are just a mass of steel all smashed and drove right into the roof."

Ted Michniak was yelling through the darkness, to no one in particular, "Get down! Get your heads down!" Then Gorley saw Bowman Maddison, in panic, grasp his water can and dump two buckets of water over his head to dispel the gas, a cascade of fresh water he would recall with poignance in days to come.

Fred Hunter had just fetched a piece of chain and was walking up the 13,400 wall with it. He heard nothing and felt nothing. When he woke up, he found himself on the ground with a mouthful of coal and blood. He tried to stand up and couldn't. "My leg is caught," he realized. "What happened? How long have I been out?"

Out of the dark and rock-storm at the 13,400 level, a man was crying.

Everyone still alive, in whatever cannonball or forced knee-bend or double-jointed posture the earthquake had left him in, recognized that it was the wailing of an exceptionally sane and good man, and for this reason it had an especially mournful sound. In the chaos of place and time, the cries came from everywhere, from out of the rock, but recognizably as the voice of Caleb Rushton. His yelps of pain and fright brought many dazed men to consciousness.

Larry Leadbetter was wondering if he was the only survivor, when he heard Caleb hollering. "All right," he thought, "there are some other men here, but I don't know how many or how bad they are hurt."

"It's Caleb," thought Gorley Kempt. "I don't know whether he's hollering at anything, but he sure is hollering." Gorley called in the dark, "Caleb! Just stay right where you are. Don't try to get out yet. Just wait till I get hold of my lamp and I'll see." He groped around and found his cord and yanked his lamp out from under fallen rock but was weirdly drained by the effort and unable to go on.

Levi Milley had been turned upside down by the bump, but was unhurt. He was by nature a melancholy man, narrow-faced and emotionally tepid, who went about his tasks with an affectless look, as if he were taking out the garbage. Finding himself uninjured, he went about his business without betraying by his manner that these chores were dramatically different. In the black sandstorm, guided by his headlamp, he abruptly loomed over Caleb Rushton and found him thrown against a pack, slashed across the face, half-buried by stones, semiconscious, and yelling. Milley, with an assist from Fred Hunter, shoved the stones off Caleb's legs, and moved off into the haze. Caleb stared after him wide-eyed and stopped hollering.

With Caleb silenced, the wails of other men were heard.

Joe McDonald woke up alone and confused, at some distance below the others. He was thirty-eight, with a solid athletic build and a clean-shaven face that looked peaceful and kind in repose, but well-lined and a good ten or fifteen years older than he was. The Explosion of '56 and prior years of alcoholism had aged him. Darkness panicked him. Since the Explosion, he'd wanted a night-light in his bedroom at night. Now he found himself in a sitting position with one leg crushed under an enormous fan.

McDonald saw a glimmer of someone's headlamp above him. "The others must be looking for me," he thought. He began shouting, "I'm here, I'm down here! Fellows, I'm here!"

No one came. He shouted more, but they were uninterested. "They're not bothering with me!" he suddenly thought. "They weren't looking for me; they were looking for a way out." As he tried to breathe between his pain and his shouting, he heard still other screams. "There's a young fellow out on the level. I've never heard such pitiful screeches and cries. Why won't they pull him out?

"Oh Jesus, why don't you pull him out?" he yelled.

"They're paying no attention," he thought again, catching glimpses of headlamps bobbing through the black fog. "They're running up and down like crazy men." The screams of the young man on the level were driving him mad. "What's going on? Why won't they pull him out?"

Joe Holloway stumbled across the head of Hughie Guthro, which nearly gave him a heart attack. Hughie's head seemed to be resting on the ground like a basketball. In terror, Holloway aimed his headlamp at the situation and saw that Hughie was intact, but buried. He knelt to scratch at the coal around Hughie's neck, but was dizzied by waves of gas and fell to his knees, gagging.

Harold Brine, with the movie-star good looks, crawled free of the trap he'd found himself in and took over the task of freeing Hughie. He was just about knocked out from the gas but he would not leave him. "If I'm going to get going, you are going to go with me, Hugh," he told him. It was friendship, it was training, it was morality, it was the Code. The Code, after all, had been made by men like him and from elements like these: decency, friendship, emergency. Brine knew that Guthro would do the same for him, for any man. Brine dug with his bare hands until Hughie Guthro was free. Hughie was filthy but unhurt.

Larry Leadbetter also was hollering from someplace, "I can't get out! I can't get out! Help me!"

"That's Leadbetter screaming at the top of his voice," said Hughie Guthro to Harold Brine, so the two of them crept toward Leadbetter, whose panic was increasing. They neared a small cranny of rock from which his voice bellowed. Then they smelled gas. "We can't get closer!" Hughie yelled into the cranny. "There's too much gas there." In a flash, Leadbetter shoved by him, running. "He *passed* us? *He* passed *us*? Jesus Christ!" thought Hughie Guthro. "He wasn't caught in there at all, he was just scared to death to move. We told him it was gassy and he goes by us like a streak of lightning." Even in these early minutes after the disaster, a sorting out was beginning, an appraisal of comrades.

No one had yet stumbled upon Joe McDonald, who was feeling utterly abandoned and grimly certain that he was going to be left behind as others found their way out. His growing sense of injustice in his own case now encompassed the injured man out on the level. He called out on his own behalf and on behalf of the young man whose sobs he could still hear. "He's right out there!" Joe called to the yellow lights in the distance. "He's only about a thousand feet out. Forget me, go get him! You can get to him!" But though he could see, in the distance, lights coming together and parting in joint actions, he could attract none toward himself, not even by this act of selflessness. What was the cruel secret to luring the indifferent headlamps? "For the love of God!" he called out, and dropped his head, moaning, unable to get himself completely out from under the huge fan.

Those moving around, picking their way over the rock, did what humans do to survive: they went in search of other humans. They limped and crawled and cursed their way toward one another. Then they stood, their blackened faces shining in the black air, with here and there the maroon gleam of a gash on an arm or face, breathing hard, swaying or staggering as gusts of gas hit them. Suddenly a couple of men dropped to the floor like soldiers at the word *incoming*. They had smelled gas wafting toward them. Between dropping and getting back up, bending over to retch, by the yellow light of the working headlamps, through the typhoon of coal dust, they began figuring out who was there, and in what kind of shape. Each noted in silence the other men he was given to work with, scrolling quickly through memory to an abbreviated conclusion: "A good man" or "a layabout," "my pal" or "never had much use for him."

In order of age, they were:

Ted Michniak, 58. "Agh, a miner's job is not fit for anyone," he always grumbled. A strong man with arms of iron and a full head of gray hair, he was growing slower, heavier, and more disappointed with his life year by year. "If you really thought about No. 2, you wouldn't work in it, would you?" He was standing, huffing, among the others, but the pain he felt in his shoulder was nearly unbearable.

Fred Hunter, 49, the twin of Frank Hunter who was trapped with the Group of Seven, had been in the mine thirty-one years and looked worn-out, with the long-lined face of an old man. Vertical creases ran from the outside corners of his eyes through the middle of his long cheeks. "Unemotional," others found him, "a stagnant type," "like his twin," "not much enthusiasm." He was, in fact, grievously injured at this moment, his leg bleeding internally, but he shuffled up to stand with the rest and was never really placed, in their minds, on the injured list.

Levi Milley, 47, a thin, rather affectless, monosyllabic man, a chain-smoker. "Had a happy childhood till my father died when I was fourteen. Left school after grade six. Worked at farming, errand boy, and in the woods till I could become a miner. There was no other job available and my mother was a widow." The liveliest thing in his life was his sixteen-year-old daughter—"I love that girl."

Eldred Lowther, 45, twenty-eight years in the mine, thought of himself as the oldest and most experienced of the group, though he was neither. As he stood looking around at the haggard crew surviving the bump, he inwardly geared himself up to assume leadership. He believed the others were thinking the same thing about him. "I went in the army A-1," he reminded himself, "and I come out A-1."

Bowman Maddison, 42, a tall quiet man, a stamp collector and songwriter, who'd mailed in some of his songs to a national radio contest. He was Caleb Rushton's work buddy and close friend.

Gorley Kempt, 39, a playful, scrawny, mischievous guy who owned a cottage at the shore; married to wry, plain-talking Margie. Father of two.

Caleb Rushton, 35, a calm and kind man, a churchgoer and book reader. He'd finished eleventh grade—nearly the equivalent, in Springhill, of a college degree. He spoke well, rationally, and with a clipped, Irish-sounding brevity and lilt, which is why his unconscious shrieks in the first moments after the bump panicked everyone else.

Joe Holloway, 35, Hughie Guthro's best friend, with whom he'd gotten lost in the woods the year before. Possessing only a sixth-grade education, he was a shy man, easily overlooked. He had been wounded in France during World War II, taking shrapnel in his left arm and leg. He enjoyed a game of darts at Miners' Hall and was very tenderly regarded by his wife, Loretta. They were raising two little daughters, but had lost two babies at birth.

Hughie Guthro, 31, the rubbery-limbed, rubbery-faced strongman, already rattled by the Explosion of '56, devoted to Margie and their children. He was full of experience and practical thinking. He talked out the side of his mouth and had a hard, round head; with his muscled arms and side-talking way, he looked like Popeye the sailor.

Harold Brine, 25, the handsome fellow with the gleaming ridge of black hair who inspired giggles when he said hello to schoolgirls on Main Street.

Larry Leadbetter, 22, three years in the mine, already married and the father of two; with a teenager's love of music. He was the son of Suki Leadbetter, a celebrated baseball player in the Maritime Provinces. He and his wife had lost a child. "I'm a mechanic, and I read a lot of mechanic books," Leadbetter would say about himself. "And I like music, old-time music, fiddle tunes. I like to play. I can't play too good, just more or less scratch away at it."

"All right, there's none of us seriously hurt," announced Eldred Lowther after they'd all finished staring at each other. (He was wrong.) "But some fellow down below us is still hollering."

Several, hearing the sad cries, slipped and squatted their way down a pitch-black slope of coal and finally found Joe McDonald. They pushed the fan off his leg. So they were a group of twelve.

McDonald, though only thirty-eight years old, had worked in the mines for nineteen years, had been exposed to poisonous gas many times, and had survived the Explosion of 1956. His blond hair was graying at the sides and his face was deeply lined. He'd been an alcoholic for nearly two decades and had had a bad temper when drinking, but he attended Alcoholics Anonymous, remained sober, and kept the temper under control. He was a decent and restrained man, devoted to his family. Now he was in the grip of raw survival again, and in agony.

More men slid down the slope to have a look at him. "You can see just by looking at him, his leg is broke," said Lowther. "He is in a bad way."

"This bone here is coming out this way; that bone goes down that way," said Hughie Guthro.

Joe, in agony from his wrong-angled leg, withstood the pain in quiet misery, sucking on his lips to keep from weeping, when the men arrived and began tidying up his area. He understood that he was in such bad shape, the others felt it necessary to talk over him rather than address him directly. "Let's see what we can do for him," said Gorley kindly. "We've got a pick and a saw. Let's prop up a roof over him, to help protect him." Joe lay back in silent, bitter vindication and began to draw comfort from the fact that, after all his hours alone and neglected, they were paying attention.

But then, talking amongst themselves, they went away again, and though he propped his head up on his hand, he couldn't quite make out their words. He was suddenly alone in the dark again! Their stupid efforts at shoring up his crevice were worth nothing to him if he was going to be abandoned. He felt as if his chest would explode with outrage and disappointment and fear. "Get me out of here!" he yelled, his throat closing up with sorrow. Due to his injury, he'd been placed on the group's back burner, he saw. They headed off with more pressing concerns. He couldn't accept it. The injustice of it was impossible to swallow. Alone again, weeping bitterly in the threatening dark, Joe McDonald realized the young man out on the level had fallen silent.

Higher up the slope, the two injured men who were still standing—Fred Hunter and Ted Michniak—also understood that there were more urgent concerns than their injuries. It was just their bad luck that they'd have to be left behind while the others searched for an exit. The whole crew of them needed to get the hell out of there before the gas overtook them.

8

"If There Are Boys Alive, They'll Be Expecting Us"

By the small hours of Friday morning, seventy-five surviving miners had been led or carried out to safety. Children kept running into the lamp cabin to see if their dads had reclaimed their brass tags from the board. A still-dangling tag meant a still-missing miner. The board was full of tokens.

Arthur, the off-shift miner who had been too jittery to remain at the pit the night before, gave up trying to sleep. His hand was shaking so badly, he could hardly take a cup of coffee before driving back to the pit. A mine manager was calling the names of men in the crowd and asking them to descend as bare-faced rescuers. Arthur made himself get out of the car and stand among them, but he willed himself to be invisible, like a kid in school without the right answer. The shift manager scanned the crowd and saw him. Their eyes met, too late for Arthur to look nonchalantly away, and his name was called.

"It may bump again," he couldn't help thinking, pushing forward underground in a knot of men, wading through the debris.

There were damp puddles underfoot, where a miner's blood had leaked out from under fallen rock. Arthur's headlamp shone down on them. The victims were unseen; only their blood came trickling out, like long, flat, prying fingers from under the rock, creeping toward freedom. He marked the spots with chalk, for the blood would soak into the earth before men could get back for the bodies—unearthing miners from a shared grave to re-bury them in shallower ones closer to home.

Nausea coiled in Arthur's belly. "My head is aching. I don't know if it's the pressure, or the gas, or what it is, but I can't stand it."

"My back just gave out," he told the men. After a respectable length of time, he exited. Ducking his head, hiding behind his black mask of coal, he slunk to his car, stayed low in the seat, and rumbled home.

"Don't go back down!" his wife urged when she saw Arthur, whiter and jumpier.

"They might not need me again," he said hopefully.

5:30 A.M.

No one else came out. As the silence was worse than the bumps that preceded it, the open, empty door of the shed was worse than the sight of badly injured miners. In the last hours before dawn, a gathering crowd waited in silence for more men to emerge. Where were the ninety-nine others?

Old-timer Percy McCormick had descended immediately, Thursday night, to help escort dazed survivors up the slope, but within the first six hours the job turned macabre and required him, instead, to try to retrieve the dead. "I've got a body here, trying to get it clear, digging it out, getting the pieces. I know all these boys but I can't recognize them. Never in my life have I had dealings with dead bodies before. But these were real good men. We need to get them out."

As he worked harder, longer hours than his usual shift, his

recent injuries plagued him. "Two months ago, I got quite a whack in the head and my side and my back. I've had headaches since that bump on September 28. I'm all over headaches and sharp pains." He worked relentlessly, took breaks to go off by himself to a crevice to vomit, and came back to work. He went home to try to sleep but the smell tailed him. He couldn't eat, and when he went to light his furnace, it was like the smell of the bodies was in it. Back in the mine, he felt himself getting dopey. "It's too much gas," he thought. "It's acting on us like chloroform. This is too hard on us." He stopped for a while, hung over his pick, trying to breathe and quell the nausea. "But if there are boys alive in here, they know we are coming. There may be one or two down and out but still alive. If we can get one man out alive, it will be worth it." A man like Percy McCormick was the Miners' Code incarnate.

The miners' wives were crumpling under the exhaustion and agony of not knowing their husbands' fates, while having to fend for themselves within jarring mobs of onlookers and volunteers. "Fidel was always the first one in the cart to go down into the mine," said Sadie Allen, wringing and wringing her hands while her children looked around desperately for a way to comfort her. "I'm quite certain today was no exception. He always joked that he hoped the 'big one' wouldn't happen on his shift." She stood her ground for hours, resisting orders to move back, bleakly beseeching every emerging black-faced survivor to give news of her Fidel, whom folks called Paul. "Yeah, I think I saw Paul," one of the emerging rescuers finally said. "I think he's okay." The response was so vague, Sadie couldn't allow herself to believe it, though her children whirled around with happy faces, eager to see her smile, too. In pity for the children, she cranked up a painful grimace that only scared them. Finally, after an endless night of being jostled and disappointed at the pithead, Sadie, like many of the other women, found a neighbor to lean on and agreed to be guided back home. All around her, wives and mothers were being helped home by family friends along the route they'd charged down like racehorses a few hours earlier. Miserably, slowly, they moved as if they'd suddenly grown old.

The raucous TVs they found still going in their front rooms addressed an audience of an earlier lifetime, now vanished. The half-eaten piles of cold food on the plates on the table, the cold tubs of bathwater, the house slippers near the sofa, were like things unearthed from a long-lost epoch, like museum dioramas behind glass: "Coal-Miner Home, circa 1958." During the canned laughter, the ground beneath the housewives had dropped away, literally.

6 A.M.

Elaine Turnbull wrapped her arms around herself, shivering more with fear than with cold before dawn. She stood on the sunporch, looking out at the quiet street.

She and Billy had known each other since she was sixteen and Bill, twenty-one. "I was just a child. He was so outgoing that you noticed him in a crowd, the life of the party. He wasn't very big: five-six, a hundred and fifty pounds. He wasn't interested in me. That was just as well, because Pop would never have allowed me to go out with anyone that age! But when I met him again a year later, he was quite impressed with how I had matured. We started going steady. When he was twenty-four and I was nineteen, we were both ready for marriage. Our wedding was on the first day of a miners' holiday. It began early in the morning and went on all day and with a dance that night.

We didn't get away till late that night to a cabin we reserved on Prince Edward Island. And at six o'clock the next morning, there was a loud rapping at the door. 'Who knows we're here?' I thought. But there was a big group of Springhillers come to pick us up to tag along with them on a trip to New York. I was really afraid Bill was going to say yes, but he thanked them and told them that no, we had our cabin reserved, and we'd see them after their vacation.

"So we went to Prince Edward Island. We were there a day when we ran into another whole group of Springhillers downtown. We were with those people for about three days. I know they were on holiday, but I didn't expect them to go on my honeymoon with me! We came back on a Saturday night and there was a dance at the playground. When we came in, they played the Homecoming Waltz and I was so touched because that was for us.

"He's the youngest in a large, close-knit family, and devoted to his mother. I've always been very fond of her, too, and she of me. The first year we lived with his parents and saved for a down payment on a house. We moved in the following spring. We've been so happy! Happy to have a place of our own. I put up light wallpaper over the dark in the living room, and I painted the woodwork—oh, my mother-in-law didn't like that, because it was Douglas fir! But it was so dark, I've never regretted it. Life is good. We have lots of friends our own age."

Billy must have been afraid in the mine, she realized later, but he never told her. "He was so protective of me. He has never really discussed his work with me, or the working conditions. I've heard that he speaks up about it at union meetings. I think he feels that I'm still, in some ways, a child, even though we have four children! I just kind of accept it because I was the baby in my family. I think he doesn't want me to pressure him to leave the mines—which I would! He's a mechanic; he loves working on cars. But he loves the men he works with; he calls them his buddies.

"I gather that it is a difficult, very dangerous time in the mines. They lined up the walls or something. All the older miners fought against it and said it would cause a serious bump. And now it has."

As she stood on her porch in the predawn chill, she felt desperate to communicate with Billy. "I have friends," she thought, "who claim to be so close they communicate through mental telepathy. I always told them it was a lot of hokum, but maybe I can reach Billy." She pulled herself up the stairs which felt to her as rocky as if she were on a boat in rough weather. Feeling as if she were about to throw up, she dragged a chair to the window and sat facing the mine.

"Listen to me, Billy," she thought. "Please don't panic. Remember everything you've been taught. Keep your head up." She wondered then if she was confused, and if he was supposed to keep his head down. She couldn't remember which was the correct advice for miners and which for soldiers.

9

"Oh Dear, Oh Dear, I Would Help You if You Was Caught"

GROUP OF SEVEN
Garnet Clarke, Frank Hunter, Doug Jewkes, Herb Pepperdine,
Percy Rector, Maurice Ruddick, Currie Smith
FRIDAY, OCTOBER 24, 2 A.M.
SIX HOURS SINCE THE BUMP

Near the old 12,600 level, the six men in the Group of Seven huddled around the seventh, Percy Rector, the prisoner of the fallen pack of timber. Even if it had stood above ground, such a trap would have been difficult to pry open, employing many men, and this one had the heavy hand of the crust of the earth pressing down on it while the men slapping and kicking at it were dazed and dizzy. Percy engaged in heroic red-faced flogging and convulsions, trying to pull himself out from between the logs, and wailed with frustration and grief.

As in the Group of Twelve, the men in this Group of Seven had found and appraised each other, each man, in his heart of hearts, looking for a buddy. It was the miners' way to work in pairs. Those whose partner was dead or missing gravitated to the next best thing—the wife's cousin, the neighbor, the fellow church member—and made with him an unspoken pact, a makeshift emergency twinship.

Though no one ever had a word to say against his job performance, close friendships with his fellow miners eluded Maurice Ruddick. "Ted Michniak, him and I are pretty good pals," Maurice would tell Norma. "He gives me a sandwich; I give him a chew of gum. I had some pains coming up through my neck last week and I borrowed some aspirins from him and I told him I would pay him back and he said, 'Oh, don't bother—forget it, Ruddick.' But I took some aspirins down and paid him back."

While black coal miners did not get promoted above whites and there were none in management, at the level of laborer they were equals. Maurice's children played with white friends at school and in the neighborhood; the white children often stayed for dinner; their parents sometimes asked Norma to trim their children's hair when she lined up her own kids in the yard for haircuts. But Maurice knew he wasn't a close pal of any of the men on the job. Of course, folks naturally socialized most with their own color, and he and Norma had their hands full just raising their family. But he didn't expect to be chosen as an emergency buddy by any of the fellows with whom he was trapped.

Well-schooled in the taciturn code of the miners, cleverly watchful and a dodger by nature, and, moreover, a kind man, Ruddick withheld complaint, figured every man has been handed his personal cup of sorrow, and kept his problems to himself.

Currie Smith was trying to outshout Percy Rector. "If we had a RR jack, we could jack the pack up and get his arm out!" he hollered between Percy's screams. "Garnie, there's a jack out on the timber road. Why not go get it?"

Garnet Clarke hurried off, but was back in a moment. "Currie!" he yelled. "You better come here and look."

Garnet showed Currie that the road was gone. A fall of fresh coal was heaped up in its place. They poked about in the strange landscape in search of an exit, or at least a tool, but found instead seven bodies in ten minutes.

"Currie!" wept Percy when the two men returned. "Oh dear, oh dear, Currie. I would help you if you was caught. Can you please help me?" He wailed heartbreakingly, like a small child, his mouth a wet red oblong in the wet black face.

"If I could do anything for you, Perce, I would," Currie cried back miserably.

"It's impossible!" yelled Frank Hunter. "We can't do a thing for him unless we had a power saw. We'd have to have a power saw to cut a piece right out of the pack."

The men were making themselves hoarse shouting above Percy's shrieks. There was nothing to be done for him. They squatted worriedly nearby, looking at the ground as if trying to think of a solution or sketch one out in the dirt. They kept their faces averted from him. They scooted and edged, guiltily, inch by inch, away from where he hung until they reached the limits of the cave, which wasn't far away at all. Some lay down with their faces turned away from him. You couldn't sleep with that going on or get any rest at all, you couldn't even think. His screams— "Help me! Help me! Oh mother! Mama! Oh Jesus Christ!"— were transformed into some kind of primeval, animal tongue; they were all the more unmistakable for that. *Aaaarrrrgggghhhh* gurgled his larynx, as if the hollering throat were a separate fiery living thing, an enraged scorpion tearing and tearing at them. A few men put their hands over their ears, others over their eyes.

Within the first day, the horror of the scene and their powerlessness to help Percy had numbed the men. Maurice alone was able to stay near Percy and look at him. He talked to him softly, with fatherly gentleness, and wiped his tear-strewn face and calmed him long enough to allow him to take sobbing gulps from the water can, the sobs then like a small boy's.

Maurice asked the men for aspirin and fed a handful to Perce; the medication couldn't touch the pain, really, but it seemed that Percy's screams blasted at a slightly lower volume. Probably the engine of the man was starting to run down. He was breathing hard and staring wild-eyed from one to another of the men. The men kept their faces turned away, humiliated by their inaction. He eyed them, despite their ducking heads, and made personal appeals.

"Pep," he pleaded. "Pep. We always been good buddies, hadn't we, Pep?"

"Sure, Perce."

"Help me, Pep," Percy wheedled. "Can you just help me a little bit, help me get loose here?"

"Sure, Percy, I'll try," said Pepperdine, and he did go jiggle the pack a little while Percy squeezed roundabout and squinted up at him with a stupid, drooling grin.

"I'm about to get out, eh, Pep? You're about to get me out, there's a good fellow."

Currie Smith chose to go exploring with Garnet Clarke rather than stay near the site of such a fixed horror. Pepperdine turned from stroking Percy's pack-wood trap and quickly offered, "I'll go with you." With Percy Rector as the backdrop, twisting and begging and blubbering, the men organized themselves into a posse in search of an exit. They were almost fainting with exhaustion. Lost in time and space, they'd been awake all night, but they pushed ahead mechanically.

"Don't do it, don't get out of this air!" Frank Hunter warned them. "If we are going to get the gas, it's going to be now, following the bump." The others paid him no heed.

Maurice stayed with Percy, murmuring soft assents to his wails and periodically tipping water onto his thrusting tongue, the tongue like a small wild animal, a frantic mouse bursting in and out of its hole.

10

In Black, White, and Silver

ABOVE GROUND
FRIDAY, OCTOBER 24, 8 A.M.
TWELVE HOURS SINCE THE BUMP

A bare-faced rescuer came up for air. Women crowded frantically around him, calling out names. "No ma'am, no ma'am," he said kindly. "I don't know. I didn't see him. No, I don't know."

"Are there many people killed down there?"

"Well, yes ma'am, there are bodies. We're marking the bodies for retrieval. The ones that died, well, it is my impression that they died within a minute of that bump."

Veteran miners and filthy rescuers huddled together grimly around the pithead as low gray clouds slid in from the coast. The Indian summer ended that night, the stars were cloaked, and a cold drizzle began, delaying sunrise and soaking the gravel and dirt underfoot. The men at the pithead chain-smoked and spoke in low tones and slurred speech, so the wives and mothers and children wouldn't overhear them. They agreed on one thing: "Whoever's not out by now is going to be down there for a long, long time."

Daylight came to Elaine Turnbull with no word from the pithead. The rest of the Turnbulls were at the mine, except for

Billy's mother, who had moved in to be with Elaine and was now trying to rest in a child's bedroom upstairs. Elaine was exhausted, accustomed to a good night's sleep, but unable to make herself lie down. She walked the floor and prayed and prayed and stopped at the window and faced in the direction of the mine. "Can you hear me, Billy? I love you so much. We need you. You have got to come home to us."

12 NOON

The Red Cross and the Salvation Army set up tents near the mine and offered coffee. A fleet of ambulances stood waiting near the mine entrance. Local restaurants distributed food to heartsick, exhausted relatives of the trapped men. Boy Scouts erected a tent and a sign that read, WANT ANYTHING DONE ASK A BOY SCOUT. The Royal Canadian Legion sent men to help keep order; many of the trapped men were veterans of World War II and the Legionnaires felt a debt of loyalty to them. Queen Elizabeth notified the mayor of her concern.

Journalists and photographers were rushing into Springhill from around the world. They came from newspapers and magazines and radio and television stations in Halifax, Toronto, Ontario, New York, Chicago, London, and Paris to cover the story. Most flew into Halifax and drove up from there. The *London Times* sent a reporter, as did *Paris Match,* the *New York Times, Life,* and CBS News. One hundred and thirty-seven reporters covered the story.

"We're in the way," CBC Radio personnel were thinking. "We're disruptive. We're having new phone lines put in. We show up and say, 'Hey, we need things to tell the world the news, we need this and that, we need office space and electrical hookups,' in a community that really is just concerned about whether these men are dead or alive."

Setting up at the Springhill scene, the CBC TV crewmen discovered they could fire a signal from their mobile unit directly into a land cable a few miles away, enabling them to broadcast live footage from the pithead, a technological breakthrough in world news reporting. Television news reporting was in its infancy; viewers had never before seen such dramatic on-the-spot footage. Now every fifteen-minute North American evening news show suddenly was able to broadcast live footage from the pithead. European networks were eager to televise the story of the mine disaster, too; the film images were processed as Kinescope in Toronto and carried by freighter planes across the Atlantic. It was the biggest radio and TV network patched together in history.

One broadcast reported: *In the latest accident in North America's deepest coal mine, seven more men have been brought to the surface here at Springhill, Nova Scotia, bringing the total rescued to eighty-three.*

Ninety-two men are still unaccounted for, trapped somewhere on the 13,000- and the 13,400-foot levels. Mine rescue crews, the famed draegermen, are being hampered in their rescue efforts by huge pockets of gas, and they still have no definite indication that any of the remaining ninety-two men are still alive.

But the people of Springhill are a special breed. Many wives spent all night at the pithead. They wait, huddled against buildings, hoping against hope that their men will be brought up alive. This is Jack McAndrew of the CBC reporting to WBZ.

As such broadcasts were relayed across the globe, the immediacy of the new media hooked distant strangers into a feeling of concern and involvement. Letters and cards and gifts of food, clothing, and cash began to arrive in Springhill from across the United States, from Honolulu, Germany, Greece, Mexico, and Cuba.

Alfred Eisenstaedt, Carl Mydans, and Joe Scherschel made photographs for *Life*. Rows of plain clapboard houses on a hill appeared in silhouette against the silver light of early morning. The corrugated aluminum shed at the pithead had a single thin door opening onto the mouth of the underworld. Pale women with their scarves knotted under their chins and blue-black half-moons under their eyes stood in vigil.

The gray sky and wet black streets, the oily puddles underfoot and the black rain slickers on the running officials, the white wood churches and the polished black hearses cast Springhill in black, white, and silver. Even if the black-and-white TV broadcasts and magazine layouts could have been made in color, the town wouldn't have looked any different.

3 P.M.

The phone rang at the house of the off-shift miner Arthur, nearly stopping his heart. It was what he'd dreaded: the order to come back to work. At the pithead, he was ordered to suit up and to dig in search of bodies.

"The smell is worse," he thought as he entered the underground. "Even when they've got the bodies in plastic bags, it's bad.

"It's when I find one that it's bad. I dig, then find a body. To touch something soft, and find it in the rock. My skin is all in gooseflesh." He couldn't bite into the sandwiches offered to the underground workers by other volunteers. "I can't," he said. "The smell. You try to eat and somebody shifts a body and the smell comes up new again."

"Eat? I can eat right alongside of them dead men," said John Totten. "It doesn't bother me."

"The worst part is," Arthur thought, "I know these men. I

know them personally. That's the thing. If I had no connection with these people, it wouldn't bother me as much. But I know this guy, I know his nickname, he was my buddy. That's what makes it so hard. Especially when you find a friend you really like, and you see him." The dazed stiffness of the bodies upset him, the stunned, hollow look of their white faces, their open, stunned, blind eyes and open, unbreathing mouths full of black dust. Here they were, all dressed for work, everything in place, their shirts buttoned, their boots tied, their helmets on, their wristwatches ticking, their full lunch buckets by their sides; they were like life-size wax figures of themselves.

When the crew chief let Arthur go home, he was relieved, but haunted, unable to find rest or deep sleep for a long, long time.

"No. 2," he told his wife, "she's a man-killer."

7 P.M.

Seventeen hundred miles southwest of Nova Scotia, in the land of Coca-Cola and all-you-can-eat barbecue, pecan pie and sweet onions, alligators and gnats, citizens of Georgia followed the story. Rabbit-eared televisions snared the signal broadcast live by the CBC. The footage of pale women and coal-smeared rescuers, tin caskets, and silver rain unrolled in real time, a true melodrama such as the newsprint and radio generations never had seen. Georgia Governor Marvin Griffin, however, was not watching the news. That very week, Governor Griffin was a guest of the Canadian government. From a cabin in the north woods of Saskatchewan, he was stalking moose with a hunting party. He hoped to hang a branch of moose antlers in his office to join the capitol's odd third-floor collection of arrowheads in Victorian cases, old guns, a stuffed and mounted two-headed calf, a petrified tree trunk, a stuffed two-headed snake, the world's oldest bale of cotton, and an exhibit of taxidermy-stuffed squirrels playing poker (and cheating).

Sam Caldwell, Griffin's young public relations aide and speech writer, rarely was included in the governor's boondoggles. A tall, good-looking white man of the country club type, he had wavy dark hair and a thin, pointed nose. He showed up for work at the capitol every day in a white shirt and wide tie, the shirt on the verge of yellowing with constant use and boredom, and he circled back in the evening to the bungalow he shared with his wife, Jeannette. That Friday evening, she was fascinated by the mine cave-in. Caldwell typically was bored by any news story he didn't have a hand in, but he shucked off his jacket after work and stood behind the sofa, swirling the ice and drink in his glass and dropping handfuls of salted peanuts into his mouth from the can as he watched the evening news over his wife's shoulder.

"Look, Sam," Jeannette said tearfully. "Look at those poor people."

Caldwell had a cool manner, which led him to stand just outside a hub of activity, holding a lit cigarette with a casual knowingness that occasionally inspired journalists to spot him and yell, "Let's ask the aide!" Yet he was so far from real power, from the high elective or appointed offices he coveted, that he couldn't help but worry. On a sleepless night, fighting the oppressive air, humid sheets, and single mosquito in the bedroom, he'd get up to go have a smoke and a drink in the kitchen in his boxers and undershirt and shake his head over how much of any man's career was the result of dumb luck.

Governor Griffin, meanwhile, enjoyed growing fame—or infamy—as the South's mouthiest governor protesting the federal government's interference in "the Negro question." By October 1958, Governor Marvin Griffin of Georgia seemed to be facing down Armageddon on a weekly basis. "All attempts to mix the races," he bawled into microphones, "whether they be in the classrooms, on the playgrounds, in public conveyances, or in any other area of close personal contact on terms of equality, peril the mores of the South!" (Sam Caldwell wrote some of the governor's speeches, knowing what was required, but he was in awe of Griffin's ability to deliver them.) In 1956, Governor Griffin signed into law that the red and white bars of Georgia's state flag were to be replaced by the Confederate battle flag, a symbol of Georgia's refusal to bow to federal desegregation laws. The Confederate flag was raised in front of the capitol with as great a sense of heroic defiance as the Texas flag was over the Alamo, and has been mistaken ever since for a proud symbol of the Confederacy rather than as a snarling defense of segregation.

Governor Griffin, Caldwell knew, was the type of highly intelligent and persuasive rural Southerner bewildering to Northerners. His elongated and slurred syllables, the redneck grammatical errors he threw in for effect, and his countrified similes didn't mean he was going to let anybody get by him, and that included the U.S. Supreme Court, President Eisenhower, and the liberal mayor of his capital city, William B. Hartsfield.

Off in the great north woods, Governor Griffin didn't know a thing about the coal miners trapped a mile underground in Nova Scotia, nor could he guess that by the time he emerged, mooseless, from his Canadian vacation, his name and the state of Georgia would be broadcast alongside the surviving miners' names in headlines around the globe.

11

"There Has Got to Be a Way Out, Boys!"

GROUP OF TWELVE
Harold Brine, Hughie Guthro, Joseph Holloway, Fred Hunter, Gorley
Kempt, Larry Leadbetter, Eldred Lowther, Bowman Maddison,
Joseph McDonald, Ted Michniak, Levi Milley, Caleb Rushton
FRIDAY, OCTOBER 24, 2 A.M.
SIX HOURS SINCE THE BUMP

Gorley Kempt, light-headed with gas and shock, figured himself to be in the vicinity of the 13,000 level, near the wall, but all was changed; the old signposts had become indecipherable, like the chaotic aftermath of a tornado, stop signs sticking out of tree trunks and cows mooing from second-story bathrooms. Gorley couldn't get his bearings, and it was making him dizzy.

Joe McDonald's sad voice rose periodically from the trough in which he lay below them. He no longer called out to the men, in whom he'd lost faith, but to God.

Only half the headlamps were working. Levi Milley, gloomy and quiet in the best of times, suddenly got up and left without a word. He clambered over hillocks of coal and under felled timbers into the black mess, indifferent to whether or not anyone followed. But Eldred Lowther took it as an exhortation to get organized. "Boys, there has got to be a way out!" he called, his chest expanding to assume the mantle of leadership. "It's up to us to find it!" He adjusted his lamp and followed silent Milley, and quiet Joe Holloway went along, too, and soon cheery, round-headed, long-armed Hughie Guthro swung behind. Gorley Kempt, still fighting dizziness, got up to follow Hughie Guthro, whose good sense he trusted.

The other men turned on their headlamps and shuffled after the leaders, while Joe McDonald, in agony on his lonely slope, watched the lights disappear one by one, leaving him behind in the thickening gloom.

Ted Michniak, suffering from his dislocated shoulder, sat on the ground with his back to the rock wall, and let them pass. They hadn't the headroom to stand up, so they walked by him bent double. "If you see me boys," he said bitterly to the fellows at the end of the line, "tell them I was thinking about them." He and McDonald were left alone in the dark.

The ten pushed into the bewildering maw of black coal. It was like treacherous rock climbing on a cloudy and moonless night. No. 2 was shuddering with aftershocks of the bump. Rocks and pebbles clattered down on the miners' helmets. The men searched for a gap, an opening, a handhold, a chance, all the while hoping to avoid the misstep that would bring down the house.

Holloway was the first to feel his way around a pack, and he came upon a man crushed against the roof. "My God," he said, "look in there, but it is best not to look at all."

"I'm beat with this gas," Harold Brine said suddenly. He stretched out on the pavement—as they called the rock floor of the mine—facedown, sniffing the ground for less-contaminated air.

"When we get through, we will holler to you," called Lowther, "and you crawl up to the next pack and wait there."

The crew came upon a fellow lying over the pans. Bowman Maddison approached and shone down his headlamp. "Oh yes.

He is dead. His stomach is hanging out." As the rest said nothing, but pushed deeper into the underground, Maddison, nauseated by what he had seen, said, "We're trapped for good."

The point men were stopped by a lumber-and-stone pack.
Once it had stood as a pillar, holding up the ceiling, but now the
ceiling had tumbled down all around it and walled it in solid. It
stood before them tantalizingly like a stone door. There might
be nothing beyond it but solid rock, but there might be an
opening, a place to stand and breathe, maybe other survivors.
The men began pulling at the rocks to pry an opening. When
they'd made a ragged hole, Gorley Kempt squeezed the top
half of his body through it, looked around, and found another
miner. "He's pretty well smashed," he noted. He wriggled back
out. "Boys," he said, "when you go through, you are going to see
something you are not going to want to see. You are just going
to brace yourself and keep steady." They chopped a bigger hole,
clawed out the loosened rocks, and crawled through to new
land. Advancing on their bellies, they were blocked by a second
stone wall and began to dismantle that one, stone by stone by
stone.

Joe Holloway found two miners, but both were dead. One of
them was sitting up. "Seeing his head, the way it is battered,"
thought Holloway, "it takes the life out of me."

Like the rest of the fellows, Gorley Kempt was engrossed in a
private calculation of his chances for staying alive, how he'd fare
with these particular companions, and the odds that he wouldn't
go crazy. The notion of "going crazy" if trapped underground
was a common theme among miners. They'd adjusted to spending eight, nine, ten, hours a day in the total eclipse of the underworld, but it was with the knowledge that they'd be breathing

clean air by sunlight, or by starlight, before going to bed. If they couldn't get out, well, even the toughest of them thought that would drive a man insane.

Gorley, up top, was the life of the party, who drank and clowned and winked at pretty girls and made them laugh. There was playfulness in him, not lechery. Then he snuck into his house and to bed at dawn, elaborately tiptoeing and carrying his shoes. Margie had outgrown the appeal of his plaintively raised eyebrows and remorseful brown eyes, so, when confronted, he dropped his shoes and was straight with her. And she with him. They understood each other. He needed to carry his merriment elsewhere; she had floors to wash, laundry to hang, meat to stew, and children to raise.

"I was a little under average at school, but I always seem to be able to get along with other people," is how Gorley thought about himself. "When it comes to being a man, I wouldn't say I am too much of a man in a lot of respects—as far as fighting goes, I would probably be called a coward because I go around it if I possibly can. I back up as far as I possibly can without a fight. But if it came to something you had to meet and couldn't get around, then I think I'd do as good as the next fellow."

He had a self-deprecating sense of humor, and sheepishly took what Margie told him with a little one-shouldered shrug that said, "Yep, that's me; take it as you will." Sometimes they both just had to laugh, as at the shore recently when he was drinking, left the dance club, wandered into the parking lot, and got completely flummoxed when the great and famous tide came in over the pavement. He flailed around in the water for half an hour until the tide went out and he could find his way home.

But there would be no such mocking love or humor or forgiveness in the straits he was in now. What he wouldn't give now to have his impatient Margie shaking her finger at him and yelling at him what to do.

The de facto leaders of the group were Levi Milley and Eldred Lowther, the former silent and dejected, the latter excessively animated. Both were driven by the desire to break out instantly, by the feeling that any delay was unbearable. Gorley and the others were sucked into the wake of their single-mindedness. To pause for even a moment of discussion might allow someone to say that things looked grim, that escape might not be within their abilities; thus, no group discussion was encouraged. Milley worked in a cone of silence, as if he were alone. Lowther trotted proudly behind him, as if anointed, and sprayed the rest with pep talk—"There's always a way out, boys. We've just got to find it! I been in bumps before. There must be a way out. I'll try every trick I know, and I know lots of them. I know how to do this and how to do that. I know how to timber, I know how to get through bad spots. I'll try every one. I won't leave a stone unturned." To his silent followers, the muttering sounded unfortunately like the chatter of a man who was almost hysterical.

The group made a hole in the second pack, wriggled through it, and was instantly halted by a third pack. They searched for a way around it. The fresh fall of coal was wide and deep and solid. Milley wordlessly began climbing onto it. After a moment of misgiving, El Lowther signed on. "We've got to go right over the top!" he called as if it had been the plan all along. He clambered up after Milley onto ground known to miners as "the waste," the dangerous fall of coal left behind when miners finished the excavation of an area. "The air is coming to us very good," he reported. He was at his best like this, feeling that he was up for a physical challenge, that the other men relied upon him for leadership. "Let's try and work our way up. The air ought to blow the gases away from us."

"Yes, follow the air," agreed Holloway, but he quailed inside as he stepped up and realized that Milley and Lowther were leading them hunching and creeping up onto the forbidden waste, where the ceilings were unfortified and the ground uncertain. "It's strange in the waste," thought Holloway unhappily. "We're quite a ways in. Normally, a fellow doesn't think of coming in here. The ceiling could come down at any time."

They squatted and scraped between unsupported ceilings and unstable floors. These jaws had clamped shut nearly everywhere else in the bump, biting down on men. How long would the black tonnage of ceiling over their heads stay up? How long would the floor lie still? If the ground shook again, their bodies would never be found. The men crouched and slid on their way up the 13,000 wall, hoping to find the 12,600 level. In their fantasies, they imagined the 12,600 level would be clear enough for them to fight their way through it to the Back Slope, turn left, and hike back up to the surface of the planet.

Lowther, in front, ran into gas. The instant he smelled it, he wheeled around and threw himself backward to escape. But a moment later, sitting down, unwilling to take no for an answer, he said aloud, "Now, did I really run into gas or was I scared?"

Lowther turned to young Larry Leadbetter and said, "We ought to line up. Then if anything happens to the head guy, the second guy will grab him and the third guy could grab the second and we'll start pulling back." But he thought to himself, "Too bad it's this young fellow, Leadbetter. It's not that I don't have any faith in him, but I'd have more faith if it was another experienced miner behind me."

"Boys!" Lowther called. "Keep right close. All right, I am going to try it again."

"Try her again," said Holloway without enthusiasm.

Lowther climbed up and was knocked back a second time. "That's it. We can't get up through there."

It was impossible to progress. Where the rock was down, gas trickled in. Men began to feel woozy. "We're getting tired," Gorley said. "We're not able to put in much of an effort. And our lights are going out." They began twisting and sliding and groping in reverse, back toward their point of origin. On this return leg, they stopped beside a couple of bodies and cut the lamp batteries from the belts of the dead men. They backtracked to the long, narrow cave in which Ted Michniak lay. The cave was about four feet high and twenty feet long. The ground sloped at about a thirty-three-degree angle. Michniak was sorry they hadn't found an escape route, but he was relieved to have company again.

"Hey!" called Joe McDonald when he saw that bobbing headlamps once again decorated the distant rise. "Don't leave me down here!"

Caleb Rushton, Bowman Maddison, and Levi Milley slid down the gradient to him. "Get me somewhere safer," Joe said. "Put me up there with Teddy Michniak." They lifted him as best they could, but awkwardly, hurting him, and shuffled, hunched over, uphill with him. They couldn't get him all the way up—headspace between floor and ceiling grew too narrow to maneuver through and he was starting to holler—so they laid him down halfway and then carried Michniak down to him so the two injured men could keep each other company. "That's it, that's good," said Joe.

"I'm not going anywhere," he thought. "I'm not going to try to go anywhere. I'm going to keep cool and save my energy." He felt better. He was closer to where he'd wanted to be, though still not altogether within the circle of men. "I've known Teddy for some time," he thought. "I feel kind of happy to have him for company."

All the men rested for an hour or two, taking easy swigs from their water, regathering their strength. Then, without preamble, Levi Milley went out again, in the opposite direction; he headed down the 13,400 wall in search of the 13,800 level. Maybe that one would be clearer, offering a path to the Back Slope and an exit.

"You got grub?" Gorley Kempt asked Joe McDonald and Ted Michniak on their ledge as he, along with the rest of the men, prepared for another expedition. They showed Gorley that they had a few bites of dinner left in their buckets.

"What about water?" asked Caleb Rushton, though he had lost his water can and had none of his own to offer. The injured men showed him that a couple of ounces of water sloshed in the bottom of their canteens. "All right," said Caleb kindly, sorry to be leaving them alone again, "let me go see what we can find or what we can't find."

The explorers hit a fall of coal too ragged and dangerous for them to venture across. They sat down and tried to think of what to do next. The headlamps began to fade and to blink off and on as their batteries ran low. The men's sooty faces were visible, then gone, then visible again, as if they stood on a seedy urban sidewalk late at night, with a half-blown-out VACANCY sign buzzing on and off overhead.

"Well, let's try her again," said Lowther. "Why don't we timber the waste until we're satisfied about our safety? Then if we get down and we can't get any farther, we can have a way of coming back; we won't be blocked off." But the number of men he could rouse was diminishing. Half the men began crawling back to their clearing, already defeated. A few obeyed Lowther and tried to perform the ordinary workday tasks of propping up supports for the coal ceiling, though they were without adequate light or proper tools. They made their way across the waste, around a wall, and into the waste again. "This roof is in pretty good condition," said Lowther. "Let's see how far we can get."

Optimistic, young Harold Brine shinnied up a fall of coal and crept across the top of it. "I can see down through the stone, to the coal face," he called. "There's a hole. I think I can maybe get down there." He positioned himself over the hole and dropped straight down, squirmed between two stone walls, and called back up for the other men to follow. One by one, they dropped down after him and all emerged together onto a new and ruined realm.

"This is the worst condition of any we seen yet," said Hughie Guthro. "The waste is in so bad, there isn't much more we can do."

"But I think," said Lowther, "if we timber it, we can find a way through this one. We're going to try every trick there is in the basket, everything we know."

The men burrowed into the fallen coal through a hole about two feet high and two feet wide, and hit another stone wall. They began dismantling it, handful by handful. They passed fistfuls of rock over their shoulders, one man to the next. Then they all backed out, single file, and traded places, so the ones in front could breathe for a while. The dearth of fresh air weakened and confused them. On a normal workday, a huge fan on the surface blew fresh air down into the mine; underground workers aimed the artificial wind to the day's work sites by opening and closing wooden trapdoors. Without this ventilation, the trapped men panted, sweated profusely, tired rapidly, and grew disoriented.

Finally it was Harold Brine again who volunteered to crawl ahead into the jerry-rigged tunnel; he writhed ahead about fifteen feet and stopped moving.

"Harold? Harold? Harold Brine!" the older men hollered after a few moments. They got no response. El Lowther and Hughie Guthro looked at each other, then dove in after him, one behind the other, grabbed Harold by his feet, hauled him backward into breathable air, and squatted over him as he returned to consciousness.

"Well, boys," said Gorley Kempt after a period of silence, "if anybody comes looking for us, they are going to come through the 13,000 level from the Back Slope and not down the wall, that's for sure. We'd better gather what we have here, our tools and saws and things, and get back up the wall."

There was only one working light left. Levi Milley flashed it on for a moment and the men crawled forward; then he turned it off to save power and everyone froze, like an awful version of the children's game Red Light, Green Light; then he turned it on again and produced a sickly stream of light the color of chicken soup, and the men crawled as fast as they could; and then it went dark again and they collapsed and waited. It took them an hour to get back to the cramped, low-ceilinged slope that had become their base camp.

Hughie Guthro summarized their situation: "Twelve men alive. Able-bodied, ten." (His count would prove to be inaccurate, for Fred Hunter was hiding a grievous injury.) "There's nobody else survived," he said with finality. "We are in here, that's it."

The explorers were wearing themselves out and, whenever they returned to the cave, they were devouring the curled leftovers in their lunch buckets—sandwich crusts, meat gristle, cake icing smeared on aluminum foil, apple cores—and guzzling the water, which jingled like spare change in the water cans. No one dared suggest that the escape leaders go easy on the food and water, because to deprive them of nourishment would weaken them and hinder their effort. Also, the suggestion that provisions be saved in case of a longer stay underground would betray a suspicion that the men might not be able to engineer an escape, that they all might be down here to stay for a while.

Caleb Rushton's watch glowed in the dark. It was Friday morning. He, for one, was done in, finished with the day's escapades. He unlaced his boots. Michniak moaned in his sleep. Joe McDonald curled up with his swollen, battered leg and silently wept from hurt and homesickness. Others cradled themselves as best they could, hands curved under their faces, or clasped over their bellies, their privacy absolute though they lay in close proximity to one another, the blackness like a silent howl swirling around them. Some, near sleep, unlatched their belts and reached inside their pants and held themselves most tenderly and pityingly. Fred Hunter, trying to get comfortable on the unyielding pebbly floor, emitted an ungodly shriek of pain that made everyone else jump. "What the hell are you doing?" snarled somebody out of the darkness, for Hunter was on no one's list of injured men.

"He's just carrying on with us," someone said.

"It's my leg, my leg," he groaned.

"Ah, you're just trying to get us going."

Even relentless Milley slumped against the wall with his legs outstretched. He crossed his arms over his chest, let his head fall forward, and slept.

But Eldred Lowther wasn't finished, couldn't let go. "That's it? You're finished?" he cried. "You're ready to die? Like rats in a cage? But there's always a way out! We've got to keep looking! A fellow should be trying to make his way out. It's better than dying! There's always a way out. We know plenty of tricks. We are going to use every trick there is in the basket." He was too overwrought and antsy to sleep. He saw a sudden sputter of a headlamp among the drowsing men. It pasted a yellowish gleam onto the rock wall, so he hopped up, ready to order the man into action, but it was only the dragging of a miner off to a far crevice to urinate. Head down, the man shuffled back, found his spot, killed the light, and slept, while Lowther muttered on.

He fancied that he picked up the faint sound of rescuers in the distance. He then snarled at the men who spoke a word or snored. "Shut up!" he hissed. "Shut up, do you hear? Shut up or I'll drive my fist through you." The men didn't talk back; they just shifted their weight away from him, feeling him to be another obstacle to getting any rest, on a par with the slanted sharp floor and the sour air.

They were physically and emotionally spent. On and on chattered Lowther, a salesman of escape. "I was my mother's seventh child out of thirteen. Me and my wife have six kids. The oldest is nineteen, the youngest is just three. I was a rescuer in the Explosion, you know. In the Explosion, you had to lay right down on your stomach because the gas was down that low. The young fellow laying alongside of me said, 'Boy,' he said, 'I want to stay with you,' he said, 'because you know all about this stuff.'

"'Well,' I said, 'boy, there's no man in this world that knows all about it. We're all the same, but,' I said, 'you can stick with me if you want to.'

"'Well, I want to stay with you,' he said, 'because you don't look scared, because,' he said, 'I'm scared to death.'

"'Well,' I said, 'boy, if you're scared, this is no place for you.'"

But his crackpot harangue began to fade out for the others, like the sound of a high roof pelted by rain.

12

No Hope Whatsoever

ABOVE GROUND
SATURDAY, OCTOBER 25, 7 A.M.
THIRTY-FIVE HOURS SINCE THE BUMP

"John Totten!" a rescuer called at the pithead, knowing that John was somewhere nearby in a crew of volunteers.

"Aye!" yelled John.

The helmeted, soot-faced rescuer then gestured, with gloved hand, toward the nearby tent set up as a morgue where bodies lay on tables waiting for identification. "I think it's the wife's father, John."

Totten slowly took off his own helmet, crossed the gravel to the tent, consented to take a miserable and fleeting look, and confirmed it. "I don't want to be the one to tell the wife," he thought. "I want somebody else to do that. One of her other relatives."

He slunk home and went straight to the kitchen, then listened from behind the closed door when a minister hurried up the front steps and knocked on the door with the news. "Oh, she's upset," he thought. "He's boarded with us for twenty years. Oh, she's upset quite a bit." Not wanting to face his wife, he stepped to the sink and washed the already washed dishes and then redried them.

10 A.M.

Underground, the softly despairing, almost tender calls of "Eddie? Are you there, Eddie?" had faded, then stopped. After an indefinable quantity of time, if time still existed, Leon Melanson, with the sky-blue eyes, draped in stone, isolated and alone, heard men call from the darkness, "That you, T-Bone?"

"Yep, yep." He found himself to be hoarse and cleared his throat. It was many hours since he'd spoken. "Is that you, Perce?"

"No, it's Cecil Colwell. We're trying to get to you."

"I can't move here and I can't find my buddy. I've been calling for him."

Rescuers squatted around the pyramid of coal that was Leon Melanson. Dr. Burden, seeing the gathering of headlamps, approached. "Now, who's this?" he said. "All I can see is the top of his left shoulder and a profile of his face. Good God, it's Leon! Where does it hurt the most?"

"Everywhere," said the lovely man. He was barely able to speak. "I'm being squeezed and I'm being crushed at the same time. Is Percy OK?"

"Percy Rector?" someone said. "Haven't seen him."

"He's my brother-in-law," said Leon.

"Haven't seen him," a rescuer said again. "But that don't mean nothing—I've been down here must have been eight hours."

"I just handed a measuring stick to me buddy," Leon rasped, then breathed for a while before he could continue. "I didn't hear no bump, I didn't hear nothing...I don't think Eddie even got the sticks. Just got ahold of them and bang...I go to open my eyes and find myself pinned...Is Percy Rector there?"

"Hang on, T-Bone," the rescuers said, trying in the near dark to size up how badly he was trapped and hurt.

Doc Burden took an ampule of Demerol from his medical bag and shot one hundred milligrams into Leon's exposed shoulder. "That's all I can do for him right now," the doctor said. "You fellows keep digging him out. Come find me when you've got him clear."

11 A.M.

A manager who'd arrived as a volunteer from the New Glasgow mines made the rounds of rescue sites underground and announced, "I want these men out because the gas is almost up to ten percent."

"Can you assure us that everybody below us is dead?" asked Cecil Colwell.

"No, I can't do that," said the New Glasgow manager.

"Well, to hell with you then. As long as there's a possibility of getting one man out alive, it will be well worth our effort."

The New Glasgow manager turned to appeal to Springhill manager George Calder. "Nobody is to go down any farther!"

"If there's nobody goes down," said Calder, "there's nobody comes out. I can tell you now, there will be nobody come out."

"We're working desperately hard to try to save somebody and here's this drunk from out of town standing over us," muttered Cecil to his fellow bare-faced rescuers. "There's no reason why these people should be allowed in the pit a'tall. We will take care of our own."

Then Cecil was too tired to go on. The tools dropped from his numb fingers. On his way home, dazed and half asleep at the wheel, he stopped by the hospital to check on a few of the men he'd helped to the surface in the last thirty-eight hours.

"How is that Jack Scott?"

"Well, Cecil, he's alive," said the doctor, "but he's got a broken back."

"Did I do that, Doctor?" asked Cecil.

"No, it was the air line. The imprint of the air line is still on his back."

Cecil stopped by the bedside of another man he'd found and gotten out. "Cecil," said the miner, "I prayed and I prayed to God that he would let me see the light one more time. He let me see the light one more time and I'll tell you this: you will never, ever get me in a coal mine again."

12 NOON: FORTY HOURS SINCE THE BUMP

General Manager Harold Gordon of Dominion Steel and Coal Corporation called a press conference.

"Gentlemen," he said, "I . . ." He paused. "Regret very much to have to tell you this. There is no hope, whatsoever, for any of the men who are on the 13,400 wall, or the 13,800 wall. There is just the vaguest glimmer of hope that some men who were on the 13,000 wall may survive. There's a good deal of stone down from up, and a good deal of coal down from the working face."

Jack McAndrew of the CBC stepped away from the hut to broadcast the story.

This afternoon at a press conference by Mr. Harold Gordon, General Manager of DOSCO coal operation, said he has all but closed the curtain on the dramatic and heroic attempts to rescue the men trapped in No. 2 colliery here in Springhill. We were informed this afternoon that there was no hope to be held for the lives of the ninety-two men.

At the pithead, the word of Mr. Gordon's announcement has slapped through this crowd like wildfire, and it's put a sort of silence, a pall, over the people who have waited so patiently since last night. Some of them are still waiting, but more are leaving in ones and twos and threes. They hunch their shoulders against this driving wind and icy rain it's carrying, and they're going uptown back to their homes.

13

"It's Good Day to Him, I Reckon."

SATURDAY, OCTOBER 25

Behind the coal which sparkled silently wherever the head-lamps of hurrying rescuers grazed it, survivors frantically dug and scrabbled about. Blocked off and deafened, the survivors could not hear the rescuers. The rescuers, who were digging in search of the Back Slope and were far from the levels, detected no sign of survivors. And the two groups of survivors—with four hundred feet of solid rock between them—were unaware of each other's existence.

GROUP OF SEVEN

1 A.M.: TWENTY-NINE HOURS SINCE THE BUMP

In the Group of Seven, Frank Hunter grew increasingly deaf in the aftermath of the bump. "When she drove me down," he tried to tell the men, "when I come to meself, I had no hat on. I reached up for it and my two hands came away covered with blood. It was my ears had went."

But he couldn't interest anyone in the damage he'd incurred, though they seemed plenty interested in each other. The group of them swiveled their heads, spoke or argued, stood or squatted, or reached for the water can, in unison, it seemed to Frank. He stared at them as if he were watching a school of silverfish in a tank abruptly turn about and show its opposite flanks, wondering who was giving the signal for the maneuver. Frank yelled to his fellows, trying to get himself hooked back in with them, but they gritted their teeth at him, showed him their growling faces.

They were listening, they yelled and pantomimed, for work sounds in the distance. They looked down hard at their wristwatches, then gazed up and away, tuned in to the far-off sounds of a shift change. Frank didn't believe they heard a damn thing and told them so. "Be quiet," they hissed at him. Then they were snarling at him for shuffling his feet on the rock. "Be quiet, be quiet! There's somebody pounding."

"Frank, for the love of Pete, be still! Can't you hear there's a chipper-pick going out there?"

"For Christ's sake, Hunter, shut your mouth," said Jewkes.

"You fellows are foolish as hell," Frank Hunter told them.

"You can hear the trolleys coming down," yelled Garnet Clarke. "They're looking for us all right. I just don't know if they'll get to us in time."

"Jesus," said Doug Jewkes, "that chipper-pick's far away. They will be a month getting us out of here."

"There is nobody there," Frank Hunter scoffed from his deafness. "You fellows are hearing things."

"Shush, Frank!" said Currie Smith.

"Jesus, Currie, you are all the time saying shush," whined Frank.

Finally Frank sat still, head down, angry, like a boy being punished, and unfairly at that. "To hell with them," he thought. "I don't believe they hear a damn thing. They're fooling themselves." Every once in a while he shoved the soles of his boots hard across the gravel, scrambling the pebbles, just to annoy.

He was the oldest man down here, or second only to Maurice, and it stung him that they weren't coming to him for advice instead of yelling at him to hush up. They might have learned something.

From the cave where Percy Rector hung and groaned in agony, Garnet Clarke, Currie Smith, and Herb Pepperdine crept out onto the forbidden waste. "Oh no, oh Lord," said Pep, "there's my brother-in-law, right over there. Oh Lord, oh Lord, me and him are good buddies, going fishing together, one thing and another all the time." It took the air out of Pep and he crept back to the group, leaned his head against the coal, and tried to shut his eyes and ears against the sight and sounds of Percy's writhing and begging. In misery, he took his forty winks, though it was like trying to nap at the site of a car wreck. Sleepless, weeping, he crawled off to join Garnie and Currie again. He found them tiptoeing across the waste. Currie had found his own lunch can and inside it his watch, the kind you could read in the dark. "It says 2:10," he said, and they all sat back on their haunches to calculate.

"Saturday morning, I figure," said Currie.

Pep got up and immediately stumbled over another old friend. "Here's my buddy, then!" he said, aiming down his headlamp and recognizing Barney Martin, who was sprawled facedown on the waste. "How you feeling there, Barney?" But Barney didn't answer, and his hand was cold to Pepperdine's touch and there was a red mark on the back of his neck. "Well, then. It's good day to him, I reckon."

When the men returned to the group, the fact that they'd found life was their lead story. "We saw Barney Martin. He's doomed. He's either dead or just about done."

Sore and sad, and chafing against the rock of their prison cell, the men hunched inside their jackets, curled up on the floor, and tried to sleep. The howls and gurgles of Percy Rector penetrated their dreams.

Unlike men separated from their families by disasters such as dam break, flood, hurricane, or tidal wave, the coal miners knew precisely where their wives and children were, and that they were safe and dry and well-fed. The stores would be open, and all the citizens free to come and go as usual, their collars turned up against the damp. Though everything was utterly changed and ruined, and men lay dead and dying and moaning underground, the town would look the same, unbroken, under a windy gray sky. The fearful visions which plagued the survivors were of the future, of the women's and children's lives without them.

Herb Pepperdine, Garnet Clarke, and Currie Smith left again in search of an exit. They reached the spot where they'd tripped over Barney Martin, lying spread-eagled and cold as death. "Hey, Barney is gone!" they yelled. "He ain't in his spot!" They felt around with their hands and feet. "Oh, he's gone in that stone pack there and died, likely," said Currie.

"Well, I'm going to look for him," said Garnet.

"Garnie, don't waste your strength, my boy, you'll need it," Currie said.

"All right then," said Garnie.

Their headlamps were giving out anyway. "That's it for my lamp," Pep said. "Even if I wait half an hour to turn it on, I'm getting a light not much more than a cigarette butt."

"Let's take a battery off one of these guys that got it."

Nervously they approached a corpse whose identity they couldn't tell. "Can you get the battery off?" Currie asked Garnet.

"*You're* right alongside," said Garnet. "You do it."

"Well, you're right there yourself," said Currie. "Oh, all right."

"I got to do it," he thought. "The body is all wet and awful. But there is a battery here."

"Got that knife?" he asked. He took a penknife from Garnet, cut the belt, and pulled the battery off the corpse. Then he patted the man's pockets and found a key. He turned it thoughtfully in his fingers, was about to toss it into the waste, then pushed it back into the pocket. It might help identify the man, if the lot of them were ever discovered. He scooted over to another body and was less timid this time. He patted the poor man down and hit the jackpot: a few sticks of gum loose in a pants pocket.

Pep, meanwhile, was gingerly plucking a treasure from a third man's pocket. He'd found a chocolate bar. "I could eat this all by myself," he thought. "But I'm not going to do it. I won't."

"Looky here!" he said to his buddies. "A candy bar! It's lovely. Oh, it smells good!"

When the three returned to the group, they had a happier report. Pep called, "Looky here, boys, what I brought you." He unwrapped the candy bar and twisted it into seven wads. He put two in Maurice Ruddick's fist. Maurice pocketed his own to enjoy later, and turned to Percy Rector. Percy's mouth dangled open as if the period of primal screaming had left his jaw detached; with two fingers, Maurice inserted a cube of chocolate into it, trying to stick it on the dry tongue.

"Well, that made me worse," complained ungrateful Doug Jewkes. "I'm already so thirsty, I'm about to go crazy, and that chocolate made me thirstier."

"Mmm, that tastes *good,*" smacked Pepperdine, with the pride of gift giving, ignoring Jewkes. "It's like having a big fine turkey dinner, ain't it?"

Time passed.

"If I could just go home," someone spoke sorrowfully in the darkness, probably unaware he was speaking aloud, "and see my dog being fed."

14

Hard Times

Bespectacled, slight Doc Burden, with the high-pitched voice, was working deeper in the mine; the sheen of sweat on his face looked like fury, the coal dust clinging to his cheeks like a beard. The rescuers were uncovering only dead men. Then a runner arrived from out of the darkness. "Doc! They want you back over with Leon Melanson because they want you to cut off a leg."

"What do you mean, cut off a leg?"

"There's a dead man trapped with Leon and the dead man's leg is up under Leon's armpit, crossing his body. They can't get Leon out till they get that leg out of the way."

Traveling back through the debris, Dr. Burden stooped to cut a cord from a dead miner's battery, for use as a tourniquet. Leon's head, shoulders, and chest had emerged from the coal, but a strange leg coming up out of the pile at a bizarre angle was jamming a boot under Leon's armpit.

"I can feel the man around me," Leon was saying to his team of rescuers. "I know he is dead, from the cold." Leon was moaning, so the doctor gave him a second injection.

"He's still fully buried from the waist down, so his legs aren't visible," the doctor said. "Now, I have seen people trapped in bombed buildings overseas in the war and I'm telling you, this could be Leon's leg, and not another man's."

The rescue workers scoffed.

"Pull the boot and sock off," said Burden. He peered close to examine the exposed foot. "Well, it is white and cold, but I can't guarantee that it's the dead man's foot. These feet can be in very queer places." The doctor tried to push the foot down under Leon's chest but Leon cried out that his chest hurt. "That still doesn't tell me," said the doctor. "It could be the dead man's leg pushing against Leon's chest, or it could be his own leg. Just keep on digging. Don't do anything drastic."

"This is heartbreaking work," he thought as he traveled back to other disaster sites, "them chipping away at hard-packed coal with one live body and one dead body underneath."

Within the hour, the rescuers sent for the doctor again. He'd been proven right: Leon's partner, Eddie, was dead and wrapped around him, but it was Leon's own broken and crushed leg twisted up across his chest and under his armpit. He stood encased in coal, performing an inhuman split. Dr. Burden gave him another shot of Demerol and waited for it to kick in. Then several rescuers bent down so that Leon could be pulled up and out and laid across their backs. The doctor tied the length of cord around the leg as a tourniquet, and Leon was extracted. "Watch for a rush of blood," the doctor warned. "He's not bleeding right now, but there's no telling what will happen once we move him." They got Leon onto a stretcher, straightened out the leg, and cut away the pant leg so the doctor could have a look. "He's still got circulation in it," Dr. Burden realized, "but I have no hope that he'll regain use of it at all." Leon was sent up to the surface. He was admitted to the hospital with two black eyes, a broken nose, and a leg full of compound fractures and lumps of coal. He floated in and out of consciousness for a week, then little by little came to himself. Someone had laid his harmonica on his bedside table, and he blew a few tunes to amuse his fellow patients.

"Was it Percy brought it?" he asked his wife.

"No," she whispered, "he's still underground."

Finally he was driven by ambulance to a hospital in Halifax, where the leg was to be amputated.

"I've had some hard times," he said, before going under anesthesia. "But life is hard anyway."

4 P.M.

Dr. Arnold Burden drove home for the first time since the disaster. He sat in his driveway a long time, too tired to move. Inside, moving slowly, he ran a bath, got into pajamas, ate breakfast, and went to bed. He slept about two hours, until the phone rang—a reporter looking for a quote—and, unable to fall asleep again, he got up and dressed. "There are more important things to do than sleep," he told his surprised wife. At the pit, they waved him on to the hospital; there was no work at all for him, or for his colleague, J. Carson Murray (whose pretty daughter Anne was going to grow up to be an internationally acclaimed country music star). There was no work for doctors at the pit; only bodies were emerging.

"The house is full of people!" Bev Reynolds thought in confusion. Only two days ago she had called Doc Burden to ask if four-year-old Danny had recovered sufficiently from the chicken pox to play outside, and then he had ridden his bike behind his dad, Wes, to the end of the sidewalk. Bev stayed in her house waiting for news. Her small road was busy with traffic, and friends and relatives visited, bringing food. They talked too loudly, and they ate with gusto, and they knew what day it was, and they knew what to dish out and what to refrigerate, but she drifted among them, timeless. "I do not know where these people came from," she thought. The only anchor in her life was her brother, Art, who showed up every day on his way home from his rescue work at the pit. She had taken him aside on the first day, her nails digging into his upper arm, and told him, "I don't want anyone to tell me anything except you, Art, because I'm not going to believe it. There are all these rumors, people saying they found parts of men, that sort of thing. I don't want any of it. I want you to tell me the truth."

Art lived down the road, and Bev looked out the window every day to watch him go by, heading toward the mine, or walking back home for a bite of dinner and a few hours' sleep, then walking back to the mine. He kept his head down. He knew she watched him.

At the urging of friends, Bev sent Danny to stay at a neighbor's. He kicked and wailed at being taken away. She was so weak, she nearly gave in and let him stay home, but relatives all assured her it was for the best. The child was calmed somewhat by being permitted to bring his tricycle and wagon, which his daddy had knotted together for him on that last morning home. The boy's rage faded and his thin chest coughed with sobs of defeat as the neighbor led him to her house with one hand and dragged his trike with her other.

MIDNIGHT

"He'll be back," Norma Ruddick told herself, slowly finding her way back to bed after the baby's night feeding. "God won't take him away from me and leave me to bring up twelve children." She lay down, sighing, and pulled the covers up. "Because what will I do with twelve children?"

15

When Sleep and Waking Feel the Same

GROUP OF TWELVE
SUNDAY, OCTOBER 26, 6 A.M.
FIFTY-EIGHT HOURS SINCE THE BUMP

After a few hours of sleep on the stone slope, the twelve survivors stirred and realized that the swarming oily blackness was now outside their eyelids rather than inside—thus, they must be awake and their eyes must be open. Lowther, their wacky sentry, was still going. "I am the oldest guy of the crew that is doing the work," he was saying. "I'm experienced. I been in four different mines and through a lot of bumps and everything. I kind of feel responsible for you fellows."

"I don't know if I'm in gas or I'm still asleep," thought Joe Holloway, coming slowly awake, "but I hear this friend of mine calling me and calling me. He's a long way off..."

Joe Holloway, Levi Milley, Hughie Guthro, Gorley Kempt, Harold Brine, and Caleb Rushton pulled themselves together, checked their failing headlamps, stood up, went off to urinate, and reconvened, gearing themselves for another day's work. They passed around the two water jugs in their possession, the water clinking like charm bracelets at the bottom of the tins.

From their ledge twenty feet below the rest, Ted Michniak and Joe McDonald began hollering for water. "Hey! Hey! Hey!

What about us?" yelled McDonald. Caleb slid down to share what there was.

Then the half dozen men felt themselves adequately fit to start the day. It was early morning up top, and there was fresh work to do; they hadn't yet tried to penetrate their own level. However, before they had even gotten out of sight of the injured and resting men, the explorers were blocked by a wall of caved-in coal. They'd walked to work along this alley on Thursday afternoon and the roof had fallen down behind them. It was a simple material problem of removal. They pawed at the coal wall in search of loose chunks.

There was bright daylight up top now, a blue and windy day fanned by the dry, fluttering orange leaves. Not a sparkle of sunlight fell to the miners. The light squandered itself upon the dirt and gravel driveways and parking areas around the pithead; it warmly patted the heads of the wives, mothers, and children gathered there.

"Don't all burn your lights at the same time," warned Gorley in the gray half-light below. "Take turns." He shut off his lamp every few minutes and waited. "Let it build up a little. Them lamps are only charged for twelve hours. Turn them off and then back on and you'll get a dim light for a minute."

With picks and shovels, they began to tunnel through the vast fall of coal blocking the 13,000 level. It was slow work, in unsafe, unventilated holes. In no time, they felt thirsty and hot. It took hours to make a few feet of progress.

What is the point? they asked themselves as they fell back and mopped sweat off their black faces with coal-covered shirtsleeves. If the coal was in solid from here to the Back Slope, it would take days to reach it; and if it were solid up the slope...

well, they were two and a half miles from the surface. They wouldn't live long enough to dig out.

"I didn't realize it was this bad," Hughie Guthro was thinking. "Every place is blocked off solid. How is anyone going to get to us?" He kept clearing his throat, thinking he was getting hoarse, but it was the first tickling of thirst. His throat had dried out so much already that no phlegm sprang up when he cleared it; instead, it made a sticky gulping sound.

When the men unearthed the body of a dead miner, they wordlessly cut his belt and removed his battery, then used it to replace one of their own. It gained them another couple of hours of light.

They rounded a pack and tunneled farther, carving out a hole the size of a man on his belly. No end was in sight. Of course, there would be no light at the end of this particular tunnel, only more darkness, whether the glittery blackness of fallen coal or the blue-black darkness of the sunless underworld.

"I don't want to be the bigmouth one of the bunch," said Gorley when they took a rest, the long line of them bunched up in the long hole, perspiring and hungry and dizzy and all beginning to swallow hard, thinking they were getting sore throats. "But what about a vote on getting out of this spot? I don't figure it's a vantage point."

The others grunted in agreement and retreated back, back, back to the only clearing with any air and headroom, where their comrades lay.

"My God, we have got to have some water," Gorley hoarsely said. No one had spoken for a while. His throat and nostrils burned with dryness, as if he'd breathed in smoke. "I'm going to go look for some." Caleb Rushton and Harold Brine got up and followed him up along the wall.

"Caleb," Gorley said, as they felt their way, "you were working up this way. Maybe you have some idea about where your water cans would be located." They kicked and groped around and earnestly aimed the tremulous lightbeam, as weak as skim milk. They located Caleb's water cans, but they were crushed and filled with coal dust.

"You know, there was a chap who had a habit of setting his cans over near the waste," said Caleb, his upward-turning, lilting sentences sounding like a list of questions. "The waste isn't as heaved up, there might be a chance." His boot unearthed a water can with a bent spout and water still in it. "I figure," said Gorley, "that we're entitled to a little something out of this, since we're the ones made the trip."

One of the men dug from his pocket a four-ounce aspirin bottle and poured the tablets back into his pocket. Gorley took the bottle to use as a dipper. They wrapped their big, rough mitts around the bottle as gently as if they held a daughter's toy teacup. Each man took a miniature sip of water into his raw and burning throat. They then stood and took mournful note of how brief the swallow was, how their searing throats still raged.

Gorley said, "We could do the whole thing in and say we found nothing."

The three stood gazing down at the water can. It sat on the ground in the sad fall of light from the dim headlamp.

"But," continued Gorley, "we ought to take it back to the boys who need it." The others nodded. The Miners' Code stood among them like a school principal.

"Well," he said next, "maybe one more bottle around." They took careful turns gathering their sips of aspirin-bottled water again. They moved with the utmost seriousness, in silence, with trembling hands, like altar boys assisting at their first Mass. "It lowered the can some," said Gorley, jiggling it. The water rolled against the deep sides like a bucket of pearls. "But then again, it didn't seem to take too much out of it. All right, listen, this time just enough to wet our lips."

With hands shaking from eagerness and need, they dipped and passed the half-filled aspirin bottle around a third time and took turns bathing their swollen and splintered lips. The dampened coal dust made a paste and they rubbed it around on their lips like Vaseline, savoring the absorption of every molecule of H_2O.

When they carried the water can back to the others, Levi Milley oversaw pouring it into the aspirin bottle, treating it as reverently as an after dinner liqueur.

"That aspirin bottle's a good thing," thought Larry Leadbetter, "because if you pass the can around, some of them can't resist taking a good big swig." But after he'd had his turn, he felt worse; the few drops on his lips only seemed to make the rest of his mouth and throat swell and burn more savagely.

"Hey, what about that fellow they called Rabbit?" said Hughie Guthro after a time.

"What's that?"

"That fellow Rabbit, ran the long-wall engine. Somebody brought a carrot down one day and tied it to the bell of the engine, just playing with him. What about that carrot? Think we could find it?"

Hughie felt his way down the wall—it wasn't far to the mess of machinery that had been the long-wall engine. Waving his hands ahead of him in the dark, Hughie actually found the dusty, shrunken hanging carrot. He came back flapping it triumphantly and carefully broke off a tiny rubbery nub for each of the twelve men. He rolled his tidbit around in his mouth a long time.

"I never had a carrot tasted so good," said Hughie Guthro, sucking on his morsel till only a string of it was left on his tongue. "Old Rabbit Reed," he observed, in brief eulogy. "Lester was his right name. Used to call him Rabbit."

16

"What on Earth Will I Do without Him?"

The families of the ninety-two missing men led a surreal life, days and nights of mingled sleep and waking. Prepared meals appeared unbidden on their tables—the work of kind neighbors—steaming dishes of soup or stew materializing like bewitched bowls in a fairy tale, the children of the house sitting round the table spooning in the food; then, in the blink of an eye, it was 2 A.M. and the kitchen was clean and dark, or 4 A.M. and the housewife found herself wearing a nightgown and galoshes, standing on her back porch and listening to the night rain and icy wind.

"What on earth will I do without Currie?" thought Mabel Smith. "Roger's thirteen, he'll be OK. David's eleven. Marilyn's only seven, and Carolyn's only two and Currie's afraid she's going to be a cripple. She's not moving around like she's supposed to be doing."

Sadie Allen had felt deeply that her beloved Fidel was gone ever since she raced down Main Street. Harold Gordon's statement on Saturday confirmed what she knew. Still, she felt she ought to try to wait at the pithead and keep up the appearance of hope. At home, with her four children, all she did was cry. "Maybe Pa will come up today!" the children would say to her as she put on her coat. She was at a complete loss as to what to say in reply, so she left the poor children standing in the hall with their mouths open and got back on the treadmill of walking to and from the pithead.

2 P.M.

Mixed reports about the journalists and hundreds of out-of-town volunteers began to circulate among the townspeople. Some were considerate and sympathetic (a couple of them were to stay in touch with Springhill families for many years), but one photographer leapt in front of a victim's small son, who walked among the pallbearers with his hand on his father's casket. "Hold it right there!" the photographer barked. Another asked Norma Ruddick to assemble all her children and sit on the sofa looking at the TV, as if it were the moment of the bump.

"Ministers are coming from the Island and from Halifax and they're preaching to all of us that we should expect that our men won't be brought up alive," said Mabel Smith to her older children. "They say, 'You might as well face it now.' I don't believe it. They can preach and have sermons and everything, but I'm going to think positive until the very end."

"I let one of them photographers into my house," humble Margie Guthro told her neighbor. "He asked me to sit at my kitchen table and cry. I," she said proudly, "showed him the door."

But then an elderly woman carrying two suitcases showed up at Margie's door and announced "God sent me to comfort you."

Confusedly, good churchwoman Margie Guthro opened the door. The strange woman in an old-fashioned hat put down her suitcases in the living room and looked around expectantly.

Margie withdrew into the kitchen. Her brother followed. "Is she bothering you?" he hissed. She nodded yes. He returned to the woman and asked her to go.

"But God sent me," said the woman.

"No," he said, "He didn't, and it's time for you to go."

She took up her things huffily and exited. She crossed the street to the neighbor's house and knocked, but they wouldn't let her in. "They say she tried the Salvation Army," the neighbor later told Margie, "and they didn't have any room for her, so eventually she went to the train station and I guess she went back to where she came from."

Gentle Margie Guthro attempted a sarcastic remark: "Wherever that was." And even in the middle of this horrible week, she had to wipe her eyes with the tip of her apron after a moment of laughter.

8 P.M.

On Sunday night in New York City, comedian Shecky Green was scheduled to appear on the Ed Sullivan Show with an eight-minute routine.

As he prepared to take the stage in the live broadcast, Sullivan suddenly approached him and said, "Shecky, we don't have time for the whole routine. You've got two minutes."

"You mean, you're cutting me down from eight minutes to two minutes?" Green cried.

"Well, I just said we don't have time for the eight."

Onstage, unable to do the bit he'd prepared, Shecky Green grabbed the microphone and began to fiddle and improvise with it. He'd done this kind of stuff before, in Las Vegas. He took the microphone apart, examined it, blew through it a few times to test it, then sounded the racehorse call from Churchill Downs.

Clutching the microphone stand, he became a drunk whose car was coming apart until nothing was left but the stick shift. Then the stand became a hollow tube through which he could talk to someone under the stage. "What's that?" he called. "You say the canary died? That's a gas!" The audience was to understand that he'd made contact with coal miners trapped under the stage.

"You say you're hurt? Nah, you weren't hurt. That was soft coal!"

If he'd heard anything earlier that day about the Springhill disaster, it hadn't registered; the shtick seemed the creation of the moment. It got some laughs. He wrapped it up in two minutes, stood up red-faced, waved, and headed off the stage.

Ed Sullivan was waiting for him backstage with a look the comedian never had seen before. Ed Sullivan's placid, baggy face seemed disfigured by disgust and fury.

"You are sick, sick," he said. "You are the sickest son of a bitch I've ever known in my life."

Green laughed feebly, thinking it was a sort of joke, some kind of odd compliment; he'd never heard Sullivan swear before. Sullivan shoved past him, introduced the next act, then found him again backstage.

"You dirty son of a bitch," he said again, and Green had the first glimmer that Sullivan wasn't kidding. "You're sicker than Lenny Bruce."

"What did I do?" asked Shecky Green.

"You lost me Canada," Sullivan snapped. "You'll never set foot on this stage again."

"I've got a contract for twelve more shows. What are you talking about?"

There were coal miners trapped underground that very

night in Nova Scotia, he was told, and the likelihood of their survival was slim.

"How sick do you think I am?" Shecky Green cried. "I had no idea! You think I'd deliberately make fun of trapped miners?"

"Get out."

"Sullivan's memory of it only got worse over time," says Shecky Green. "You know, it became [impersonating Ed Sullivan]: 'You caused the mine disaster. You did that.'"

17

The Lost Lovely Sky

GROUP OF SEVEN
SUNDAY, OCTOBER 26, 10 A.M.
SIXTY-TWO HOURS SINCE THE BUMP

Each man in the Group of Seven had found his niche. At first it was just the spot on the pebbly incline where his sore body got as accustomed to the slag and rocks as to the knobs and seams of his old mattress at home: "Ah, I'll put my shoulder here and then I can lean my head upon that bit of sediment . . ." And then he got more used to it, because even sick he'd never spent as many hours in bed as he did lying here, on his side, his back, his belly, aching for relief from the stone.

Percy Rector continued to weep and moan, though he couldn't sustain the volume. Maurice Ruddick was staying near him, murmuring over him like a mother administering cool washcloths to a sick baby, the words meaningless but the kindness in his voice and touch were of some use to the patient. Percy no longer begged them to try the saw blade against the pack timber; he'd seen it twang like a rubberband when they tried it. He'd thought of a better use for the broken blade: his own skin and bone.

He offered it, offered his own white shriveled upper arm to them, if only one of them would play the role of butcher and sever it. They dangled their heads toward their laps and affected deafness like Frank Hunter, whose eardrums had been blown out.

"Jewkes," Percy wheedled. "Jewkes. Come here. I need you to take my arm off. Jewkes!"

"No, Perce," spoke Doug Jewkes finally. "Stay right where you are. You wait and hang on now. Help will come to us. They'll get you out, because we can't." But Jewkes thought to himself, "I know damn well they never will. I'm just telling him that to try and calm him down."

The men looked from one to another trying to figure out what to do for him. "He's a big man, fat," Garnet Clarke said. "He's got a mile of earth on top of him. We got one saw with a broke handle. It would take us three months to get him out of there. With tools, all right. With no tools, no."

"Pep! Come here, Pepperdine." Rector was gasping. "I need you to take my watch. Can you get it out of me pocket?"

"What for, Perce?"

"You give it to me wife, eh?"

"Perce, I ain't getting out of here myself."

"Yeah, you will, you'll get out."

Pepperdine stood and shuffled over to Percy. Unwilling to make eye contact, he dug from Percy's pocket the watch wrapped in its little velveteen bag. "You took good care of this watch, eh?" Pep said. He thought, "We were always hollering, 'What time is it, Perce?' and he'd haul it out. Didn't make no difference how many times you ask him, he hauled the watch out. We'd tease him, just to make him stop working. 'What time is it, Perce?' and he'd haul the watch out." Pep pocketed the watch most tenderly.

———

"You know, Garnie," Currie Smith whispered to his pal, "I had told you on Wednesday to let's go hunting and you said, 'Oh my gosh, Currie, no, we can't, I had took Monday off.' And I said, 'That's right, you did.' And you said, 'So I can't. I have to work.'"

"My God," Garnie replied. "I wish I had listened to you and took the Thursday off. Oh, it was a lovely day, that Thursday, A lovely sky, eh?"

Of course, the miners had not brought with them the provisions they'd have taken if they'd known their visit underground would be of indefinite length. Each man had headed down with a tin pail holding a couple of sandwiches, a gallon can of water, a lamp battery good for twelve hours, the clothes on his back, and the pit boots on his feet. A well-prepared caving expedition, by contrast, would have backpacked in with bedrolls, first aid kits, bottled water, dried food, extra batteries, walkie-talkies. But these were no teenage spelunkers, boys and girls clammily finding one another's hand in the dark; they were simply miners hiking down for a day's work, and that day's supplies were long gone.

Garnet Clarke and Currie Smith kept trying to pierce through the piled-up 13,000 level. They had one pick. They came up against raw roadblocks of rock and coal at every turn. "You take pity on the older ones," thought Garnet when they sat down to rest for a minute, "because they're older and it's harder for them to get around." Patting the coal around him in desolate search for an opening, he suddenly felt a piece of pipe sticking out of the rock. "Look here!" he yelled. "Look at this pipe broken off. Let's holler into it."

"Help! Help" the men shouted, their lips pursed together like a duo at a microphone.

A response came quickly: "Hulloo!" a low voice said. "Hulloo!"

"Oh my God, we're rescued!" yelled Currie. "Hello! Hello! We're down here!"

"Hulloo," came the same low voice.

"There's seven of us, can you get to us? We're alive down here! We got one injured real bad! Boys, we're saved!"

"Hullooooo."

"Well, shit," said Currie. "It's Barney Martin."

"Where are you?" they called dutifully, their hearts still pounding from happiness, but slowing now.

"Hulloooo." They crawled over the waste in search of Barney, but stones started falling on them and they froze. "Just stay still," Currie hissed. "The good Lord's with us, surely. Stay here and I'll go ahead a little bit, and if I fall, pull me out." Crawling a few feet farther into the grayness, Currie tumbled into a hole and landed on top of Barney Martin. Currie let out a yell and Garnie crawled rapidly after the sound and dropped into the hole on top of Currie.

"Gee whiz, kid," said Currie. "Get out of here, Garnie. Stand up so we can get some air in here."

"Water?" Barney whispered from underneath the two men.

"No, Barney," they replied, "we ain't had any for a while. You?"

Barney gave no answer.

"Well, Barney," said Currie, as he climbed out of the hole and prepared to depart, "the only thing we can do is pray to the Lord that somebody will come."

Barney still did not reply; he seemed, at best, semiconscious. There was nothing they could do for him. They lacked the means and the strength to extricate him, and would have had nothing to offer him even if they freed him from his hole.

On their way back to the group, Garnet and Currie got lost. "To dickens with the pick," said Currie, "leave it there."

They crawled aimlessly over the coal, sweating and anxious. They stopped to rest.

"Well, boy, I don't know, it don't look good," said Currie. "I don't believe we'll make it."

Garnie said, "No," and started to cry.

"Garnie, look, I got a wife and family at home. Don't cry. We need all our strength. I think I got strength enough yet for a couple more days. Maybe more."

"All right, Currie, I'll stop."

But then Currie Smith broke down and began to weep.

"Well, Currie," said Garnet, "we'll get out. Like you said."

"Yes, you're right," said Currie, "but it builds up inside you."

They lay still and listened for Percy Rector's screaming. When they heard his wails, they crept in that direction till they found the clammy room where the other men lay.

"Boys," said Currie Smith. "There is no possible way of getting down through. If we had lights, if we had the power, we could."

"Do you suppose there is any way we can get Barney up with us?" asked Maurice, upon learning the man was alive.

"We are too weak," they said. "We were just barely able to make the grade to get back here ourselves. There's no way we'd get him out of that pit."

"If rescuers come," said Maurice, "Barney will be the first one they will get."

"Well, if we ever do get out," somebody said, "we'll get a big pension."

"Like fun we will," said Currie.

18

A Malevolent Factory

ABOVE GROUND
MONDAY, OCTOBER 27, 5 A.M.
EIGHTY-ONE HOURS SINCE THE BUMP

"The work is turning gruesome," the rescuers complained when they came up and threw themselves on the ground to gasp for fresh air.

"It's warm in there," Dr. Burden explained. "The bodies that have been compressed by coal balloon out as soon as they're uncovered. They stink from decomposition."

"The corpses are dripping on us," said the rescuers. "It's slow going. We got to clear the rockfalls and collapsed levels, and we got no trolleys to do it with. The trolley rails are flat up against the roof. We got to move the debris, but there's no place to put it. We got to timber the new tunnels we're digging, but we got to carry in the timber by hand."

Floyd Gilroy, a member of the group of rescuers who called themselves the Wrecking Crew, was working nine-hour shifts, mostly on his hands and knees. He was finding one to four bodies a night.

"We done all the hollering and talking and chewing, everything we could think of, to keep our minds off them," he told his wife when he went home in the middle of the night to sleep. "We knew what we was under, what we had to go through."

"What is it, Floyd?" she asked him hours later. He was heaving about in bed and loudly sighing.

"Well, I hate to tell you. But every body we struck, we always got them out, brought them with us, see. But when we struck Johnny Jackson's body last night, it was too late to carry him, we couldn't get him out, we had to leave him there. Well, every time I go to roll over, it's like I can see the body. I'm just thinking about him."

"It's a nightmare," thought Mabel Smith, with her dear Currie among the missing. "The TV's on all the time. I have to look after the children. I can't just sit around and cry all the time, that's not doing any good. I can't sleep at night, so I've got to ask the doctor for pills. Currie's brothers want to go ahead and dig his grave, but I'm saying no. I'm not going to believe anything till I hear for sure. I'm not going to start digging graves. You have to think positive because you have the children and everything."

6 A.M.

A car drove into the yard at the Turnbulls', where Elaine paced sleeplessly day and night. A priest came into the house, followed by the rest of Billy's family, looking over his shoulder. "It's over." Elaine knew then. "He's gone."

She took in the news in silence and went upstairs to look at the sleeping children. They didn't know yet. "We are on our own," she said aloud.

———

One by one coffins emerged from the door of the shed covering the mine entrance. The mine seemed like a malevolent factory operating in reverse: hoisting the dead in their coffins out of their graves, one by one.

Each coffin was carried to the ambulance garage at the mine and opened by a mine official, a union official, and Dr. Burden. All three witnesses had to agree on the identity of the man. They then signed three tags: one for the body, one for the aluminum case, and one for the mine office. If the victim was unrecognizable, the team relied on the lamp identification number. They called a minister and waited an hour or more before informing the press. Raymond Tabor, a Little League coach and father of four, the husband of sweet Ruth, who made the best fruit pies in town, was identified, and the coffin was moved to his dining-room table.

Garnet Clarke's parents sat at their kitchen table and bowed their heads for a moment of silence. It was their only child's twenty-ninth birthday. They hadn't been told yet if he was alive or dead. They were poor people, and barely literate, so rather than besiege rescuers and reporters at the pithead for news, they sat humbly at home, chain-smoking, waiting to be told their fate.

Dr. Noel Murphy, a psychiatrist from Halifax, moved to town to try to help the wives and mothers manage their grief. "It's the saddest thing I've ever seen," he told a colleague. "There are two principal types in need of help," he noted. "There are those who scream and pound the walls, and those who sit and stare at the ceiling and say nothing for two or three days." He was obliged to hospitalize some of the wives, including one who spoke of killing herself.

The international news story grew thin; even the most innovative journalist was unable to crank a new emotion out of it. Coal and Death—it was an old tale. With no new dramatic findings to relay, the reporters decamped. They left behind the hollow-eyed women in scarves and their worried-looking children, standing at the pithead, standing by open graves, or standing on their porches, staring off into the night.

19

"Ruther've Done Chicken Farming"

GROUP OF TWELVE
MONDAY, OCTOBER 27
FOUR DAYS SINCE THE BUMP

When the last battery failed and the water supplies dwindled dangerously among the Group of Twelve, the urgent hands and big, hurrying, booted feet of Eldred Lowther fell into disuse; he lost his pick in the waste. Levi Milley gave up and retreated into himself, his knees drawn up, his mouth pulled down.

"I have a feeling in my stomach as if I want to cry," thought Joe McDonald, immobilized by the swollen leg on which the fan had fallen. He tried to lighten the feeling by shouting once into the blue-black space, "Let me out!" But the sad feeling in his stomach, like a lump of raw dough, remained cold and heavy. "It's from shock, I figure, or being scared."

"There were eight of us kids in my family. I never expected to be the first one to go," he thought. His father had died when Joe, the seventh child, was two years old and his mother was in the eighth month of pregnancy with the eighth. "Many a day I was hungry. Lots of winters we barely had shoes to put on our feet." As a young man, he boxed. "I went in for boxing to learn how to hit. Out of a Jack Dempsey book, I pretty well got the knack of it. I had about thirty knockouts in addition to street fights. I beat some pretty big men. They were big fellows but they weren't worth two cents. When *I* hit a fellow, he stays hit. I don't look for a fight, but I don't walk away from one either." In his twenties, he excelled at ice hockey. "For a few years there, I was the best skater in Springhill. I'll still take off a day to go skate if it's clear." He tried to think about the ice, and not about his wife and three children and precious seventy-six-year-old mother.

"My leg is about four times its normal size." He began to have a feeling of pity for his puffed-up leg, as if it were an old friend lying beside him. "There's nothing holding it together but the skin, poor old leg. It's like it's not a part of me any-more." The thought of how he'd be nursed at home by his tender wife and children, how they'd bring him soup and tea and arrange his blankets, thickened the feeling in his stomach. "Poor old leg."

Men stuck close to their buddies, if they had a buddy alive and walled in with them. Caleb Rushton lay near his good friend, Bowman Maddison, and shared reminiscences with Hughie Guthro, who had lived across the road from him when they were kids. Hughie Guthro lay close to his best friend, Joe Holloway. Joe McDonald and Ted Michniak had made a new alliance out of injury and pain. The singletons worried about their lost partners or emitted tears made more of salt than of water, trying not to recall the sight of a friend's smashed body. "I dreamed about me buddy," spoke up Lowther at one point. "We set there and had a bottle of beer. Him and I set there and drank seven bottles of beer." That's all he said. Then he rolled over and felt awful.

The miners had followed Levi Milley and Eldred Lowther in the attempts to escape. The time to escape was over. There was no use in following those men anymore. Although Lowther, even in repose, figured he was the indispensable leader, he was the only one who felt that.

Levi Milley spoke once in a low voice. "I'd ruther've done chicken farming."

There was no headroom for standing, nor mood for socializing, nor light to see each other's faces, so they didn't mingle and josh like they did at the pithead, waiting their turn to shoulder into the arriving trolley. Only their voices circulated in the coal-dust dark. From one man came a story, from another a joke, from another a complaint and a whine, from another the first words of a church hymn; there were dreaming mumbles and uncontrollable belches and farts as the engines of their bodies chugged on empty; there was the spatter of scarce pee onto the coal floor, a sigh, a zip. Each man took the measure of all the others by sound alone. Their voices and noises lulled others to sleep and woke them up again, like children in their sleeping bags on the floor of a tent, dawdling in the twilight of consciousness between whispers and sleep.

As their canteens went dry, batteries failed, and hopes of escape expired, a couple of new leaders arose. Somehow Caleb Rushton and Gorley Kempt took over. Men in their loneliness found Caleb's optimism to be a source of hope, and Gorley's geniality to offer a bit of company.

Underground, despite his best intentions, Gorley retained his lightheartedness. Of course, it was a grave situation they were all in, he acknowledged with clenched brow and droop of shoulders, yet this jaunty fellow seemed to feel that he'd been in bad scrapes before and had escaped by the skin of his teeth. Who better to be trapped with than Br'er Rabbit?

Though Caleb Rushton privately leaned on round-headed,

plain-talking Hughie Guthro, others were looking to him. He held to his faith in God. He had book learning. He spoke with a calm, low-timbred voice. Other men—jittery, perspiring, all over goose bumps, cranky, parched—calmed themselves when Caleb spoke, as if he were offering dippers of water from a serene internal lake. "If the Lord had meant for us to die," he said, "He could have taken us a few days ago when our buddies were killed. He has a different plan in store for us."

Caleb, with his fine, kind voice, became not only the pastor but also the choir leader. He'd start up a hymn and the others, lying around him in discomfort and pain, chimed in as best they could. Or another began it—Bowman Maddison offered, "And the oil lamps were burning"—and Caleb took the lead. It was an easy membership in Caleb's underground church: you could sing or not sing, and you didn't have to get up, shave, and dress on a Sunday morning to be there; nor did you have to ferry your girdled wife in her hat to church and then slouch behind the steering wheel of the truck for a snooze, enduring the sidelong looks of the righteous as they hurried past.

Isolated in this way, plucked out—arguably by the hand of God—and assigned to this limbo between life and death, it was natural for a man to turn his thoughts to the state of his soul and figure out the odds of his getting a heavenly reward.

"Church," thought Ted Michniak. "Now that's one place I haven't been for years." He was a Catholic who had married a non-Catholic outside the church, and his wife had moved out ten years ago and now was living with another man. "I am an outcast from the Church," he thought, unsure whether he should or should not join in the Protestant hymns. In Springhill, the priest always warmly shook his hand and invited him to re-turn to church. Michniak often walked a couple of blocks out of his way to avoid passing the father's house and risking another friendly encounter. "I don't blame the priest," he'd think, huffing uphill in the wrong direction. "That's his job."

Joe McDonald, also a Catholic, prayed fervently. He was using his fingers for a rosary. Michniak rested his head on the stone floor and took some comfort in listening to Joe pray.

Bowman Maddison, the tall stamp collector and songwriter, quietly brooded upon his status in the community. He was never certain who knew the truth about him: he had been born out-of-wedlock. He had always kept himself at a slight remove from others. "It has kept me from going and mixing with people. I hate to mix with people that their mothers and fathers were married."

Bowman knew there were people who would say his brothers were not fully and truly his brothers. "I always call them my full brothers. Some people call them half-brothers. But that's ignorance, isn't it? We came from the same mother." He wondered whether the men with whom he was trapped knew he was a bastard. Who knew what his place in the afterlife would be? "Surely God cannot say it is my fault, what I am," he thought.

20

"You Know He's Bad People, but You Can't Help But Like Him."

"Governor Marvin Griffin of Georgia was a charmer, a real political animal. Therefore, he had no principles," chuckles Joe Cumming, a sixth-generation Georgian and former Atlanta bureau chief for *Newsweek*. "I think of him as that throaty voice, red face, big smile. Marvin Griffin played politics the *old* way. I stopped by the governor's office soon after he was elected. I was a salesman then, trying to sell the state a tourism film, and the aide mistook me for a campaign contributor. The aide said, 'Guv'na? This Joe Cumming. He hadn't got a thang since we got in.' I loved that! Naturally, they assumed I was a supporter looking for my kickback. I loved what it told me about the way he was planning to run things.

"He was a Willy Stark. My brother-in-law used to say about Griffin, 'That man is *primitive*. He reminds me of raw meat.' He was the kind of man—you know he's bad people, but you can't help but like him."

Griffin ran for governor the summer of 1954 in the pig-roast, stump-speaking style of the late, legendary Governor Eugene Talmadge whose motto was "Retreat, hell!" In his navy blue suit and polka-dot tie, standing in the back of a pickup truck or on the steps of a county courthouse, dabbing with a flag-sized hanky at his red face, Griffin promised country white folks what he—and they—thought they still wanted to hear: that the Old South would stand forever. In Moultrie, Georgia, he yanked dried animal pelts out of a feedsack, introduced them by the names of his opponents, then nailed each fur to a piece of wood. He encountered less jubilant crowds when he first campaigned in the hills of north Georgia. "First time I ever spoke at Cleveland, Georgia, in White County, I had about four hundred," Griffin reminisced, "and I made 'em the foot-stompingest, double-barreled, old wind up stump speech you ever heard in your life, and they never changed expression and I told my benefactor, 'My friend, I did not sell any calico here today.'"

Under Governor Griffin's administration, state revenues paid for his hunting and fishing trips; private land, including the property of the governor's supporters, was worked by prison labor; and the state parks department bought boats that couldn't float for parks without ponds. "In spite of its many merits," writes historian Robert W. Dubay, "the Griffin regime is fully deserving of its reputation as one of the most corrupt, amoral, mismanaged, and inefficient administrations in Georgia history." In time, twenty-four state officials, employees, and businessmen would receive grand jury indictments on fraud, conspiracy, and embezzlement charges.

"Never in Georgia history," reported Lester Velie for *Reader's Digest,* "had so many stolen so much."

Tourism was not much of an American industry yet in the 1950s, but it was heating up. Folks in rural Georgia could see there was something in it. When a man stood to stretch his back in an onion or soybean field, or looked out from the loft of a tobacco barn, he saw late-model Oldsmobiles, two-seater Thunderbirds, Buicks with wraparound panoramic windshields tiptoeing down his country road. Searching desperately for the state of Florida, the fancy automobiles swatted at gnats and flying ants with their windshield wipers and crunched in their white-walled tires over the armadillos. By the time the Yankee cars slowed to a stop in downtown Statesboro, or Alma, or Waycross, you knew the tourists thought they'd never get out of Georgia. You knew they were going to look at their atlases when they got home and confirm their dawning impression that Georgia was the biggest state east of the Mississippi River.

If it was a black family that had mislaid the highway to Florida, they rolled up their windows and glided on through town, the children looking sadly out the windows, wishing for a clean place where they would be welcome to eat or to use the facilities, the wife looking modestly down into her lap so as not to accidentally make eye contact with a cracker, the father keeping his shirt buttoned to the collar, both hands on the wheel, and eyes fixed on the road. No, they'd have to ease on down Main Street, up and over the train tracks, and thud onto the dust roads of the colored section before they could comfortably disembark. There they might find a meal served family style in a boardinghouse, and, if they were lucky, indoor plumbing.

But even the white tourists stepped out of their insect-splattered Studebakers and Packards cautiously, smiling nervously, grateful to have found some semblance of civilization, but uncertain whether the natives spoke the King's English.

It didn't take a rural genius to figure out that the Yankees were on vacation and eager to spend their money. Confederate flags on little sticks, rubber alligators, cloth pickaninny dolls, salt-and-pepper shakers in the shapes of an old field hand and a kerchiefed mammy, Indian bead belts, rubber tomahawks, postcards of grinning black boys eating watermelon, china plates with pastel scenes of plantation life—the tourists would buy just about anything displayed on the glass shelves under the cash register next to the cartons of chewing gum. The Southern way of life was cheerfully packaged and marketed along with the sweet iced tea, the country-fried steak, and the sacks of fresh peaches as warm and fuzzy as kittens. There was no need for white families to cross over the train tracks into the colored section, where different stories, or the same stories with different points of view, might be told. They could purchase white Southern perspectives on the Negro way of life right there in the dinette.

But Georgia didn't have a resort. And the locals in the southeastern counties weren't the only ones watching as the Yankees paid for their lunches, poked toothpicks between their lips, punched their purchases down into their already over-stuffed trunks, and tootled away south on Route 1 out of Baxley, Georgia, toward Jacksonville, or down 41 from Valdosta along the Gulf Coast of Florida, across the Everglades, and into Miami.

The governor of Georgia didn't like the feel of this thing, either, letting perfectly good revenue go steaming bumper-to-bumper out of the state. What did they see in Florida? The Florida beaches were as hard and hot as big-city parking lots, weren't they? And Florida's white people were about as brown and leathery as parking lot attendants.

Georgia's coastal land, by contrast, was lovely—untamed and tangled, exotic and peculiar, with a salty, aromatic, woody haze after a summer rain. Americans just didn't know about it.

"It is easier to milk a tourist than a cow," Governor Griffin opined and ordered state funds to prepare Jekyll Island, one of a string of Atlantic barrier islands, to be a national tourist destination.

21

Birthday Party

As the six survivors trapped with Percy Rector choked for a taste of water, they also ached for companionship. They couldn't seem to get much solace out of men as bereft and weepy as themselves. They seemed to multiply each other's misery rather than lessen it. Everyone said it was worse to be trapped alone. Lone survivors of the Explosion of '56 recalled an almost unendurable panic, unrelieved by the calming presence of a buddy. But these survivors, trapped together, it was aggravation that gnawed at them, frustration at the stupidity of their fellows and the stupidity of getting stuck and dying with such men.

The largest portion of depression is loneliness. Each man felt that he was alone in the world. Each married man thought with deep homesickness about his wife. Hadn't his wife loved him almost like his sweet mother had? Or at least, in this loneliness, it seemed that was how much his wife had loved him. Every one of them also yearned for his mother. Some of their mothers had been lost to early exhaustion and death, and these men had the unsettling thought that their mothers were younger than the sons were now. Others had a tough gray-haired mother still living, and it broke their hearts to picture the women weeping over them.

But the women couldn't reach down to them here, couldn't cluck over them, or order them with mock sternness into the bath, or shake a cookpot at them, or frown and turn away smiling when offered an off-color joke or tidbit of gossip. From deep in the pit, the survivors loved their mothers and wives more tenderly than ever and promised God they'd show the women how much they loved them, if only they could be released from this hole and permitted to walk, once more, up a little blacktop street toward home.

The everyday world of the women—stove top, washtub, back stoop, clothesline—looked, from where the men lay, like heaven. And it was directly overhead. One mile up. Under a blue and white, windy sky.

Frank Hunter sadly felt his stomach. "There's no stomach there at all," he thought. "I have no stomach. It feels like a bunch of worms in there. I feel me hip bones and, Jesus, there is no flesh on them."

Garnet Clarke's birthday was on October 27. He turned twenty-nine. Maurice Ruddick located a piece of a sandwich as dry as a piece of burnt wood. He snapped it apart seven ways and led the singing. "Happy birthday to you," the big filthy sad men sang in the pitch-dark, and passed around the splinters of sandwich hand to hand.

On Currie and Garnie's last foray, when they'd agreed that escape was hopeless, they had brought back a final prize: a water can full of coal and dust. Garnie pulled off his undershirt and strained the black water through the shirt, and the men sucked a few drops. But there had been no water since then.

"What they do in the desert, I hear tell," offered Currie Smith, "is drink their own water. It tastes all right after, you know, you wait till it cools a bit."

A couple of men went off to the shadows to pee into a bucket and try it. Some couldn't trick their tongues, which reared up and warded off the urine.

"I can't drink it, too salty," said Garnet. "Look at Frank go, though! He likes beer, so I guess maybe he likes it."

"We got oil down here," one of the men remembered one night. "What about trying to drink that?"

Maurice Ruddick's low voice rose to them from his spot beside Percy. "No. Don't go drinking no oil. Listen, just chew up some bark, chew it fine to get the juice, and then when it gets too dry, take a swallow of your own water to juice it up a bit."

"Listen, fellas," said Pep, "I've been thinking about cutting my leg to get some blood to drink. Would that do any good?"

"No, Herb," said Maurice.

As the days dragged on, the thirst was such that a man felt like a splintery wooden stake was sticking into his throat. Hourly it was twisted, and twisted.

Whenever Percy Rector woke up, he strained and strained against the trap. Delirium and unconsciousness glazed his eyes and drugged his brain for most of the hours out of every twelve circling around on the men's luminous watch dials. When he woke up, he pulled against the log wall, with a moaning so deep now it came from his belly, his bowels. The men heard him jerking forward, with a hernia-deep grunting, *unh, unh, unh.* They knew he wet himself and beshat himself.

Then he was chattering and swearing and shouting in excitement, sunk in in some garishly lit-up realm between agony and hallucination. They no longer had water to give him, and he had flinched violently away, snarling, when Maurice dribbled urine from a bucket into his mouth; so his brain invented water, bubbly blue-white cascades of it in a waterfall just out of reach. He pointed to it, just over their heads, with a trembling finger. His grinning, yearning, panting face was horrible to see. He stuck his tongue out a long way, craned bizarrely with it, to catch the rainy moisture drifting off the falls from where he stood on a slick mountain ledge. When they aimed a headlamp at him, they saw him rapt with attention to the thrashing falls and mountain stream. He closed his eyes to savor the spray.

"He's delirious," said Herb. "I don't think he is in any pain, do you? I think when a man is delirious, he can't feel any pain."

"All right, boys!" yelled Percy once with such clarity, so much like the voice of old Perce, that it woke up and scared the men. "I got me horses hooked up. I'll go down to that brook and haul up a barrel or two of that water. We'll all have plenty of fresh water to drink then, ho *ho*!"

It was driving them mad. They hunched forward and clamped their hands over their ears to block him, for they all were almost insane with thirst.

22

Day-Glo on Velvet

As hours passed, religion was mostly displaced by obsession with thirst. Each man had but one thought in his mind now, and the thought was, *"Water!"*

The drought was going to be far worse than the famine. Their stomachs had shrunk into fists, but the men's tongues grew thick and black. "This must be what it is to die of thirst," they thought. They could hardly close their dry mouths, which of course made the dryness worse. As a man's tongue dried out, he felt as if he were holding between his teeth a thick, splintery chunk of burnt wood, which scraped the lips in front and jabbed the pharynx in back. On the surface of the tongue, the papillae had petrified; no longer lubricated and quiveringly sensitive, they scraped against the roof of the mouth like short bristles on a hairbrush.

The aspirin bottle was passed for the last time. Hughie Guthro slid down the incline to share the water with Michniak and McDonald. The droplets of water were as precious as beads of platinum. Rolling through the dry papillae toward the throat, the droplets were like silver balls bouncing down the slope of a pinball machine.

———

"What time it is?" someone gasped into the darkness over-hanging the Group of Twelve.

Caleb Rushton propped himself up to lean close to his still-faintly-glowing watch. "Three o'clock Saturday morning," he said one time, and, "four o'clock Sunday evening," the next time, the time leaking away from them blackly and soundlessly and dangerously, like oil from an engine.

"What time is it, Caleb?"

"Nine in the morning, Monday morning."

"Well, Judy's off to high school, then," thought Levi Milley and felt happiness in the thought that life as he once knew it was still rolling along. But then, in a whiplash of sorrow, he remembered, "Oh, school might be cancelled because of us. I don't know where Judy is!"

On the fifth day, the stone-roofed vault that held the Group of Twelve lit up like a Day-Glo painting on velvet. Baubles and streamers of light frolicked before the men's amazed eyes. Orange, purple, red, yellow puffs bloomed in the black air, expanded, and burst like silent fireworks. Unseen by their fellows, men swatted and grabbed at the bouncing globes, but their hands tore through them as if through mist. Some guessed that the light show was a feature of their own brains going haywire in the long dark, their own blank neurons misfiring, doodling random hallucinations. Since everyone's greatest fear was of going insane, no one spoke up about the lights, in case the response was that his mind was starting to go. Finally, Bowman Maddison said, "I can see lights between my eyes, yellow, blue, green. They're going up and down in the dark."

"Yes!" said Caleb. "I'm seeing them flashing in front of my eyes all the time. Mine are like those kaleidoscopes, you know?

With cut glass in them? It's like one of those going all the time."

"I see yellow and blue lights flying by," said Eldred Lowther. "And I'll tell you what else: I can see the packs and the stone walls just as nice as can be. My eyes are shining on them, like headlights."

"Every time I try to fall asleep," said Harold Brine, "I feel like somebody's shining a light right into my eyes. Everything is all lit up."

"You see that red and yellow glow? Right now?" someone yelled.

"Yeah, I see it," said Milley. "It's probably because we want to see it. We're so long in the dark we're persuading ourselves we can see a yellow glow."

"My headlights are on again!" shouted Lowther.

From Monday on, they didn't move much. The deprivation of food, water, sunlight, and fresh air left their limbs fainting with lassitude, their hearts banging, their skin shivering and covered by goose bumps. After a man got up to go urinate farther down the incline, he slid groaning back to his shallow hollow on the rocky floor like a schoolboy returning to an assigned seat. When all the batteries of all the headlamps were dead, there was no confusion about location, for the rough circle of bodies—ten higher up, and the two injured men several yards down the gradient—stayed imprinted on the mind's eye of each like a photographic negative.

"The trick they're doing, I wouldn't do that to anybody," Joe McDonald fumed, lying with his swollen leg as his closest comrade. He was certain that water was being sloshed among the able-bodied men higher up and that his share and Michniak's were being stolen. "I always try to be kind and help somebody else. When somebody does a dirty trick like that, I don't like it and I'll never forget it, either. If I was on my feet, things would be different."

"They think we're going to die," he growled to Michniak. "The way they're treating us. They're thinking, 'To hell with them.' They don't care if we live or die. I been watching them close. They say they *just* run out of water and we haven't had none since Saturday, so they gave themselves away right there. They're dirty, I'm telling you."

"Jesus," he thought, "I don't know what I'm going to do with them when I get out of here."

"Well, boys, you know what they tell you in basic training," rasped Gorley Kempt after a long spell of silence in the dark. "We got to drink our own urine."

"Boys," said Harold Brine, "we have to survive. That is what we will have to do, drink it if it makes us sick or not." He and Gorley went off, peed into their buckets, tried it, and couldn't swallow. "It is right salty," said Harold, grimacing.

"I can't drink it. I can't get it down," said Gorley.

"I am so dry that I have to," El Lowther said to himself. He had held on to his empty lunch pail and an empty sheet of wax paper—"it might come the time that I eat that," he had thought. He peed into his piece can, then twisted a bit of the wax paper to make "a little wee cup" and dipped that in the urine. He lay back, opened his mouth, and let drops fall to the back of his throat, to avoid tasting it. For a short while, it sustained him. "I'm not getting enough like this," he said. He reached over and tried to take a swill straight out of the can, but spat it out. "My water's too strong."

Others were discovering the same phenomenon: they couldn't drink their own urine.

A few more hours passed in darkness, till a man had a thought. "Pass your can, eh?" he said with a bitter laugh. "Let me try yours." It was discovered that a man could better stomach someone else's water. They made a communal bucket, blending their output. Now when a fellow got up to pee, he emptied his bladder into a bucket, and passed the clanking bucket to the next man who needed to urinate or needed to drink.

"All right, pass it over," said Lowther. He shut his eyes, held his breath, and gulped.

"I'm thirsty, but I'm not *that* thirsty," said Hughie Guthro. "Joe, you want to try it?" Joe Holloway reached for the warm can and took a sip, but gagged and retched and couldn't swallow. "Wait, let me just wet my lips with it," he said, reluctant to pass it on. He dipped the tail of his shirt into it and took a few swipes across his cracked lips.

They handed down a bucket sloshing with urine to the two injured men.

"I can't get it in my head to drink it," said Ted Michniak.

"Put some bark in it, cool it off," someone called.

Larry Leadbetter discovered he had half a roll of Tums, for stomach upset, in his jacket pocket, so he crumbled a tablet of Tums into the bucket of warm urine, to kill the taste a little. As the dark hours passed unseen, the communal urine grew increasingly sour and salty. The few pints of liquid, recycled over and over through all their bodies, became ever more concentrated. It grew dense and briny, like ocean water. It no longer quenched thirst, and no one urinated very often anymore. Still, they passed the bucket around and dipped their shirts and swabbed their lips with it, lips cracked and breaking in the drought, beaten raw by the wooden tongues. Or they swilled a burning salty gargle of pee through their teeth and spat it out if they couldn't make themselves swallow it anymore.

Handsome Harold Brine, with his rugged four-day beard, was remembering that someone had said, "It's an awful death to die of thirst." He wanted to know more about it, but didn't want to remind the men of it by asking. "What will it be like? Why is it worse than other ways of dying?" he thought.

"The wife said I shouldn't be down here," someone said.

"Yeah, well damn near everyone's wife said that," Harold snapped, "that we shouldn't be down here."

"What about my little girl?" Harold wondered. "If we go, will she remember me?"

"I don't doubt there are rescuers digging to get us," said Bowman Maddison, stating what they all were thinking. "But it has done such a lot of damage, it will be a little while getting here."

"I can't help but think what our chances are," spoke glum Levi Milley, his first words in half a day.

"We're dehydrating is what we're doing," said Hughie Guthro, whose eyes were nearly swollen shut from dust. "You got to have a certain amount of water each day, or you're supposed to have, anyway."

Of course, he no longer knew when one day ended and another began. He didn't know if it was night or day up top. He didn't know what his children were doing, which reminded him that he might never know again. "I hate to think of my young fellows being left without me, at their age. It's pretty hard for children who lose their father. I was nine when Dad drowned, 1936. I didn't realize what it was, I thought he was just going away for a while. As I got older, I realized. I missed him. We was awful close. I was the baby boy of the family."

"What about that hunting trip, Hughie?" muttered Joe Holloway to his brother-in-law and best pal. "This weekend, supposed to be."

"It's about to kill me thinking about it," said Hughie Guthro. "I was ready. Even had the grub ready."

"When we was trapped in No. 4, we had a hunting trip planned for that weekend, too," said Joe.

"I know it, I know it."

Joe Holloway, lying in the dark beside his friend, realized he couldn't think about his wife and sons; every time he began to think of them, his chest filled with grief and tears spiked from his eyes. He tried to think about hunting instead. But every trail led back to his wife. "You know that old pair of hunting boots I've had for two years and never wore because they're too small and they hurt?" he said quietly to Hughie. "Well, would you believe Loretta bought me a new pair of insulated boots for this trip and they came Thursday morning?" He couldn't say any more, but scooted lower down on the sloping floor and commiserated from afar with his poor new boots, still in their box, which might never get a chance to go into the woods. Long after he was a dried-out pile of bones down here, the handsome leather hunting boots with fuzzy insides would still be there, in their tissue paper on the shelf of his closet, waiting for him, waiting for their first adventure.

———

"First you're warm, then you're cold," said Gorley. He had dug up a couple of old shirts he'd found lying around and wrapped them around his shoulders like shawls.

Joe Holloway rolled over and his arm fell against his brother-in-law, Hughie Guthro. "God, I can hear your heart. I can feel it, it's tapping so hard." He put his hand on his own chest. "Mine's doing the same thing."

Lowther felt it, too. He thought, "My heart isn't beating right. It's beating so hard, I think I can hear it. When I just sit up to reach for the urine pail, just that little bit of exertion, I feel an awful difference. It's more like a pound than a beat. It's not a real heartbeat anymore."

His stomach felt like a little ball. "I feel like my stomach's gotten so small that my backbone has come forward," he said aloud.

He couldn't get the scene out of his mind of a fellow he found crushed into the roof. "Everything was hanging out of him. It was horrible."

"I'm feeling foggy and not too bright," thought Bowman Maddison, lying in his spot near Caleb. "I learned about gas in the war." When he felt the goose bumps rise along his arms, he thought to himself, "There it is. It's the gas."

23

Good Night, Sweetheart

ABOVE GROUND
TUESDAY, OCTOBER 28, 3 A.M.

Margie Kempt kept all the lights on in the house, even when she went to bed. "If I turn them off, it'll look like I don't expect Gorley home. Somebody down there has got to be alive." Then a neighbor stopped by to say that the Kempts' vacation pal, Alfred, Margaret's husband and father of ten children, who always said he'd borrow Margie if times got tough, had been found dead.

Norma Ruddick, whose sisters and sisters-in-law had moved in to help care for all the children, said, "Don't let me hear the TV or the radio. Different times somebody will come on singing like a quartet and it sounds like him. Turn it off, turn it off."

Two wives phoned the Amherst radio station to complain: "The music you're playing between announcements, it's no good. What do you mean by playing 'Good Night, Sweetheart'?"

4 A.M.

New to insomnia, Elaine Turnbull knelt on the floor of her living room and, with scraps strewn about her as her four children slept, upholstered a chair. The phone rang long past midnight. It was her friend Olivia, who'd lost both her husband and her oldest son in mine accidents.

"What are you doing?"

"Upholstering a chair."

"Put the coffee on. I'm coming over."

The two women worked till dawn on the chair, sitting back on their heels from time to time to admire their handiwork. Neither mentioned Billy, nor why they both happened to be awake in the middle of the night.

8 A.M.

Bev Reynolds, who watched her brother Art pass up the street and down the street and refused to hear any reports but his, looked out the window and said, "It's all over. Art is coming to tell me it's all over."

Her sister and her friends were with her and protested, "Oh, don't say that, Bev! He comes up this road every day!"

"No," said Bev. "He's coming to tell me."

Art turned off the road and came up the yard and through the front door. Bev stood waiting. "It's all over, babe," he said.

Danny, with his tricycle and wagon, had been boarded at a neighbor's in the immediate aftermath of the bump and wasn't brought home till after Wes Reynolds's funeral to spare him the raw emotions. He would come back home with his little trike and wagon to find everything in the house exactly the same, except that his father was gone and would never come back. His mother would regret the way she handled it for the rest of her life.

24

Could a Mouse Escape?

The roads and alleys were blocked by coal, debris, and dead miners. The survivors of the Group of Twelve, resting together under low-dangling rocks, were too big to get past the barricades of disaster. But could a rat have gotten out? A bat? Could a mouse find its way to the surface? A beetle?

Caleb Rushton, Gorley Kempt, and Harold Brine began pondering the iron pipes and rubber air hoses of the compressed-air system. Power tools underground ran on compressed air rather than gasoline. Hoses, like air hoses at a gas station, wove around and through the rock, connecting to ever-thicker pipes and hoses, the ganglia connecting finally to the compressed-air machine on the surface. It was conceivable to a few of the pinned men that a very small mouse could scamper from hose to pipe to hose all the way up to light of day, if the network weren't crushed. But the men had no message-bearing mouse to release.

But sound traveled, they thought. If they could find a pipe, they might be able to detect sounds of rescue. Then they could bang on it, a rhythmic hammering to signal life. In August 2000, the same thought would occur to the Russian sailors trapped in their sunken submarine, the nuclear-powered *Kursk*. They knocked out SOS against the flanks of their ruined craft from the bottom of the Bering Sea. The SOS was heard, but rescuers could not reach them in time.

Harold Brine and Gorley Kempt blindly went exploring until their patting hands hit upon a broken-off air line in a niche not far from the home cave. They could feel that a six-inch metal pipe was joined there to a three-inch hose by a shut-off valve.

"You suppose we can take off that shut-off?" asked Gorley.

"I don't know, but I'll try," Harold said. He chiseled with a pack-wedge at the two nuts on the shut-off valve; he worked off one and loosened the other. He backed out of the hole, saying, "I can't stay here much longer. You had better come in."

Gorley dove in and pulled off the second nut. "That gives us a full six-inch air line to listen at," he said, and Harold snaked back in to listen with him. They heard a motor running far away. "It's afternoon shift, isn't it?" said Gorley.

"I don't even know what day it is," said Harold.

"They're working hard."

"You can tell they're getting farther in because the tugger is running longer each trip."

The two men huddled in the dark and listened to the distant but human sound of machinery being operated until the shift ended, and then they heard nothing. Why hadn't another shift come on? They waited hopefully for a long time, afraid to cough or speak lest they miss the sound of comrades working to find them.

"They figure we're gone," said Harold finally, and the two crept back to the group.

"I know what they are doing out there," Harold glumly told the waiting men. "They are setting up that new loader. They figure we are all gone in here. They're setting that new loader up and they're going to clean out that level."

Lowther agreed with Harold Brine. "These fellows are thinking there's nobody alive, there just can't be. So instead of digging a hole to get in to us, they're timbering the place all up, getting ready to bring the bodies out."

"They'll never get to us that way," someone cried. "It will be weeks and weeks, and we can't survive that!"

"They're making a passageway to bring the coffins in and out," said Lowther. The others found him to be as irritating a doomsayer as he had been an optimist.

"Shut up, Lowther," someone said.

"What if they should give up and seal her up?" Caleb Rushton was thinking. "Not knowing, of course, that we're in here. They have no way of knowing we're in here." What he said out loud was, "Surely in other cases they would get every man out that they could, and the only way they can know for sure is to dig through and find out if there is anybody alive."

"Let's all have a go at the pipes," Gorley proposed. "We'll do it in shifts, boys. We'll bang on that thing till they hear us. Let's keep it going, then. Round the clock, eh? Two boys at a time."

Caleb stepped up for the first shift. He wriggled into the crevice and began to tap at the end of the pipe with an empty lunch bucket. "Hey! Hey!" he hollered. "There are men alive here!"

He held the place for an hour or two, until his urgent calls faded to a rather mechanical regularity. "Of course, the spirit falters when the digging and working out there seems to stop," Caleb thought. "We can't seem to get through to them. Now it's gone quiet again. What the heck are they doing out there?"

"We're getting an answer!" he screamed once to his fellows,

waiting on their slope of ground—he'd heard voices through the pipe! He banged and shouted with renewed vigor, but it was not, after all, an answer, and the voices drifted away from the other end of the pipe, out of earshot. There was silence for a long time. "Boys," he said stoutly, when he crawled back out, "as far as I am concerned, we *are* going to get out of here."

"I can hear pounding," reported Harold Brine when he crawled back from his shift. "I hear it on both sides of us."

"It's up the wall," someone said.

"No, it ain't," said someone else. "It sounds like it's at our level."

"It sounds like miles away," said Harold.

"It's an awful long way off," said Lowther. "It's all over. Look, we done everything we could. It has to be this way. It must be or we wouldn't be left. This is the way it's going to be."

"Be still, Lowther."

"How are my wife and children going to make out?" thought Lowther. "How will they go through life now? Will the company look after them and see if they've got enough money to get by on?"

Hughie Guthro returned from his turn banging on the pipe. "I can hear them pounding, but they can't hear us."

"I've been on rescue work in different places," persisted Lowther. "I know what they should be doing and I tell you, they ain't doing it."

Levi Milley was out of hope, not that he possessed much of it in the best of times. "What way will I be when I die?" he wondered. "Will I be melancholy? Will my breathing get irregular? Or will my heart just stop? Will death creep up on me or will there be pain?"

Eldred Lowther was thinking about his twelve brothers and sisters. "We've been together all our lives, but all at once one fellow died, and my sister in Toronto has cancer and she is down to sixty-two pounds, and Mother is not in too good shape, and one brother moved to the States, and another brother went to Halifax. We're all split up. And now I'll be leaving, too. I'll be splitting with them, too. I always wondered if we all meet up again when we die, and now it won't be too long before I find out for myself."

"I dreamed," Hughie Guthro told Joe Holloway, "I dreamed I was in the store at the corner of my street drinking a bottle of Pepsi-Cola."

"Yep," said Joe. "I heard you licking your lips."

"I dreamed I was fishing in a big brook," El Lowther said. Later he reported, "I dreamed that I was laying in the hospital and they were bringing me long glasses of ice-cold milk with ice cubes in it."

"My leg is asleep," Fred Hunter said aloud. "My leg is all numb and my foot is numb."

"Rub the circulation back into it, Teddy," said Harold Brine.

Fred Hunter started rubbing, but let out a holler at his own touch.

"Come here," said Brine. "I'll rub it." Fred made his way in the dark to Harold and stood over him, leaning against the wall for support. Harold hiked up Hunter's pant leg and rubbed vigorously.

"It's still getting cold," said Harold. "I can't do nothing for you, Teddy."

"Hold your foot up," some of the boys said, and Hunter rested his foot up on a prop and tried to say no more. He felt scared about the leg, about what it meant that he couldn't feel it anymore other than in moments of searing pain.

Gorley was increasingly tormented by an outstanding debt. "I got a couple of pieces of hose the other day to put on the heater of the car," he remembered. "As a rule, when I do anything like that, the boys at the auto shop let me take little things like that and pay them later. It was a dollar-forty, and I didn't pay them yet. I didn't leave no note for Margie to see that I owed them." As he shifted on the coal floor, trying to find a posture to sleep in, he twisted and tried to evade the thought of those hoses that it now seemed he had stolen.

"I can't get no ease with the leg, no matter what way I put it," Fred Hunter said some hours later, not knowing whether to suppress or relay his rising panic about it. He lay on top of some timber with his head hanging over one side and his legs hanging over the other, and stayed there, just trying to make it from one minute to the next.

25

Unnecessary Humiliation

The state of Georgia desperately needed investors and industries, so Governor Griffin went trolling for them through northern cities, the luncheon speaker at Chambers of Commerce and Kiwanis Clubs. In his Panama hat and seersucker suit, red-faced Griffin harangued that there was no place on earth where the peaches were sweeter, the watermelons redder, the fish hungrier, or the girls prettier. (His detractors would point out that there was also scarcely a place where the taxes were lower, the right-to-work laws tougher, and the chief executive more willing to send in state troopers to intimidate labor unions.)

Griffin was canny at luring northern manufacturers south to Georgia, but sometimes, back home, he turned petulant, as if he'd come to his senses and realized he was trafficking with the enemy. Like a rubber band stretched too far, he cracked back into the Bainbridge-born son of his KKK newspaper-editor father. As the Atlanta business community winced, Griffin sometimes lost his temper too early, before he had his investor snugly tucked into a Georgia county, and he scared the Yankee away.

The words Griffin spoke, when a fit was on him, were not intended for civic and business leaders in the North, nor even in Atlanta where Griffin felt hemmed in increasingly by Negroes, Northerners, liberals, and journalists. His harangues were hand-cut for broadcast by radio and distribution by small-town newspaper, like the paper his daddy had owned and he had taken over after "Pat" Griffin died; his words were meant to wing their way out over the cotton fields, peanut fields, tobacco fields, chicken farms, and peach orchards, and to float through the two-story redbrick downtowns where men sat at their desks with their shirtsleeves rolled up, beside their oscillating fans, perspiring.

Governor Griffin would speechify as if he'd never left his hometown newspaper office where he sent the secretaries scuttling away from the spray of spittle and epithet, and then sermonized further at the dinette down the block over his fried pork chop and three veggies lunch, dampening his sputtering words with sweet iced tea. And it wasn't even the case that the majority of Southerners held such raw and profane views about "miscegenation" and "mongrelization of the white race" as the governor did.

The 1950s was the era of moderates holding their tongues and looking around themselves cautiously; and it was the era during which civic leaders—World War II veterans among them—began to warm to the notion of racial civic justice (though not *social* equality) even if for no other reason than that it was better for business in Georgia than scenes of inflamed white mobs lurching through the streets with flaming torches.

Even at lunch in the dinette in Bainbridge, as Griffin ranted, there would have been a few diners weary of the racist cant, who wiped their mouths, slid coins under their plates, and left. Though it was on their behalf that a governor of Georgia was still mouthing off in the mid-1950s, there were hundreds of thousands of southern white citizens who sighed over their evening newspapers and wished the stalled state would move on.

In 1955 Georgia Tech won an invitation to the Sugar Bowl for the third year in a row. Their opponent, the University of Pittsburgh, fielded a black fullback. "The South stands at Armageddon!" Griffin brayed when he heard the news. "The battle is joined! We cannot make the slightest concession to the enemy in this dark and lamentable hour of struggle."

The governor was hung in effigy by thousands of rioting Tech fans. ONE TIME WE ARE FOR TECH, read banners held aloft by two thousand Georgia Bulldog fans protesting in Athens. (Unfortunately, 250 of those demonstrators detoured on their way home and engaged in a massive panty raid on coed dormitories, spurred on by female students pitching undergarments out their windows.)

"I am for segregation," Griffin shouted to the press during what some were calling "the Sugar Bowl nigger controversy." "I am for it 100 percent. I am not for it 90 percent. I am not for it 75 percent or 66 percent. I am not for it on Monday and against it on Tuesday." It was front-page news across America. *Time* described Griffin as a "pinhead"; Pennsylvania newspapers urged him to take his bigotry back into the piney woods from which it came; and even the Jackson, Georgia, *Progress-Argus* reminded readers that Georgia schools had "played against Negroes before without any earth-shattering consequences." "A football game isn't a social event. No tea will be served," said an *Atlanta Constitution* editorial. "There are no females on either team and there is absolutely no danger of intermarriage as a result."

The Board of Regents voted to permit Tech to go to New Orleans. Retreating slightly, the governor announced that he would boycott the game, "but if other people want colored folks sitting in their laps," they were welcome to it. Tech won the Sugar Bowl 7–0, but Governor Griffin retaliated by closing dozens of state parks and recreational facilities rather than see them integrated.

In 1957, Governor Orval Faubus of Arkansas signaled his intention to peacefully desegregate his state school system. Arkansas was being portrayed as a model of racial civility, when Governor Marvin Griffin of Georgia took it upon himself to fly to Arkansas to intervene. "If [the federal government] tries to tell us ... to integrate the races, I will be compelled to tell them to get their black-eyed peas and soup pots out of Georgia!" he roared to an assemblage of White Citizens Council members in Little Rock. The audience stood and cheered and offered rebel yells; the Arkansas citizenry was electrified.

Thousands of white protesters threatened eleven well-dressed high school students with violence; President Eisenhower federalized the Arkansas National Guard and mobilized a thousand troops from the 101st Airborne "Screaming Eagle" Division; and Faubus and Little Rock became the indelible symbols for blithering bigots. What had gone awry? "One of the South's most effective prophets of massive resistance [had] hurtled into the picture," writes Faubus biographer Roy Reed. "Gov. Marvin Griffin of Georgia, a failure as a chief executive but a first-rate rabble-rouser, came to Little Rock...."

Others labeled Griffin "a roving ambassador of turmoil."

The *Atlanta Constitution* had more than one occasion to lament: "How can we expect this state to attract anything except ridicule when its chief executive so constantly seizes upon the slightest excuse to make political capital? It is our hope that reason will reassert itself ... and that Georgians will be spared any further unnecessary humiliation."

26

Percy's Brook

Percy Rector had passed out again and was breathing heavily, raggedly, moaning and begging in his sleep. His chin hammered his chest. Occasionally his head would stagger halfway up and he'd look bleary-eyed at the men in the Group of Seven, with a hoary, hurt look, a thick-browed bewilderment with a face like a speared buffalo. "Help me," he whispered hoarsely. "Why won't you help me? Please. Please. Currie, will you? No? Garnie? Pep? Help me, boys. I just need a bit of help here, you see."

"Listen," someone said, finding it unendurable. "Maybe we should do it. Maybe we should cut off his arm."

"Help me! Oh God! Oh God! Oh God! They won't help me!"

Someone grabbed an ax and jumped up, ready to cut.

"No!" said Frank. "No, don't cut the man's arm off. You'll kill him. Let the man live as long as he will live. There is such a thing that somebody might come along and get us out and they might save him."

"The way I see it," said Currie Smith, "if we cut him and that starts the blood, and what if we have trouble with him? Maybe he'll go out of his mind, see, and if anything does happen and we cut his arm off and he dies that way, well, they'll kind of blame it on us."

"They won't! they won't!" cried Percy in a moment of lucidity. "No one will blame you, I swear, it was the bump done it, not you, I'll tell everybody, and I'll be all right then, see, so it'll be all right. I swear it!"

They pounded the sides of their heads with their hands in the combined torture of their scorching thirst and Percy Rector's screams. His screaming was like the sound of a man's thirst, raw and ruptured and unnatural. Then his head pitched forward and he slept again, twitchily, noisily, and they tried to sleep in the clammy air, on the jagged ground.

"Listen, boys," said Jewkes. "I believe Perce is gone."

They heard Maurice scoot to Percy's side. "No, there's a pulse," he said quietly. "But it's very faint."

Finally the blackness over the men was opaque and thick and shining. Whether their eyelids were open or shut made no difference. All the batteries were dead. A man could sit slack-jawed, he could dig into his nose with his forefinger, he could scratch his butt or his scrotum, because the utter darkness was as solid as the waxed exterior of a new shiny black Buick. As if heavy polished doors were slammed shut on both sides and a hard black roof curved over his head, each man was locked in alone by the darkness.

They slept. Percy Rector must have found his way to that brook of his, and left his horse on the bank and taken a canoe onto deeper, bluer seas, because he didn't speak again. Instead the men, when awake, had to listen to his anguished, labored gagging. It sounded like someone was choking him. They forgot how to breathe normally themselves, listening to the battle of it, as he gasped and gagged against an invisible strangler. It was Death strangling him. He worked so hard, it seemed he would pull in all the oxygen in the cave, and yet it didn't satisfy him, and he choked and sucked for more air, the epiglottis going *eh-eh-eh* with each long, abrasive, unrewarding inhalation. This went on for a day, in and out...and in...and out, the flaps of his throat as dry and rough as a sun-dried old flag. There were longer and longer pauses between the last exhale and the next inhale, and they couldn't help but feel on edge, the suspense of it, wondering if each was the last breath, if the fighter in him had finally tired. They held their own greasy air in their lungs, listening. He hauled the air in with a rusty sound now, like an old pump, and then let it go with a creaking noise. And then there would be silence, and they'd think, "That's it," and pause for a memorial thought. Then here it came again, the squeaking, grating, rusty *eh-eh-eh* as some force within him yanked on the nerves and jangled the muscles and set things in motion one more time, the mad, blinded little commander of Percy's brain— or, if that was gone, of Percy's heart—not wanting to be cheated out of life so soon because of one stupid pinioned arm.

"Cut it off," he had begged them, eager to be rid of the mutinous limb that had gone off and gotten itself in a jam. "Cut it off," let it go, it was but a fraction of his life, just an arm, he could live without it, the AWOL arm. He disowned it. He disinherited it. They mistook him utterly if they thought he wanted to swap his life for an arm, that he'd rather die whole than live amputated. Plenty of one-armed veterans of the World Wars had married women, begat children, held down jobs. They played cards, too, and some of them fished. Cut it off, cut it off, I won't mind, I won't hold it against you, just free me from it. Leon, where are you? I need you now, chum. I always carried you the months you come up short, and you carried me when I was short. I toted home sacks of groceries, enough for both our families. "Hamburg tonight!" I'd yell, and the kids would come running, my kids, your kids. "What'd you bring us, Uncle Perce?" "Well," I'd boom, "only some ice cream, but I know you kids hate ice cream." "Ice cream! Ice cream!" they'd dance, and the wives, your wife and mine, leaning out of the kitchen to smile at me. "Oh Percy, that's so nice, you didn't have to, you'll spoil them."

Take it, take the arm; let old No. 2 swallow it. I don't mind burying me arm here if you'll get me out of this. I'll walk over it in future years and give it a thought. I'll tell the grandchildren I don't have yet, "Guess what's right underneath where we're standing. Grandpappy's arm! Yep, yeah it is. My arm. See, a long time ago, before you was born, there was a mine. . . . Please, boys, I don't care for it anymore, really, the arm. Take it off. You boys are wrong to think you can't live reduced, that the worst thing in life would be to lose an eye, a foot, a leg, a hand. You'd still be breathing, wouldn't you? You could still drive a truck onto a dirt road to hunt for deer; you could still drink, I'll warrant, and manage to hoist a mug of beer and yell out for more at a house party. Just sever it, it's no good to me now, I'd ruther live.

"He's gone," Currie Smith spoke suddenly into the dark space. "I seen him go. A light just shot off through the dark."

"Well, that's funny," someone said.

"I didn't see nothing."

"It's the truth," said Currie quietly, in awe. "If I drop dead right now, it's the truth. If I put my right hand to God. Because I seen it."

"Yeah," Maurice confirmed, dropping the lifeless hand. "He's gone."

"I seen it," said Currie.

"Thank God," someone said. "Maybe can we finally have some peace and quiet."

27

Gas Like a Night Nurse

The air blowing across the dead bodies was stinking and made the Group of Twelve men retch.

"My skin feels like the skin of a corpse," thought Levi Milley. "I can feel it. It feels exactly like a corpse."

"I hope when it comes, it will be gas, and not because of no air," thought Eldred Lowther. "I think I know what it would be like to be suffocated, but the gas will hit us so quick, we'll never know what happened. Let it be the gas."

The men could feel a stop in the airflow the instant someone higher in the mine closed a trap door. Larry Leadbetter would holler, "Oh! Getting warm! Getting warm!"

"When the air stops, first you start sweating," El Lowther thought, so whenever Leadbetter yelled, "Getting warm," Lowther braced himself: "Here it comes."

"The miners are saying this is the worst bump they ever heard tell of," thought Larry Leadbetter. "We don't know what the obstacles are like, or what the gas is like out there, or what the air is like. They think the whole place might have fallen in. They're saying they never heard tell of a bump like this."

"Things are getting real serious," thought Lowther. "There's more and more times where there's none of us talking or anything."

"My grandfather died here before I was born," Lowther said aloud. "He's still in this mine. I guess it's in the family to end here."

"Quiet, Lowther."

"I figure it's going to be the gas that gets us," thought Joe Holloway. "I'm hoping it's going to be the gas. As far as death goes, it will just be the matter of going to sleep. No pain to it or nothing. The gas will start from the high side and it will keep closing in."

One night, the gas felt heavier. "This is it," thought Fred Hunter. "We're done for."

"This is it," he said aloud in the dark.

"Just lay down and go to sleep," someone said.

"Just relax," somebody else said. "Just lay down and try to relax."

"If the gas comes in, I will get pneumonia," Joe McDonald thought. "My stomach has kind of a sickly feeling. I'll get pneumonia and that will be the end for me."

"Well," thought Gorley Kempt, "if I'm going to die, I figure it will be either starvation or gas. It will probably be slow and more like a dream than anything. It might not be too bad. It might be a very easy way out."

That the gas would kill them quietly was the most they could hope for. Perhaps the gas would kill them one by one, moving among them like a frighteningly serene, yellow-eyed night nurse, gliding among hospital beds, offering from her tray one last serving of pills to be swallowed before lights-out.

———

The men began to say good-bye to each other. "We're not getting out of here," Ted Michniak said to Joe Holloway.

"We're finished," thought Fred Hunter, picturing his wife, in the kitchen, bending over their little girl at the table. "She'll get compensation," he told himself. "She'll be able to stay home with our little girl. Please, Lord, look after them. Please let her stay home with the little girl."

Every once in a while the silence was broken by a tortured yawp, an anguished nauseated "Oh God!" as one and then another of the men faced the fact this was it, this was really it, this was death. The loneliness and homesickness and sorrow swallowed a man alive every bit as much as the coal mine had; "Oh God," or "Oh Mama," or "Oh Margie," was the heart's hopeless attempt to claw free of the trap.

Most of what men did in life was a piling up, a hoarding against life's end. Before their shifts, the coal miners had tilted ladders against their gutters and climbed up and renailed a few shingles, or rebricked a chimney; at a wife's urging, a man would lie belly-down on the cracked kitchen linoleum to peer under the stove and try to see why it was smoking. Money couldn't be saved on miners' wages, but a child's bike could be bought brand-new at Christmastime from the hardware store and walked home, the dusky winter trees reflected in the tin fenders, the shiny bike itself reflected in the wife's happy eyes as the two of them wheeled the thing into the woodshed and hid it under a tarp. A heaping-up of goods, a hedge against death.

But when they lay on their sides and backs, below ground, forced into idleness, with their belches and farts and their hacking for water, there was nothing earned and nothing set aside. Once they lost hope in escape, they had no interest even in doing a bit of housekeeping, as a group of trapped women might have done (surely there were rocks that, if rolled up against this wall out of the middle, would make the hole a bit homier, and the center area could be swept, and couldn't the unused jackets be banked against this wall as a shabby kind of sofa?) Not a single word or movement added up to anything anymore for the trapped men, because there'd be no one to tell, no one would benefit. The realm of productive activity was closed to them.

Gorley Kempt and Harold Brine squeezed side by side into the crevice that housed the open end of the six-inch air pipe. They were like lost dogs at the animal shelter pushing their long noses through the wire mesh. The men's faces were pressed together, up against the pipe, listening, listening, knowing that somewhere in the blue-black beyond there was life, there was humankind. Like stargazers at a telescope, they stayed at their pipe, praying to be contacted by life from a planet far from the one they were on.

28

The Boxer

In the dark, in the Group of Seven, silence rustled like static against their sore eardrums. Rector's body slumped unseen. The survivors lay fatigued, dropping pounds, losing hair, mad with thirst in this nonplace, this nowhere, this clammy anteroom, tormented by itches and swallows, aggravated by every fart or snort of their fellows, furious at their own stupid need to pee and the stinking burning froth of it if they raised a can of it to their desiccated lips.

"You think gas is coming in on us?" someone asked.

"Nah, if there was gas it would have had us by now," said Garnet. "There's a small hole at the top of the wall you can go to breathe. The air is just whizzing by there, but you'll get the smell off the dead men."

The most active men slid into the bitterest surrender. Currie, Pep, and Garnie were done in. They had tried their hands at every ledge and crevice; they had crawled coughing across the waste; they had estimated to the cubic ton how buried they were. Their initial optimism and determination soured into foul anger and disgust. Garnet Clarke got mad at Frank Hunter about Frank's feet, which, in the cramped space, kept touching

Garnet's head. "Move 'em, Frank," he warned softly. "Move 'em or so help me God I'm going to have to hurt you. Get... them...off...me."

"He goes over to the waste to do his business," Garnet tattled to the others. "It's going right through him like diarrhea. He steps in it. Then he lays down right above me and puts his feet on my hair. You want to feel this? It feels like Brylcreem. It's *shit*.

"Frank, goddamn it!"

"Boys, we have got to get our message out," said Maurice Ruddick after a long quiet time. "We got to let those fellows know we're alive. Now, I don't mean to tell anyone what to do, but we need to start pounding on pans or pipes or whatever we got."

Like the bristly silence that arose after Percy stopped wailing and died, Maurice Ruddick's voice was something new. Hearing its low timbre and soft huskiness, the other men noticed that Ruddick hadn't really said much since the bump, other than the occasional gentle question—"Is there any way we could get Barney up here with us?"—or quiet response— "Yes, there's still a pulse." The arguments, complaints, suggestions, and bickering among the white miners had been rowdier than Ruddick's voice, and he, a colored man, had deferred to them, as was traditional.

There was plenty the miners didn't know about Maurice Ruddick. They didn't know his education exceeded most of theirs, that he was on the level of a Caleb Rushton. They didn't know he had been a competitive amateur boxer. They had never seen his dancing footwork or his jabs, and they didn't know that he watched his weight and still worked out. They didn't know that, for Ruddick, making his way among them was sometimes another type of defensive footwork.

"Boys," he said, "I know you're tired. And we're hungry and thirsty. And I don't mean to tell you what to do. But I mean to start banging on everything we got. We got to let the rescuers know somebody's alive down here."

From the disarray and filth in which they lay, stuck somewhere between hell and Nova Scotia, and with odors of death beginning to swirl around Rector's hanging corpse, the men tried to pull themselves together. They needed to stop scrapping with each other, Ruddick said, as if he alone were consulting the mythical volume of the Miners' Code. They needed to stay vigilant for sounds from abroad, and they needed to pound on those pans and pipes. Though far from the youngest in the group, he sounded like he could back up his suggestions with muscle.

"I want to live as well as the rest of you boys. If the good Lord spared us through the bump, we must be going to get out. He spared us for a purpose."

Within his own realm up top—the colored church, the colored house parties—Ruddick was a confident, almost strutting fellow, with cash in his pocket. He was liberal with unsolicited advice. With his kids, his word was law. Since the bump, he had waited in the shadows of this cave for one or another of the white men to display leadership, though he couldn't guess who would. He didn't figure they'd turn to him. While Pep, Garnie, and Currie organized escape attempts, Maurice devoted his energy to doctoring Percy Rector, a job for which, as a father of twelve, he felt qualified.

But now, in total darkness, with the men no more than voices to each other and with self-discipline falling to shreds, he asserted himself. Invisible now, he opened the musical instrument of his voice; no longer the acquiescent Negro they knew on the job, he spoke to them in the voice of a kind and experienced father, the way he would reassure and tease and coach his children through a night of thunderstorms.

The fellows heard Ruddick wearily get up, stagger slightly from weakness, and feel his way toward the crushed pan line. In a tin explosion of sound, he brought a supper pail down upon the pans—*bang!* Then again—*bang!* It startled the others. Their hearts jumped. In threes he made percussion: nine bangs to build an SOS, an elemental human message.

It was the mathematical order of it that made it human, separated it from the random mineral noises of the mine. Three short, three long, three short. No one who heard it could say, "That's just air in the pipes." No, they would have to say, "There's men below."

Ruddick switched to pounding with a pick handle, stayed at it for a quarter hour, for a half hour, and then his aching arm stopped midair.

"Boys? I need to sit down. Who wants to take a turn?"

Garnie got up to do it, and when he was done, Currie, then Pep, then Frank Hunter. Doug Jewkes's leg was paining him, so he couldn't contribute, other than at the times the men all hollered in unison, "Help! Help!"

If somebody sulked, muttering that it was useless, they heard the gentleman in Ruddick's corner stir himself and get up, shuffle carefully up the uneven slope, feel his way to the pan line, and start to bang.

"We're pounding and nobody hears," someone would say.

"Our object is to get out, to live," said Ruddick. "That's my persistence, to live as long as we can. We got to keep rapping on the pipes. If those fellows just once hear us, we are saved."

"I guess I'm kind of taking over," he thought. "I'm not try-ing to show authority or anything like that, but the boys are minding me pretty good. In a roundabout way I'm saying, 'Do this, do that,' and all the boys seem to be quite cooperative. Once in a while they're getting disgusted, I hear different things, but they're going along."

Maurice Ruddick was becoming more high-spirited, it seemed, as the others tilted into despondency. When he went to bang, he did it with a bit of wit for anyone who was listening, though mostly, it seemed, to please himself. He swung the beat. He played surprising rhythms; he improvised as if he were playing bongos and the men could hear his low chuckle. He stopped pounding for a moment and sang scat of his own invention until the men, laughing, begged him to bang instead. He made up a little song about himself and his wife, a countrified rhyme. But privately, he worried. "They don't seem to give us our signals back. That is what kind of has me worried, not getting our signals back. I've had a couple little sniffs myself. Anything like that breaks the tension. I think nearly all the other chaps have had a couple sniffs."

"Currie? Currie?" said Maurice.

"What?"

"It's your turn."

"It's no good because the sound won't carry," said Currie. So Ruddick took Currie's turn, until Currie got up and went.

Later Ruddick attempted a more mournful minor-key church hymn and waited for them to join in. They didn't. "Jesus, Maurice," one of them said. "It's bad enough being stuck down here without you singing junk like that."

29

A Particle of Light

On Wednesday, October 29, rescuers crawling on their bellies down into the mess reached the levels. The rockfall was so dense at the entrance to the 12,600 level, they detoured around it and went deeper, scratching forward down the slope in the dark. They were virtually without hope of finding anyone alive. No coal miner ever had survived underground this long. The rescuers removed debris a bucket at a time, and passed it back along the line of prone men poking forward into the earth like a centipede. The first man filled the bucket with stone and coal and maneuvered to get it to the man behind him, who shoved it back to the third man, and so on down the line till the bucket emerged from the mouth of the tunnel and was emptied by another miner into a waste area, and everyone inched forward.

When the first man exhausted his strength, the others crawled backward and let him out of the tunnel, and the second man in line slithered back in and took over the lead. All day and all night, some pulling twelve-hour shifts, they pushed forward by inches, by buckets, by handheld lumps of coal and stone, lying on their stomachs, pausing sometimes to listen or to call, "Hello? Hello?" Percy Hunter was among the rescuers. His brothers—twins Frank and Fred—both were missing. Then the man at the head of the line angled toward the right and nosed into what once had been, what should have been, the 13,000 level.

Volunteer Earl Wood, when it was his turn to go first, dug into a section of rock that dissolved into dust. "Hey!" he yelled behind him, "this may be the opening we were hunting for." Poking out of the soft landslide, as the black dust cleared, was the stump of a broken-off steel pipe, six inches across.

"Did you hear that?" Gorley asked after he and Harold Brine had lain in silence for many hours with their faces mashed close to the pipe.

"I did," said Harold. "It sounded like a steel pipe dropping."

"That's what I figure," said Gorley.

They pushed forward another millimeter, trying to wedge their faces into the pipe. "I hear a voice," said Gorley.

"I hear it," said Harold.

The section that fell open was dusty and gassy, and the rescuers drew back, to let it air out. The men sat near the mouth of their tunnel and rested, heads down, breathing hard. Then one of the men startled. "I heard someone speak. I could swear I did!"

"I heard it, too!" said another. "Just a piece of a word, very faint."

"Is it coming from where that pipe's broken off?" One stuck his head in the tunnel and peered down the long hole with his headlamp.

"Don't go back in there," others warned, "till the air quality gets checked out."

"Nah," said the man, withdrawing his head. "You just heard the voice of them out in the slope."

A volunteer out-of-town manager looked in on them and offered, "Don't make a spark." Then, "Good day, boys. I'll be seeing you."

"Gee whiz, that scared me to death," said local rescuer Bobby Jewkes. "I was OK till he come in and said that. I wonder if we'll ever see *that* fellow again."

"Right," said another, and sarcastically mimicked the out-of-town volunteer: "Try not to blow yourselves up, boys, and good luck to ye!"

"I'm ready to go home," one of the volunteers said in earnest.

"If we go home, there's someone else got to come in our place," said Bobby Jewkes. "What in hell's the use of going home?"

Then word came to him that the body of his brother Billy was found. Bobby was told to go up to the surface to wait for it. "Be seeing you, boys," he said glumly, and shoved off. His shoulders drooped with the knowledge that he would have to deliver the news to his parents that, of their six sons, one was killed and another, Doug, was still missing and presumed dead.

The other men waited for permission to continue to excavate the new fallen-in area. Chief Surveyor Blair Phillip, accompanied by an engineer, arrived to check the quality of air coming from the uncovered, broken-off pipe to determine the extent to which poisonous gas was loose in the mine and whether it was safe for the rescuers to push ahead. Blair Phillip ducked into the new section and felt for the pipe. He held a glass jar to the stump of the pipe to gather air.

A strand of light from his headlamp reflected off the glass jar and angled into the pipe.

In the long dusty black tube, for half a second, a particle of light danced.

For Gorley Kempt and Harold Brine, with their faces at the far end of the pipe, the effervescent sparkle was like a meteor shower. It was like Grandma's one-hundredth-birthday cake, like fireworks in the night sky. There was no other explanation for a glitter of light inside this telescope of darkness. "My God," choked Gorley. "We're saved."

He tried to nose farther into the pipe, toward the now-vanished mirage of light and yelled, "Hey! Hey! Hey! We're in here! Hey, there's twelve of us in here! We're alive in here! Come get us!"

And they got an answer.

"Who's speaking?" came a metallic voice from the far end of the pipe.

"Gorley Kempt!"

"Who's in there with you?" Blair Phillip called back.

Harold Brine slid back away from the pipe, dropped his head, and cried into his stiff shirt. It was the first time he'd broken down. He sniffed deeply, got a grip on himself, and slid close to the pipe again.

"How many is in there?"

"Twelve of us. There's twelve of us in here," Harold called, crying.

"Can you name them?"

"Yes! I can name every one: Harold Brine, that's me. Gorley Kempt, he's right here. Caleb Rushton, Joe Holloway. Hughie Guthro, Larry Leadbetter, El Lowther, Ted Michniak. Levi Milley, Bowman Maddison, Joe McDonald."

After a pause, Phillip hollered, "I get eleven."

"Who'm I leaving out?" Harold asked Gorley. "Oh, I know! It's Teddy Hunter, Fred, we call him Teddy."

"Did you say Fred Hunter is in there?" said the voice.

"Yes, that's it, that's the twelve."

In his excitement, Blair Phillip yelled into the pipe: "Stay where you are! We'll come as quickly as possible."

Gorley slid back to the trapped men, almost hysterical with happiness, hiccupping and coughing. "They said they want us to stay put."

Rescuers scrabbled backward out of their hand-dug tunnel and crawled and hobbled out to the slope, and sprinted, hunched over, till they reached a still-working underground telephone. The winner knocked the receiver off the hook and screamed into it.

In the office at the pithead, a manager took the call and then nearly kicked down the door to shout out the news: "There's men alive below!"

The few listless reporters who'd lingered in Springhill for lack of another assignment leapt to their microphones and the roll of names poured out of radios and TVs in town and began to interrupt television programs all over North America.

The CBC's Jack McAndrew reported by radio:

About fifteen minutes ago . . . the message [was received] that there are twelve men alive at the 13,000-foot level. . . . Apparently the word came through a six-inch air pipeline encountered by the rescue workers approaching the 13,000-foot level. The workers were electrified by the message, "There are twelve of us here. Come and get us!"

Reporter Jeff Deon said:

It's almost unbelievable! I looked toward the mine a few moments before the announcement. It was quiet under a shroud of mist, and below me a hearse was returning from one of today's funerals. It was a scene of quiet, of hopelessness. And now this!

A phone call to the elementary school sent secretaries and teachers running through the halls. The teachers told the children, and the children slid out of their chairs and started jumping. "Dismiss school!" ordered the principal by intercom.

"The children are so excited," Grace Gilroy saw. "They're not even waiting to be dismissed. They're just flying."

"Let them go," the teachers said to one another.

"Let them go in any way they want to go," Grace thought. "They are so keyed up and so happy that somebody has been found. They're flying in all directions as fast as they can go." By the time she gathered her jacket and purse and exited the building, the children were gone. "I don't know whether they went home or out to the mine, but there isn't a sign of one of them."

Alden Maddison, the son of Bowman Maddison and the new big brother of a four-month-old baby, ran straight to the pithead and found himself the subject of a television interview. "I never gave up hope!" he yelled at the camera. "God wouldn't give us Constantine and then take Daddy away."

Margie Kempt was tuned to the radio news when she heard, "'There's twelve of them there and the man we spoke to was Gorley Kempt.'"

"Well!" she thought. "You see? After there was no news for so long! Everybody figured it was a complete loss! After the reporters left town! I told my sister, I *told* her, 'Somebody is alive down there. Somebody in all that mess *has* to be alive.'"

The phone rang and it was Margie's sister, crying.

"I told you! I told you!" scolded Margie, starting to cry herself.

And her sister scolded back, "Oh, you crazy thing!"

Margie hung up, put her hands on her hips, and—a practical-minded gal—looked around her, aware that her house was about to become an epicenter of activity and media coverage. "Now, this house has a great coal stove—it draws well and that's for sure a miracle—and it's got a floor covering and a bathroom, but it hasn't got much furniture. And the TV has to be turned on and off with a pair of pliers ever since we had that fire. My *God,* I can't have people coming to the house looking like this! I need to go buy some furniture!" She packed her handbag, backed out the car, and drove down the hill to Letcher's Furniture on Main Street.

"Gorley's coming home, we cannot look like scruff," she told Lorne Letcher. "They'll think all the miners live like that." She purchased a chair, a floor lamp, and a chesterfield, for delivery that afternoon.

Norma Ruddick was on her way upstairs when she heard the television report of survivors. She froze, listening. Six names into the list, she knew. "I know he's not in the bunch. Something tells me Maurice is not in the bunch." He wasn't.

"All right then," thought Mabel Smith in her country farmhouse. "They didn't find Currie. But there might be more down there. They said there was no one and then they found twelve."

Retired miner William Moss, Sr., heard from his daughter-in-law to turn on the radio. He was hoping for news of his brother and didn't get it. But he got down on his knees on the kitchen floor anyway. "I thank you, God," he said, "for what you've done for the men. Even if it isn't my brother, I am thankful for all that you have spared."

4 P.M.

Arnold Burden was at home in his bathrobe and slippers, filling out death certificates. Next to the names, he wrote, "MSCC," for multiple severe contusions and crushing. Then Merle McBurnie was stamping and banging at his front door. "Get your clothes on, Doc!" he bellowed. "They found twelve men alive in the pit!"

Burden ran upstairs to dress, and called down to his wife to bring in the pit boots from the car. He phoned the company office from his bedroom, in case it was a rumor. "Is it true?"

"Yes," said the office man, "there are men alive but there is no grand hurry to get here, because we haven't got to them."

"Well, if you can hear them, I might be of some use."

"I know most of the men down there," Burden was thinking as he drove toward the pithead, "but some of them I have a special interest in, if they are alive or not." He stamped into the pit office just as a mine manager, on the phone, was writing down and confirming the names of the twelve. The man tapped his pen next to one of the names for Burden to note: it was Caleb Rushton, the ex-husband of Burden's sister and a respected friend.

He tapped again to show the doctor that next to two of the names he'd written, "Severely injured."

Rescuer Floyd Gilroy and his Wrecking Crew were having coffee and sandwiches at the Sally-Ann before going down. "Did you hear that?" the miners said to each other, and they tore out

of the diner. "We're going to work like we never worked before," thought Floyd, half running back down the slope. "Boy,
that puts the energy back in you! Just puts new energy."

A phone call was placed from New York City to the mine office.
It was from the *Ed Sullivan Show,* an act of damage control, not
to "lose Canada." "We'd like to invite some of the trapped miners to come visit the show this Sunday!" the man told Arnold
Patterson. "We'll treat them to a weekend in Manhattan! May I
speak to one of them?"

"Not right now," said Patterson. "Seeing as they're still
underground."

"Would you relay my message to them when they get out?"

"Will do."

30

Home Cooking

WEDNESDAY, OCTOBER 29

SIX DAYS SINCE THE BUMP

Jack McAndrew of CBC Radio reported:

The crowds are almost deliriously happy in spite of the tragedy that many of them have suffered. At the Salvation Army tent, I talked to a woman who buried her own husband yesterday and who is almost as happy as her friend whose husband is among the group of twelve sending word to the surface that they're there, just waiting for the rescue workers to come and get them.

Now the crowds are all back again, and there are cameramen there, and I hope they will be able to record so that people all over the continent will be able to see the jubilation on the faces of those who have heard from their loved ones—and even on the faces of those who are still sharing a very deep, private grief—a sense of miracle. That's the word that's been used over and over again.

One CBC reporter had seen a certain woman at the pithead day and night since the disaster. The reporter checked in at the mine manager's office and got the list of twelve names. As he stepped out the door, perusing the list, she was there. She waited for him to look up. "Is he on the list?" she asked flatly, without hope.

"No ma'am, I'm sorry, he is not."

GROUP OF TWELVE, 4:40 P.M.

"We need water!" yelled Gorley Kempt through the compressed-air pipe.

"We'll get there," called a rescuer. "Just lay down and take it easy."

"Look here," said Gorley. "We got to have water. If we don't get water, you might as well quit digging and go home."

"The doctor says you can't have it."

Doc Burden actually was prescribing that they take just a mouthful at a time, and count to five hundred between swallows, but the subtlety of his cautious instructions was lost in the pipe.

"What doctor? You put the doctor onto the end of that pipe till I talk to him."

Dr. Burden's flutelike voice played through the pipe.

"You had better get us some water," ordered Gorley, "because we have a couple of fellows who are hurt and they need water, and we need water, too. We just have to have it."

"All right," said Doc Burden. "We'll run a tube through this pipe." He thought, "The fact is we have no idea how far we have to tunnel to reach them, nor how long it will take."

An extraordinary restlessness was unsettling and upsetting the men huddled on the black slope. After the first brilliant moments of relief and joy—"Oh boy, oh boy, oh boy," said Hughie Guthro—they were suddenly like bundled-up travelers in line, sweating and delayed behind a closed door at the bus station, awaiting departure, shifting heavy packages and squirming children achingly from one arm to another. The impatience to get out was almost worse than the hopelessness that preceded it. They had rapidly, eagerly pulled themselves together in readiness to depart, and the expenditure of the energy to sit up, to tuck in, to smooth back the hair, to slick away the tears, was more than they could afford. The very effort of looking forward to life again weakened them, and they fell limply back.

"They're not putting no pipe through!" someone protested.

"They don't care," said another. "Why should they? *They're* OK."

"Yes, they promised to put it through," said Gorley, who had become the middleman, with its attendant mistrust. "I'm going to stay at the pipe till we get it. Don't worry."

Volunteers slid into the crevice with fifty feet of copper pipe from a supply store in town, and inserted it into the broken-off end of the compressed-air pipe. Shoving and hollering, they inserted the entire length of it and then called, "Do you feel it?"

"No!" came back Gorley's answer.

The fifty-foot length of pipe was too short. God only knew how thick the rock was between the survivors and their rescuers. Doc Burden, working with steady hands despite the exuberance and impatience all around him, taped a length of plastic pipe to the copper, and tried to push that through. "It's too snug," he said to the rescuers. "I'm afraid it will get stuck and we'll have no way of getting food and water to them. Send a runner up for a hundred feet of copper pipe."

Harold Brine weakly crawled to the crevice to wait with Gorley for the water. "Do you think they'll put it through?" he asked.

"When Doc Burden comes back, I'll beg him. He won't be able to refuse me."

A runner finally returned with a hundred feet of copper pipe.

"Push it through, keep pushing," the rescuers said. They felt it stop, and felt Gorley give it a shake on his end. They sawed off the excess piece sticking out into their tunnel, measured it, and realized with horror that eighty-three feet of solid coal and rock stood between them and the trapped miners.

6 P.M.

"Get ready now!" Dr. Burden called to Gorley. "Shake the pipe to let us know the water is getting through. We won't be able to talk while the water is going."

"Gorley!" called Doc Burden again, before the transfer. "You tell them to take a mouthful and swallow and count to five hundred before taking another mouthful. If they drink too fast, it will make them sick."

Working in the cramped space by the light of headlamps, using a new five-gallon pressure pump of the type for spraying trees, the rescuers slowly pumped fresh cold water into the new copper pipe. It spat into the horizontal tube and whizzed away. At the other end, with hot, swollen lips and barking chests, Gorley Kempt and Harold Brine waited to receive it. Prayerfully, in the blackness, they held out a water bottle.

As if glass marbles had been released by the handful from the free end of the pipe, a gaudy, rolling, silvery sound rushed straight at them and scattered from the copper tube. Working frantically in the pitch black, the two men could not get the water bottle positioned right to catch the water. It was ringing and slapping onto the coal floor around them. They held out their buckets desperately. They were like blind beggars who hear silver coins flung by a rich man ringing on the sidewalk and rolling away.

For the first time in the six and a half days, Gorley Kempt lost control. His mouth veered open sideways. "Mother of Jesus, we're wasting it! We're wasting it! What the hell are you doing?" he snarled at Harold. "Mother of God we're wasting it!" The tube sputtered, the last drops fell, and Gorley dropped to his stomach and licked the coal as the moisture was absorbed into the dust.

"Hey! Hey! Where's our water?" yelled the trapped men from the slope, suspecting they were being robbed, and Gorley could only croak, weeping, "We wasted it."

"It's gone! It's gone!" wailed Harold into the tube, but the return words were muffled by the wet copper tubing inside the air pipe. He leaned his arms and head against his end of the pipe and cried.

Five minutes passed. The trapped men grew rowdier in their anger, as if they were about to form a lynch mob and come after Gorley and Harold. Caleb Rushton and Hughie Guthro scooted up to the crevice and found Harold Brine with his mouth on the pipe, half licking half shouting, and Gorley on the ground coughing and sobbing.

Voices blew in from the pipe: "Did you get it? Did you get the water?"

"No!" all four men shouted at once. "We lost it! We couldn't see! We're in the dark here!"

"OK, boys." It was the nasal voice of dear Doc Burden. "Get yourselves ready. Don't panic. There's plenty of water. We've got more water for you. Get organized and tell us when you're ready."

This time the trapped men cupped their hands around the end of the pipe and guided a bucket toward it. After long moments, at 6:08 P.M., six and a half days after the disaster, the trapped men heard the sweet, sizzling rush of water again. Like children on a warm night scampering to catch fireflies, the dusty men shimmied and maneuvered and captured the singing rivulet, which seemed to carry within it sparkles of light and fresh air and the scent of sunlit grass.

They dove onto the bucket and choked down messy, grateful, weeping swallows, ignoring Dr. Burden's cautions to count to five hundred between sips. Gorley passed the bucket to Hughie. "Here, take a good slug of that." Then, in the dark, all hands on the bucket or hovering protectively near it, as if it were a crystal goblet, they slid back to the cave. "Go ahead," said Gorley, deliberately omitting Doc Burden's advice. "Here, make a pig of yourselves if you want to."

"Caleb, say grace for us," called one of the men.

Caleb cleared his throat, near tears, and spoke. "Lord, we thank you for the pipe and the blessed water that came through it."

"Amen!" shouted the unshaved, unwashed men, and then they threw themselves upon the water, snorting and guzzling it, clutching the water bottle with two hands and biting into it as if it were a hoagie sandwich, grabbing it greedily back and forth from each other. When it was gone, they bleated woefully into the dark for more. When it wasn't immediately forthcoming, they hurled angry accusations again about the rescuers and about Gorley and Harold.

The rescuers were eager to get moving, to start digging through the wall of rock separating them from the men, but here was Gorley again at the far end of the pipe, begging for more water. "Can you wait?" someone called down. "We're trying to get organized to come get you."

"If you don't give us water, there's not going to be anybody to come get," yelled Gorley from below.

So a crew was formed to attend solely to liquid transfusions.

Within the hour, the trapped men, calmer now, were sucking in coffee sweetened with sugar. The first swallows of coffee from the sloshing lunch pail had washed away the sediment of coal, bark, and urine from their teeth. The second swallows they balanced on their tongues, like toffees. The novel sweetness and heft and deliciousness filled a man's mouth like a melting-warm, cold-spraying bite from a county fair caramel apple on an autumn day.

When they devoured the water, tearing at it with their teeth, they had been beastlike in their need. But as they handed round the coffee, as if they sat relaxing beside a campfire, their souls returned to them. They were men again.

Then tomato soup made its way from the kitchens of Springhill by dozens of cookpots to the pithead, went slopping under jiggling lids down the slope, and was pumped into the copper pipe. The trapped men then smacked their lips upon almost-tepid soup. As the water had carried to them a breeze of the open air, the tomato soup bore a smoky taste from the coal-burning stoves of the small kitchens of Springhill, with an ambience of rubber boots dripping onto rubber mats by the kitchen doors, and a hint of the Ivory soap that had bubbled over the rough hands of the housewives. Life returned to them, and the remembrance of life, and the taste for life.

ATLANTA: 7 P.M.

"Look, Sam!" Caldwell's wife told him that evening when he came into the living room from the kitchen with his whiskey on the rocks and salted nuts. "They found survivors. There's twelve of them still alive under there."

And that's when he was hit by his brilliant idea.

No matter how it played out, no matter that he later would

say, "There came a time in the fall of 1958 when I had an opportunity to prove my inexperience in politics," it was a brilliant idea, the cleverest, sneakiest thing he'd ever come up with. For the first time in too long, he felt like a young man of promise again, the whiz kid he'd once been. Almost tipsy with sudden energy and excitement, he paid another visit to the bottle on the kitchen counter and then needed to step outside. He remembered he hadn't looked at his own backyard since summer. He wrested the swollen kitchen door open and stood on the soft doorstep admiring his tenth-acre of crabgrass, crickets, galvanized fence, and metal clothesline, all of it vibrating with the tinny buzz of cicadas. He breathed in the leaf-moldy tepid air as if the land, too, held promise. He leaned back in the doorway and reached for his cigarettes and lighter on the counter and lit up with shaking hands, trying to organize his inspiration.

If his wife was glued to this story, and it was all the rage of the secretaries at the capitol, and men in the downtown bars after work exchanged a few words about it, then the whole damn country must be tuned into it. This country and Canada. And God knew where else. It was a big, big story.

So, he suddenly knew how to boost tourism in Georgia: if the whole damn world was praying and crying over these miners they had just dug out of the cave-in—they'd been down there, what, a week, a month?—well, what would everyone say to the state of Georgia inviting those men to pack their bags, grab hold of their wives and children, and come on down to Georgia for a week of sun and recuperation? Why not put them up in the just-finished motel on Jekyll Island, the island upon which floated Governor Griffin's hopes for a state tourism industry? Wouldn't all the journalists pack up and follow? Wouldn't they broadcast coastal Georgia's beige beaches and blue sea and palm trees, and the coal miners pale and sloop-shouldered in their brand-new bathing suits, half-blind in the subtropical sunshine? "Lookit where those coal-mine families are having a vacation," women in Missouri and Michigan and Indiana would say. "Whyn't we go there, honey? It's closer than Florida and look how pretty." "Well, damn, it's right off U.S. 17, probably cheaper than Florida, too," the husbands would reply. And here would come America!

Caldwell chain-smoked with jittery hands on his back step while he tried to get a good look all around this thing. For the life of him, he couldn't see a damn flaw in it. He drank too much that night and his wife, giggling, had to push him off her in the kitchen and say, "Sam! What on earth's got into you?"

He couldn't sleep, but for once wandered through the house, making his hair stand on end by running his sweaty hands through it, not in boredom and angst but out of excitement and happiness. He opened up a fresh notebook on the Formica-topped kitchen table, clicked open a ballpoint pen, and poured himself a glass of ice water. The idea was as big, clean, and plain as a highway billboard to him now, and his chief thought was how to keep it a secret. He didn't want any of his colleagues to jump on it first and, more than anything he'd ever wanted, he wanted to extend the invitation to Canada before somebody in Florida came up with the same idea.

31

Last Man Out

ATLANTA
THURSDAY, OCTOBER 30
SEVEN DAYS SINCE THE BUMP

Sam Caldwell went to work early Thursday morning with the wild-eyed, uncombed look of insomnia about him. He tried to keep his eyes averted, lest someone look straight through his dilated pupils to the billboard-sized idea inside his head. But nobody was coming up with this brainstorm other than him. Everyone just kept watching TV in the governor's anteroom and wiping their eyes over the coffins and smiling through tears at reports that the trapped men were drinking coffee.

Still, there was no way to reach Governor Griffin in far-away Saskatchewan on a moose hunt. Caldwell feared that the moment would slip away, the world's attention shift away from this story, before he could hook onto the tailgate of it. In rising desperation, he confided in Tom Gregory, the governor's executive secretary. Gregory, a former newspaper editor, leaned way back in his swivel chair, closed his eyes, and tried to picture it for a moment. Caldwell stood, his lips parted, slightly out of breath from how rapidly he'd sputtered out the plan. Then Gregory bounced back up to sitting position and said, "I like it.

It's a fine idea, Sam. But we've got to clear it with the governor first."

"I've got a little research I need to do," Caldwell said, skedaddling to his office, looking—and feeling—like a crazy man. He phoned the public relations director for Eastern Airlines. "If we do this thing—and this is going to be fantastic and you could be in on it—would Eastern fly these families down to Brunswick at no cost? You'd get your money back ten times over in free advertising."

"It's terrific," the PR director agreed. "Let me get back to you." He rang back within the hour and promised free seats for the miners and their wives and children.

Caldwell phoned the head of the chamber of commerce in Brunswick, the industrial mainland city across the water from Jekyll Island. "It's a great opportunity," the man agreed. "I'll do everything I can to raise local funds to help finance it."

Caldwell and Gregory confided in a close circle of staffpersons and all were enthusiastic, but all refused to take action without Governor Griffin's OK.

GROUP OF TWELVE: 1 A.M.

The rescuers could not pinpoint the location of the men who were shouting from the far end of a broken-off airhose. The impatient and angry survivors did not know how completely the bump had rearranged the layout of No. 2.

Dr. Burden squatted in the forefront just behind the diggers, who burrowed and scuffled forward, clawing in the darkness like moles. He said to them, "If you're here, and occupying space, you have to work. As long as I'm occupying space, I got to hand back these buckets of coal, so hand me a bucket."

When it was time to change shift, the rescuers refused to leave. "Send new lights down," someone hollered out the far end of the cramped, rough-hewn tunnel. "We aren't moving till we break through. We're fresh enough. There's no use in us going up and somebody else crawling into this hole."

"Arnold, you need to back out of the way for a time," manager Harold Gordon told the doctor. "You need to rest in between these buckets. Your work's more ahead of you." So Burden squeezed to the side and stayed near the broken end of the pipe to communicate with the survivors, as the diggers tunneled deeper into the rock in search of them.

The survivors relaxed for a time with their soup entrée— pleased to have their rescue now in the hands of outsiders— and Harold Brine traveled back to the pipe periodically to negotiate for more soup and to ask, "How much longer? How much farther?" Then he stuck his head around the corner and called out in the dark, "They need directions! They're stuck at some timber and they think they went up the hill a bit too far."

"Levi," called Gorley from a reclining position, hands crossed under his head. "Levi, you're an old miner. You crawl in there and give them directions. You can steer them to us."

"I'm leaning against this coal face and I can feel every thump," said Lowther. "I expect them to stick a pick in me any minute."

Levi Milley made his way to the pipe and listened. George Calder yelled, "We come to a pack and the pipes seem to go on one side and we don't know whether to go on, on one side, or which side of the pack to go on, the high side or the low side. It'll mean a few more hours if we take the wrong side."

"It feels like you're about two feet from us!" Levi yelled

back. "Come on straight with the pipe. You'll be breaking through pretty soon! I'm going to crawl back in."

"Boys," he said when he returned. "Watch for the lights."

2:25 A.M.

Dr. Burden and a small group of men crouched by the end of the pipe in silence, waiting, as the point group of rescuers scuttled forward. Then they felt a rush of air and a stirring up of coal dust. "That's it," Burden said. "They're in." The doctor sat back on his heels, took out his small notebook and pencil stub and wrote, "2:25 A.M. Breakthrough." Then he pitched forward onto all fours and hustled into the tunnel.

The hole had been punched into the crevice where Gorley Kempt and Harold Brine had spent days and nights scrunching their faces up to the pipe. The first newcomer to crawl through the hole came face-to-face with gaunt, grimy, unshaven, grinning Gorley, who half stood and stuck out his hand. The men shook hands. Gorley began shivering uncontrollably and couldn't tell whether it was from excitement or from the cold air coming through the door. He cleared his throat and waved the man deeper in toward the communal cave. Then Harold Gordon, the mine manager, entered, half standing, and Gorley shook his hand, too, and directed him onward. A third man was crawling through the hole and a fourth, and Gorley squatted down to see a long line of men grunting forward with their headlamps, like bumper-to-bumper traffic in a highway tunnel.

"Hey, what about stopping these fellows crawling in here?" croaked Gorley. "You have too many in here now. Stop them from crawling in and let me crawl out."

"No," said Harold Gordon, "you stay right where you are and wait on the doctor."

———

Though the haggard survivors had known that the rescuers were close, still, when the fresh, vigorous men stumbled through with a clang of picks and a rumble of rockfall, it felt like a miracle. The epiphany of light! To see again! As the rescuers scaled the tumble of rocks they'd hammered through the wall, their headlamps painted the cave with quick white stripes—how foul and squalid it was, the survivors suddenly saw. In the total blackness, the dark had merged in their minds with the night of deep space, or with the blue-black entombment of death, something grand and noble—at any rate, not this stinking, garbage-strewn locker. And how gaunt and sickly and yellow-toothed they appeared to one another! They'd failed to reckon, in their imaginations, after the lights failed, that the whiskers would continue to grow, and the pounds of flesh fall away, and the grubby clothes balloon. It was, after all—so the nosy, roving headlamps sniffed out—a filthy grotto, crammed with blue-skinned, black-faced, gummy-toothed bearded men in baggy clothing.

The new arrivals made the rounds of the trapped men, as though they'd finally reached the head of a receiving line, where they noted the bruised faces and cut lips and hollows around the eyes, and the stench of human waste and human decomposition.

Percy McCormick marveled at the success of the rescue. "We sure never expected to meet twelve at one time," he thought. "We figured we might find one or two, but we never expected to find a crowd on their feet!"

"The fellows that are hurt are over there," someone said, and Dr. Burden approached Joe McDonald, who was propped against an overturned conveyer pan, his legs stuck out straight in front of him. Dr. Burden knelt and saw that the bone was poking through the skin.

"How you feeling?"

"Awful sore," said McDonald weakly. Burden gave him a shot of Demerol, then scooted over to Ted Michniak. Michniak was leaning against a pile of coal, his face so blackened that the doctor couldn't see his expression. He was holding his arm against his chest. Doc Burden felt his shoulder and realized his arm was dislocated from the socket. "Glad you got here," said Michniak wearily.

Draegermen were pulling stretchers through the hole now. "Take the two cripples up first," called Bowman Maddison. "We're not bad. Well, we're bad enough, but we're standing up."

The two injured men were lifted onto stretchers and dragged out. Then Burden and other rescuers gently helped the other men to the stretchers and guided them to lie down. Harold Brine's uncle crawled through the hole and found him. He held Harold's hand all the way up.

The slow, hunched-over parade of bare-faced rescuers dragging twelve stretchers departed the cave. Arnold Burden looked around and saw that he was alone. He stood for a few moments, listening. He'd asked Michniak, a few minutes earlier, "You think there are any more men alive down here?"

"We thought we heard some sounds from the top of the wall," he said.

Rescuer Floyd Gilroy, too, had reported hearing other sounds.

Burden waited, but heard nothing. As he prepared to leave, he opened the pocket notebook he'd carried with him from the beginning and logged, "Thursday, October 30, 4:20 A.M., Last Man Out."

32

That Lovely Fresh Air

Sam Caldwell loved his idea so much now, he'd have fought a man for it. But he was a mess of anxiety, concerned that valuable time was being wasted. Someone in Florida was going to come up with this plan before Caldwell could clear it with the governor. He sweated through his shirt and tie. With sticky hair and creased face, his shirt plastered to his body, he drove home at lunchtime to change. He opened the front door, saw instantly that the TV was off. His heart made a thump of disappointment. The story was over! The fast-moving world had looked away; his wife had lost interest. But no, here she came, patting her wet hair from the shower, saying, "Honey, let's put on the TV and see if there's more news about those miners. Some of them were hurt."

"I need to do something," he said. He closed himself in their bedroom, took off his shoes, stretched his legs out on the bed with his notebook in his lap, got up to redirect the oscillating fan, got up again to pour himself a drink, thought better of it, poured it into the sink, took ice water instead, went back to the bedroom, pulled off his wet shirt, and finally began to compose on the first page of his notebook. He was drafting a telegram to

Springhill, Nova Scotia. "The Great State of Georgia Welcomes You..."

Caldwell sweated out another hour, feeling like he was about to suffer a nervous collapse, before announcing to his perplexed wife, "I am not going to stand by and let goddamn Florida beat us to it. I'm going back to the office and send it."

"The Great State of Georgia invites the survivors and their families to recuperate on Jekyll Island, Georgia, for an expenses-paid week as the guests of Governor Marvin Griffin." He phoned it in; it was on its way.

GROUP OF TWELVE

Though warned against damaging their eyes by exposure to any light, the survivors couldn't resist lifting their heads and peeking out from under the bandages the doctor had pressed over their eyes. This was the only chance to see and to know the previously unknowable and guessed-at: the real shape and condition of No. 2.

Harold Brine enjoyed the tour, like a child journeying through a tunnel in a Disneyland ride. "Look at that!" he kept saying, propping himself up on an elbow, wearing his bandage at a rakish angle. "Oh my God, will you look at that? Boys," he called. "It's a good job we didn't know the condition the level was in! We never would have gotten out of this ourselves." To the rescuers he said, "We would have went out of our minds if we'd known this."

El Lowther, also sightseeing on this jiggly ride, realized he'd been mistaken about the sounds he'd heard in the distance. "I had pieced this thing together wrong," he thought. "I figured they thought we were all dead and they were just getting ready to bring bodies out. I never dreamed in the world that they were digging a small hole to get to us."

"What's all that ruckus?" he asked as his stretcher neared the surface.

"Why, there's crowds of people and reporters up there waiting for you."

"Oh, good. I was afraid it was the bill collectors."

Larry Leadbetter, feeling suddenly fit, tried to get up and walk the rest of the way out. "Let me out of here! It's time I got home." He strenuously protested being loaded into an ambulance for a trip to the hospital.

Margie Guthro and her mother-in-law and sister-in-law were among the crowd at 5 A.M., yelling and whistling and waving their hands as each man was brought up. "Here's Hughie!" she cried. "Oh, he looks a mess. His eyes are all swollen shut. Hughie! Over here!" The women laughed and cried and clapped and ran for the car, to follow the ambulance to the hospital.

This is Dave Orr of the CBC at the pithead in Springhill. Another rig has just arrived at the surface and more of the survivors are being brought out. Now a stretcher is just being passed out the door and into the back of a truck. The man is waving. Oh, I can see he's sitting up! He's sitting up on the stretcher, my soul. Oh, he fell, but he sat right up on the stretcher and waved at the crowd. He dropped his head and the crowd cheered and clapped their hands.

Ted Michniak was stunned to see his grown son, a salt miner from Detroit, waiting at the pithead. It reduced Michniak to tears to see him.

"He's a real good man, my husband," Margaret Michniak told bystanders as she stepped back and watched her husband loaded into the ambulance, " just a real good man."

This is Ken Homer of radio control. One of the men that's come up is Joe McDonald, who is the uncle of one of our technicians. He was sitting here, pretty weary, having a sandwich. When the word came that Joe McDonald was going to be on the next rake, he disappeared so fast, we didn't even see him go.

As he felt the light and cold air of the surface, Bowman Maddison inhaled deeply. "Oh, that lovely fresh air," he said, filling himself with it. An ambulance waited for him, and his brother stood beside it and looked at Bowman through the window. When Bowman saw that his brother was crying, he began crying, too, as he was driven away.

33

You Ain't Got Me Yet

ATLANTA
FRIDAY, OCTOBER 31
EIGHT DAYS SINCE THE BUMP

As if he'd thrown a rock into a pond from such great distance that he couldn't hear the splash, Sam Caldwell had to wait a long time to see if any ripples would arrive. Then, Friday morning, the office of the mayor of Springhill phoned to confirm that the invitation was indeed official, and called back two hours later to accept the invitation to Jekyll Island, Georgia, on behalf of a still-unknown number of men and their families. Some might be too weak and ill to travel. Would Georgia consider waiting a few months so that all could attend? "No sir, no can do," said Sam, knowing that for publicity purposes, he needed to get the project under way while the world was still interested in it, and that for budget purposes, a few men too weak to travel was really not bad news. Then came a call from a Springhill newspaper and then more and more phone calls from reporters across Canada, larger and larger cities. It was just the human-interest angle reporters were looking for. "It's going to be bigger than I even hoped!" Caldwell told his colleagues.

He drove home at lunchtime waving out his car window beneficently at passersby, danced his surprised wife around the small living room, showered, changed his shirt, and headed back to the office, whistling. There was, of course, the slightly nagging thought that they hadn't heard from Governor Griffin yet; any minute now he would be coming out of the big north woods and laying his eyes on an evening newspaper, and then what would he say to Jekyll Island being front-page Canadian news? He'd surely get a bang out of it. He'd know Sam Caldwell hadn't been idle in his absence. When major U.S. newspapers began phoning his office, Caldwell exulted, "We couldn't have bought this kind of publicity for a million dollars!"

GROUP OF TWELVE

In their hospital gowns and hospital beds, the least-injured men perked right up, became boyish, kicked at their sheets, acted petulant when nurses pried their lips apart with thermometers, and made vulgar, eager, tongue-wagging faces as they submitted to their sponge baths.

"I dreamed about a ladder," Gorley Kempt said upon waking up the next morning in the hospital bed, "a ladder with boards strung between ropes like they droop down over the side of a ship. I was trying to get up that, but the rungs weren't made of wood. They seemed to be made of powdered coal and powdered stone and wouldn't hold me. I kept trying to make it work."

"Yeah, Gorley?" said a buddy. "Look at your bed. You done tore all the sheets off of it."

"You were up and down, on and off that bed a dozen times in the night," said the fellow in the bed on the other side.

El Lowther was not pleased with the food. "What's this?" he asked angrily.

"Barley soup," said the attendant.

"Well, that's something I never ate in my life. Never would eat."

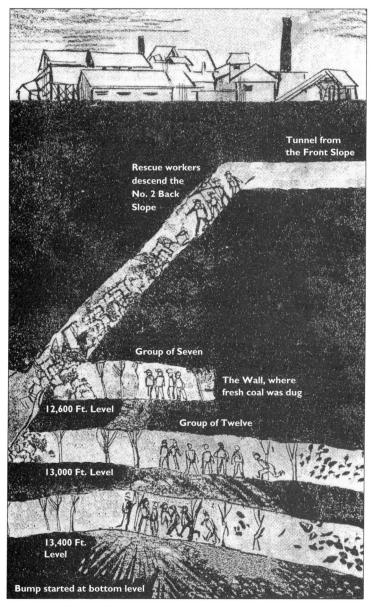

Tunnel from the Front Slope

Rescue workers descend the No. 2 Back Slope

Group of Seven

The Wall, where fresh coal was dug

12,600 Ft. Level

Group of Twelve

13,000 Ft. Level

13,400 Ft. Level

Bump started at bottom level

In the No. 2 slope, coal was extracted from three levels. At the moment of the bump, 174 men were caught underground. Coal miners said: "If you really thought about No. 2, you wouldn't work in it, would you?"

Volunteer rescuers race to the pit; they will change into pit-clothes and wait to be chosen to descend in search-and-rescue missions. *Carl Mydans/TimePix*

Norma Ruddick and her children, three weeks of age to twelve years old, await news of husband and father Maurice Ruddick, missing since Thursday night. *Sun Media Corp.*

Nearly every family in town has someone in the mine; family members, friends, and journalists wait for news. *Joseph Scherschel/TimePix*

A makeshift morgue was established in a tent near the pit-head; in other tents, the Salvation Army, the Royal Canadian Mounties, and the Boy Scouts offered food and solace to the families of the trapped men. *Carl Mydans/TimePix*

Trained rescuers and first-aid workers arrived from mining towns across Nova Scotia, as citizens of Springhill had traveled in times of disaster to other coal mines. *Joseph Scherschel/TimePix*

Garnett Clarke is one of the last survivors to reach the surface. His rescuers fear that after his week in total darkness his corneas will be damaged by exposure to light so they have bandaged his eyes. *Joseph Scherschel/TimePix*

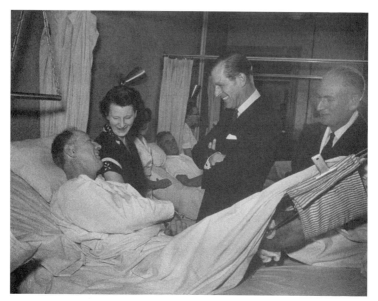

A royal visit by Prince Philip assures Nova Scotia, and all Canada, of Great Britain's and Queen Elizabeth's concern and compassion.
Joseph Scherschel/TimePix

The survivors from Springhill begin their beach vacation; Georgia state troopers enforce separation of the races by escorting the Ruddicks to a house trailer rather than to the motel.
Carl Mydans/TimePix

Maurice Ruddick performs "Aren't You Sorry?" and other songs to an audience assembled by the Negro Chamber of Commerce of Brunswick, Georgia. *Carl Mydans/TimePix*

Maurice Ruddick and his family find themselves handsomely entertained at a house party—held by a member of the Five O'Clock Club—in the segregated neighborhood of the Brunswick African-American community. *Carl Mydans/TimePix*

Springhill's white survivors and their families enjoy shopping, fishing trips, beach picnics, and dances. Life Magazine's headline reads: "Segregated Spree in Georgia." *Carl Mydans/TimePix*

"Well, that's doctor's orders, that's all you can have."

"Well, damn," muttered Lowther, and he ate it.

"Can I have another bowl of that?" he called the next time the attendant passed his bed.

"I thought you said you didn't like it."

"Can't a man change his mind?"

When he tried to let his guard down and act less hostile, Lowther couldn't stop weeping. "I don't get what's the matter with me," he thought. "The minute someone says something to me, I immediately choke up and break down. I'll turn my head so they won't see. I know I'm a harder man than this but I can't seem to stop."

Ted Hunter was taken to a hospital in Halifax when it was determined that his leg was damaged beyond restoration and the internal bleeding was threatening his life. When he rejoined his fellows on the hospital ward, he gave a friendly wave. "I was awake during the whole time they amputated my leg," he called. "I never felt them cutting the flesh. I felt them sawing the bone. I said, 'There she goes.'"

On Friday, October 31, 1958, His Royal Highness Prince Philip, on a visit to Ottawa, made a detour on his homeward journey and directed his jet to touch down in Moncton. Nova Scotia Premier Robert Stanfield and other officials met the prince at the airport and drove him straight to All Saints Hospital in Springhill, where Mayor Gilroy waited to escort him to the beds of the survivors. Dr. Murray was on duty, but, being a modest man, shy of the limelight, he withdrew to allow others to bask in the royal presence. Prince Philip moved gently through the wards of injured miners, leaning down to exchange a pleasantry with each man and to shake his hand.

For over an hour and a half [reported the CBC] *His Royal*

*Highness Prince Philip brought to the town of Springhill the sympa-
thetic encouragement of his cheery presence. In All Saints Hospital, the
twelve men miraculously recovered from the shattered depths in the
small hours of Thursday morning waited expectantly with some of
their injured comrades who were among the eighty-one rescued earlier.*

*His Royal Highness spoke to each and every man, sometimes seri-
ously, sometimes flashing his famous smile in response to the touches
of humor which is part of a miner's stock-in-trade.*

Following his tour of the wounded, Prince Philip asked to
see the mine site before leaving Springhill.

"It was rather nice, you know, to do that," said a woman still
waiting at the pithead for news of her missing husband, watching as the prince was driven away.

CBC reported:

*There are still fifty-seven men for whom there has been no ac-
counting. The company still has a disaster on its hands.*

The mine officials stated that they held no hope of more survivors. An uncle of Norma Ruddick dropped by and said,
"They're all dead down there. There's nobody alive."

Norma left the kitchen, saying to an older daughter, "He
doesn't know. He's just going by what he heard."

"Every night the news comes on and it isn't good news," said
June Jewkes, waiting for word on her husband, Doug. "That
was great when they got the first twelve out. But now it's another day and the same thing and no good word."

ATLANTA

On Friday afternoon in Atlanta, a tight-lipped secretary handed
Caldwell a note to phone Eastern Airlines. "What?" he asked
her. "What?"

"Just call," she said.

"Mr. Caldwell, listen here, I have got to apologize," said Eastern's PR director. "I honestly did not know that federal regulations prohibit us from flying anybody free of charge. We just can't do it. Now, we'll be glad to cooperate and make all the arrangements to fly everyone down to Jekyll, but you're going to have to tell me who's going to pay for it."

"Can you…is there…any kind of discount?" squeaked Caldwell, edging over to his chair to sit down. "It's for the miners. You saw what they went through."

"I sure can't," said the Eastern man. "It's going to have to be regular-price fares. That's what my supervisor tells me. Federal regulations."

"Damn, damn, damn," said Caldwell, banging his forehead with the receiver. "What is the first rule of politics, Sam?" he asked himself sneeringly, and gave the answer: "When in doubt, don't."

"Mr. Gregory, the governor is on line one," said a secretary.

"Damn, damn, damn," said Caldwell. He waited, unwilling to open his eyes and look up.

"Mr. Caldwell?" said the secretary. "The governor for you, line one."

"What in hell you do, Caldwell? I turn my back for ten minutes," Marvin Griffin hollered without saying hello. He was phoning from the Chicago airport, en route home. "You paying for this out of your own pocket or whose money exactly are you spending?"

"I'm sorry, Governor, the airline told me they were going to pay for it. I was trying to find a way to advertise Jekyll."

"You going to advertise yourself out of a job, that's what you going to advertise." Griffin slammed down the phone.

Caldwell drove home that evening, drank too much, and yelled at his wife. When the phone rang and it was Governor Griffin back in town, he wasn't surprised, although the governor never had called him at home before.

"Caldwell," Griffin said, "lay this thing out for me. How many people you invite? How many coming? Where you going to put them? We got any way to back out of this?"

Caldwell's big white billboard of an idea looked like a truck had driven through it. He tried to stretch the ripped pieces together and show the governor how it had appeared. "Well, twelve miners, but they might not all be in good enough physical condition to travel," he said hopefully. "And their wives and, uh, children. It's a million dollars free publicity, Governor," he averred, but his shaky voice didn't convey it.

"This is going to cost the state of Georgia a shitload of money," snarled the governor.

"I was thinking about it like this, Governor—"

"Go raise some money," Griffin said, and hung up on him again.

SPRINGHILL, 5 P.M.

Mothers led costumed children down the sidewalks, dressed up for Halloween. There was no joy in it. The notion of spooks and spirits was too awful to contemplate at such a time, with dead men sprawled beneath the town.

Hughie Guthro walked out of the hospital. Margie drove him over to the lamp cabin because he wanted to retrieve his tag. "CRNC 982. Yep, it's still hanging there. It's no good to anybody else, I reckon." He put it on his key chain.

———

Gorley and Margie Kempt, Caleb and Pat Rushton, and Arnold Burden accepted the invitation from the *Ed Sullivan Show*. They were to fly out the next day, spend the night in Manhattan, and go to the theater on Sunday.

"They got my grave all dug?" Bowman Maddison learned.

"Ha!" he barked, when he saw an undertaker on the street. "You pretty near had me, but you ain't got me yet. Fill 'er in!"

34

Between Hell and Nova Scotia

GROUP OF SEVEN
FRIDAY, OCTOBER 31
EIGHT DAYS SINCE THE BUMP

"I think my little daughter is a cripple," said Currie Smith into the darkness after countless hours of silence. He cleared his throat, but his voice remained hoarse and cracked. "The doctor says she didn't get enough oxygen at birth. It's looking like she's going to grow up to be a retard."

"We got no children," said Pep after a time. "I'd like to have. We lost two, and now they say we're too old to adopt any. We took care of two little girls of my nephew's when he died, but they wouldn't allow you to adopt a relative, eh? But I wouldn't trade my wife for children or any other woman in the world. We are very happy together. And the sex life? I can tell you, I'm missing that right now."

"Oh, she'll have another man in no time," someone said. "All the wives will."

No particular bond grew between the fellows in the darkness of shared unhappiness. They were like men in the waiting area of a hospital emergency room, each cradling his head in his hands, each praying to a personal god from the depths of a private disaster. The miners curled more and more inside themselves. Each was going to die alone, as if trapped all by himself. No matter that rescuers, arriving too late, might mythologize the brotherhood of the pit. What they really would uncover was a grave of bitter, disappointed, lonely men.

What would the Code have had them do? The kernel of the Miners' Code was solidarity. But they were empty. They were too hollowed out by thirst and despair to give one another relief.

"You know what I keep thinking about?" said Doug Jewkes during a quiet break. "About 7 Up. June and me, we used to make 7 Up floats and I keep thinking about them. If I ever get the hell out of here, I'm going to pour me a great big bottle of 7 Up."

Frank Hunter had lost so much weight, he could no longer keep his pants up. He opened his belt and cut new holes in it with a jackknife. "If that bump went out to the slope," he said, "it'll be right near impossible for them to get to us."

"There was nine of us, six brothers and three sisters," Pep said. "My mother went through hard times, the hungry thirties. My father left the railroad and gave over fifty years to the coal mine. He got an award for being the steadiest worker in all that many years. But he went blind. I had a brother killed overseas. I was kind of a favorite of my mother, I guess. Of both of them. I wonder how she's handling this now."

"If I could just get me a nice cold fresh bottle of 7 Up, I believe I could last another week," offered Jewkes.

"Jesus, Jewkes, you told us that already. Drop the subject."

"Leave him be," said Ruddick. "He's doing wonderful. You will last for another day, boy."

"Currie?" Doug Jewkes whispered.

"What?"

"You still got hopes?"

"Yes, I've got some hopes."

"By Jesus, you're some boy. I don't understand you."

"Doug, I got good hopes and I will until I draw my last breath."

The rescuers calculated that if any others had survived, they would have to be in a spot parallel to where the twelve men were found; and that would be the intersection of the 12,800 level and the wall. Though the 12,800 level was two hundred feet closer to the surface than where the twelve had been found, it was completely impassable. It would take a week to clear it, the shift managers estimated.

CBC Radio reported:

The last word, the last informed word . . . [is] that it would take at least a week to bore through to the juncture where men might possibly be.

35

Angels, Angels

GROUP OF SEVEN
SATURDAY, NOVEMBER 1, 4 P.M.
NINE DAYS SINCE THE BUMP

With jubilation and talk of miracles ringing out overhead, underground rescuers pressed on. Each dead body they uncovered was another weight on their hearts. With the 12,800 level crammed to the roof, the volunteers began to dig a new tunnel alongside it, bucket by bucket, handful by handful.

One rescuer stumbled over a hole at the bottom of which lay a man. The rescuer plunged in nearly on top of him, and the man moaned. "He's alive!" called the rescuer. "Man alive here!" They pulled apart the dry well and revealed Barney Martin, squeezed into a tiny spot with his legs cramped against him. They called for Dr. Burden to hurry.

"He's barely breathing, but his eyes are wide open," said the doctor. "His body is stressed from sitting in such a tight position for so long."

"We can't understand what he's telling us," said a rescuer.

"His sounds are unintelligible," the doctor said. "His mouth must be full of coal dust." The men gently extricated Martin and laid him on a stretcher. "He's in a semi-coma and severely dehydrated," said the doctor. "Keep pouring that coffee into him and get him out of here; there's no point in my checking for internal injuries down here."

Maurice said hoarsely, "Currie?"

"I'm awake, Maurice, just laying here and praying."

"Suppose we got up and pounded on them pans. We could, you know, get an answer."

"The only way we're ever going to know is to pound," agreed Currie Smith, who wearily got up and began banging.

Instantly a man from just outside the cave called, "How many's there?"

"Seven!" answered Currie with a gasp. He looked beyond the pan line and saw rods of light from headlamps crisscrossing like sabers in the darkness.

Ruddick suddenly felt Garnet Clarke grab him by the head and kiss him.

CBC Radio broadcast the news:

Somehow or other, during the night, progress was made and pressed forward to such an extent that sounds had been heard, the sounds of voices, somewhere in the depths. It's an official report; it has been given to us by Mr. Ernie Patterson, the public relations manager of DOSCO, who is in direct contact with the workers at the mine.

Then there were lights all around them, white, white spot-lights, floodlights; it was like looking up at the white sun on a July day at seaside. The men threw their arms over their pained eyes and wept with happiness. "It's like angels, angels," said Jewkes. The white lights swept over them, back and forth, whitewashing them up and down, and piercing their eyes like flashbulbs. Barely able to look up over their shielding arms, the survivors felt themselves showered by light, irradiated. What few colors there were in the pit—a blue-green shirt collar, a patch of yellow rain slicker peeking out from under a muddy coating, the ripped brown candy-bar wrapper—suddenly leaped to life and glowed. The hale, strong-voiced rescuers were invisible behind their incandescent headlamps.

"Ruddick? You in there, Maurice?" called one of the rescuers, John Calder.

"I'm here."

"Man, the workmen's compensation board sent me down here specifically to get you out."

"Why is that?"

"Why?" said Calder, in high spirits. "They said they'd have to pay so much for your wife and twelve children, if we don't find you, there won't be enough left over for the others."

It has now just been learned that they have reached seven men at the 13,000-foot level. I'll repeat again: The rescue workers have now reached seven men.

Herbert Pepperdine's wife fainted when told he was coming back. She woke up confused on her kitchen floor, surrounded by grinning relatives.

Mabel Smith had taken the children trick-or-treating for Halloween the night before. Her mother-in-law, who was staying with her through the crisis, shook Mabel awake at six the next morning. "Wake up! They've found Currie!"

Disoriented Mabel asked calmly, "Oh, did they?"

"Yes, they did! Get up! We're going to the hospital."

Mabel went into the kitchen, leaned on her refrigerator, and cried until she choked with the frightening thought that she would never stop crying.

———

June Jewkes was in bed when her son came and stood by her bed and said, "Mum, they found Dad."

"No, Randall, don't fool about things like that at a time like this, dear."

"No, it's true, Mum. It come on the telly. They found him."

A minister stepped out of his car and moved up the walkway to the Ruddicks' house. Norma, who was waiting for him at the door, cut to the quick. "Is Maurice alive?"

"Yes."

Dr. Burden, having sent Barney Martin up to the surface, now crept forward with other rescuers and glimpsed the group of survivors standing in their cave.

"There's ten percent gas here," a rescuer was saying. "We better hurry up and get them out of here."

"Well, they been here for quite a while," said Doc Burden. "I guess they can stay another half hour."

"Hey, Ruddick, you the one they call the singing miner?" called one of the rescuers.

"I reckon."

"How about singing us a song then?"

Recalling that in the world to which he was about to be restored, his voice was valued more highly than his judgment, Ruddick managed to croak, "Give me a drink of water and I'll sing you a song."

"We need water! Give us water!" the men clamored, and Doc Burden poured out an ounce for each of them.

"That just sunk into my tongue. It didn't even go down my throat!" said Jewkes.

"I think we could use about a can of water for each man,"

ordered Ruddick, not yet dispossessed, by daylight and the return to society, of leadership.

The fanning lights hit upon Percy Rector's corpse then, and everything stopped. "Oh Jesus, oh Perce," the men said. He was wilted and shriveled, his face stiff in agony.

"Good God, we couldn't see him before," said Jewkes.

"Jesus! Terrible, terrible," rescuers said.

"That is an awful-looking sight."

"I never seen anything like that before," Jewkes kept saying. "I ain't never going to get this out of my head."

"Sit," the rescuers told the men, "and drink this. Build your strength up before we go." They served them hot chocolate and tomato soup.

"Can you boys walk down the wall?" the rescuers asked after a few moments of noisy slurping. Ruddick lingered paternally toward the rear of the cave to make sure that nothing and nobody was left behind, other than Percy's grotesque corpse; then he hobbled behind his fellows out of the hole to where stretchers waited. He lay down and felt bandages pressed over his eyes. Doc Burden, behind him, jotted again in his pocket notebook: "Last man out, 8:45 P.M."

Doug Jewkes pulled the bandages off his eyes as he neared the surface. "I never been so happy in my life!" he cried. "I have got to see that sky." His brother Bobby rode up in the trolley with him and pulled his pit boots off. "You'll never need these again," Bobby said, and pitched them back down the slope.

There was a crowd of photographers at the pithead, with flashbulbs snapping.

"I never thought all that stuff was going on," thought Pepperdine. "Flashbulbs and all them folks, never thought about them being so many around the mine, never even dawned on me about that."

"What you want, Doug Jewkes?" a reporter called when his stretcher bobbed out the door of the shed.

"All I need now is a bottle of 7 Up and a scoop of ice cream!" he called, and the crowd laughed happily and nobody yelled at him.

ATLANTA: 9 P.M.

"Honey?" called Caldwell's wife from the living room Saturday night. He was sitting by himself in the kitchen, trying to think. "You better come see something."

"The seven men discovered alive last at the 12,600-foot level are being brought to the surface," said a reporter. "They are being loaded into the ambulances to be driven to the hospital . . ."

The phone rang. "Damn, Caldwell!" the governor barked. "I thought you told me the ones you invited were the only survivors. We inviting these boys to the party, too?"

"How can we not, Governor?" whispered Caldwell.

The governor watched the coal-covered men emerging from the pithead. He laughed: "Shit, they all look like niggers."

36

Wives and Husbands

On the propeller plane carrying the Kempts, the Rushtons, and the Burdens toward Boston, the Springhill contingent was invited to visit the cockpit. The pilot shouted that they were cruising at about the altitude above ground that the men had been trapped below ground. "Well, sir," said Burden in his high, pinched voice, looking out the small window, "I didn't get out of the mine till nine last night and I don't even know if I packed a fresh suit!" No one could hear him above the engine noise. "And Caleb and Gorley have only been out of the mine a couple of days," he thought, "after being trapped in that hellhole for six days."

Burden was beginning to sag. "I've had two hours sleep out of the last thirty-six. I don't know whether I'm more excited or more exhausted." Back in his seat, he leaned his head against the window with a small sigh and fell asleep.

"Who would have thought we'd be tripping off to New York together this weekend?" Margie yelled to Gorley, but his gaunt face was thrown back and he was snoring with his mouth wide open.

Pat Rushton also was considering that, three days earlier, the last thing on earth she imagined was a time of whispering and giggling in the dark of the early morning with a miraculously restored husband, much less agitating over what to wear in New York City and to the *Ed Sullivan Show.* Caleb had come out of the bathroom jiggling his too-large pants around his starved stomach. He cinched his belt and double-knotted it like a shoelace.

In Boston, the shaky new heroes descended the staircase to a throng of journalists, photographers, and TV cameramen. "Good Lord," thought Burden, as they hurried to catch the flight to New York, "Caleb, Gorley, and I are going to be televised internationally on the most popular TV show on earth. Millions of people will be watching. And this will be within twenty-four hours of crawling through rubble a mile underground. Yes sir, we're about to become faces in an international news story."

As they headed toward the Park Sheraton Hotel in taxis, the sightseers saw a Broadway theater marquee with the lit-up words, MORE MEN ALIVE. Papers hanging from the newsstands reported the evacuation of the last seven survivors from No. 2. Photographers milled in front of the hotel, awaiting the group's arrival. "Excuse me, guys!" called one. "Can I get a shot of you looking up at the big tall buildings?"

"They want us to look like country bumpkins," Burden said to his friends. "Don't look up!"

In their small, hot, handsomely upholstered rooms, they phoned for room service and dug into sirloin steaks on wheeled tables draped with white tablecloths. At seven-thirty that night, they were shown to seats down front in Ed Sullivan's theater. He crossed the stage at eight o'clock. "Today's show is in honor of heroism," he said. "We want to commemorate the heroism of the individual, like these brave men from Springhill, Canada, and we want to commemorate the heroism of the small nation of Israel." He then introduced the first act, the Mormon Tabernacle Choir.

"Everyone is talking about the Springhill Mine Disaster," said Sullivan when he returned to the stage. "The escape and courage of these men have captured people's imagination. Tonight we have two of those heroes with us in the audience. With them are their wives and the town doctor. Let's give them a round of applause." The group stood up, looking rueful, and Caleb and Gorley waved. The audience cheered. Sullivan mentioned the Springhill Miners' Disaster Fund and solicited contributions. Later, backstage, he gave Burden his personal check for a thousand dollars, and his on-air appeal would help raise two million dollars.

Monday morning in the hotel was Caleb's first chance since rescue to have a long soak in a bathtub. The ground-in dirt floated out of his skin and hair, and left such a gritty black ring in the hotel tub that he and Pat were mortified and got on their hands and knees to scrub it clean.

Out on the streets, the small group attracted attention everywhere they went: "Aren't you the people from the mines in Nova Scotia?" Monday night they enjoyed free tickets to *My Fair Lady.* On Tuesday, they flew back to Springhill. Dr. Burden, exhausted, returned to the identification of bodies.

SPRINGHILL

Mabel Smith bustled into the hospital ward to visit Currie, but stopped short in misgiving. "Oh my! He looks so different. Well, I can see it's him, but he looks like someone who just came down off a mountain. He's all dark, and he lost his teeth down there, his false teeth; he's got no teeth." In her pretty dress, squeezing her pocketbook, she drew hesitantly close to the gaunt, hollow-faced man. His eyes moved and his gums showed in a grin, and she saw that it was him. She removed a white glove and patted his arm with her soft hand. "There there, dear," she said.

The most happily married couples—the Smiths, the Pepperdines, the Ruddicks, the Rushtons, the Guthros—reconnected in gentle joy like the chiming together of wineglasses in a toast. They resumed their lives together. The wives picked up the frayed ends of their husbands' psyches to commence the work of knitting them back together.

For a few of the fellows, the visiting wives put a damper on the fun. These women arrived already used up, sleep-deprived, aggravated by such a life. They had plenty of their own complaints to unload—it had been no picnic up top, either, but here these fellows were shooting lewd remarks from bed to bed behind the nurses' backs and acting like they were too good for their hand-delivered food trays, as if the meals weren't quite up to their high standards. More than one of the men encountered a tired wife, who wished for anything other than being expected to wait adoringly upon her man, posing for a newspaper snapshot—slender in a belted dress with a Peter Pan collar, girlishly lifting one leg as she hugged her brave survivor—then trudging back out to the parking lot and driving the rattletrap back to the half-finished house and the unwashed children.

The wife of one of the survivors had left him well before the bump. In the hospital, he learned that she had moved back into his house while he was trapped. "She thought I was dead," he thought. "She came to collect her widow's money. But I disappointed her!" She came once to see him at the hospital, but manners remained stiff between them. By the time the miner was discharged, she had moved out of his house again and disappeared from his life.

"Hey!" yelled Garnet Clarke, soaking up the attention of his parents and siblings. "I've still got shit in my hair! Can you believe this? It's turning my hair gray; that's what it's doing."

Herb Pepperdine lay in his bed quietly enjoying a smoke and a bottle of Pepsi when he heard Doug Jewkes say to his wife, June, while pointing out Pep, "You see that fella there? Well, you go down and anything he wants, he gets. He can crawl in bed with you. If it wasn't for him, I wouldn't be here today."

Garnet Clarke, meanwhile, was feeling grateful to Maurice. "That dark fellow who was with us," Garnet told his mother about Ruddick, "as soon as I heard them coming, I reached over and kissed him."

"Doug is just a bunch of nerves," thought June Jewkes. "I can't hardly talk to him. He's just jumping around all over the place. He can't seem to stay still."

Grinning reporters were jostling around Doug Jewkes's bed to nab another 7 Up quote. He was more than willing. He posed for photos, lifting the green bottle that glittered in the sunlight from the window. He himself was several shades lighter each day. "I was so black, I was just as black as that box over there," he told reporters who visited later in the week. "It's going to take them days, they've been two or three days just getting the dirt off me.

"Yeah," he said magisterially reclining, manufacturing quotes, "thinking about that 7 Up and ice cream, and them floats me and June used to make, thinking about that near drove me crazy. It near drove me crazy, I'm telling you. I think that is all that kept me going. I kept saying to meself, boy, I'm going to get the hell out of here and I'll have another bottle of that 7 Up. I don't know yet whatever kept me from getting scairt down there. I wasn't scairt, not from the time that it happened. Well, I got out and the minute I landed at the hospital, it wasn't an hour or so I had two great big bottles of 7 Up on me stand."

It made for great print. And then a man from Moncton, New Brunswick, introduced himself as the manager of a soft drink bottling plant and said familiarly, "Doug, I'll be in touch with you."

Sure enough, another man appeared, representing Seven Up, and said, "Doug, we got you a job in Toronto. And we're going to start you away at seventy-five dollars a week."

Jewkes, flustered, sat up straighter and explained shame-facedly, almost inaudibly, that he'd never finished school.

"That's got no bearing on it at all," the man said grandly, as journalists took notes. "The job is there for you."

"Well, I have had some different jobs offered to me," he told the man. "I could have went sea fishing. Over on Prince Edward Island a fellow has offered me his cottage over there to live in it for a dollar a year. A man from New Brunswick wrote and said I could go half with him on a fishing deal, go out deep-sea fishing with him. I figure I might as well go down in the mines as go out on the water."

"Well, we got this job waiting for you, Doug," said the Seven Up man, talking out the side of his mouth as photographers snapped the two men facing front for the cameras.

"I'm scared they'll get me up there and want me to do some-thing," Jewkes told his wife later—the fact was that he couldn't read very well—"but the man said, 'That's got no bearing on it at all.'" He was to repeat the man's encouragingly dismissive comment for eight weeks, up to and through the time his fam-ily pulled up stakes and moved to Toronto.

When Barney Martin's wife arrived at the hospital soon after his rescue, she protested that the gaunt nearly unconscious man was not her husband. But he'd nearly lost his ear in a mine accident in 1952. Now, in the hospital, she went hesitantly closer to the coal-blackened fellow and saw the marks on his right ear. "Oh my God, it is Barney," she said.

Barney Martin recovered slowly, confused about what had happened to him, and nearly deaf. "I heard that they did have water for a certain number of days, but those boys never gave me no water," he told an interviewer in the hospital. "When I talked to them, they said that all I was saying was, 'Water, water, water.' They said, 'We got no water, we'll give you some urine. Will you drink that?' And I just kept saying, 'No, no, no.' But now I hear that they did have water for a few days. I needed it bad if not worse."

"Hey, Garnie, here comes another cake!" someone yelled down the ward. As news reports appeared of Garnet Clarke's melancholy birthday in the mine, well-wishers sent cards, cash, and cakes. He scooted up higher in his bed. "This one's from Ontario!" he called out, opening his card. "The last two came from Halifax!"

"What?" cried Leon Melanson, the once-suave blue-eyed dancer, still in agony in his hospital bed, learning of the fate of his brother-in-law, Percy Rector, as the first survivors of the Group of Seven were carried in. "You mean to tell me they couldn't save him? They couldn't do anything for him?" He was roiled by grief on top of the unending pain in his leg, and arched backward. "Jesus, they couldn't find an ax or something to chop the pack away? They couldn't give him any relief? He just stood there till he died?

"I can't understand it, no way can I understand this. This is my wife's sister's husband. This was my close friend. Percy's a good man. He'll do anything in the world for a person. And they wouldn't help him? This isn't right, this isn't right." He himself would be taken to Halifax for amputation of the leg and would have to fight his way back to life. He was a sweet and lovely man. But he never would forgive the men trapped with Percy, never could really stomach being around any of them again.

37

The Singing Miner

Eddies of journalists, psychologists, sociologists, mothers, sisters, brothers, and wives lapped outside the closed doors of the hospital ward, waiting for visiting hours to commence. When the doors opened, there would be a polite footrace to the bedsides of the survivors. The reporters, naturally, were hoping for a scoop, the inside story, tomorrow's headline. Professors of sociology and psychology from Dalhousie University and the University of Halifax recognized a remarkable opportunity to learn about individual and group survival in a disaster scenario. In this Cold War era of nuclear threat, the possibility of human survival underground was a subject of pointed interest to millions. The professors already had lined up graduate students to assist them with extensive interviews, psychological assessments, and I.Q. testing of every one of the rescued men. The wives simply wanted to understand what had happened and what had saved these few, when so many good men were lost. When a woman saw her friends, the scores of widows, daily on the street: "Oh, my husband...," she would say. Then what? "Just happened to be...." "It was just his luck that...." "I'm so, so sorry about your son, Mrs. M——, I was praying for him; it just happened that my husband..."

Norma Ruddick wondered about it all. The nights standing alone at her bedroom window, the chest of her flannel night-dress damp from falling tears, prayerfully twisting and twisting her fingers, saying, "Please God..." Did that save Maurice?

Or, he always wore his helmet, even when eating his dinner, so when the rocks began falling... Had that saved Pep?

His grandfather and his father both survived disasters. It's just a bit of fine heredity, a twist in my husband's genes that placed him just beyond where the rocks were smashing...

Everyone connected to the miners had, or wanted to have, a story to tell—everyone except the miners, in their cotton gowns, in their hospital beds. For them it was plenty to have glasses of ice water on their trays; to blink stupidly at the tall windows at the far end of the ward, glazed by the sun into opaque panels of shimmering whiteness; to hop up and tiptoe, buttocks jiggling under the short back-opening garments, across the cool floor to the john and then rush back to bed past the hoots of their fellows. Wives came and went in their little hats, with their snap-shut handbags crammed with letters and some cash from far-off well-wishers. Toddlers were lifted only to wriggle away from a kiss from their gap-toothed, bluish, grizzled pops. And then the men napped, and if they jolted awake in the daytime, they were reassured instantly by the wall of windows, the streaming whiteness of the air, the daylight that poured across everything like a spring wind. But if they awoke with a yelp from a bad dream in the night, and the ward was dark, terror choked them. Men dug their fingernails into the sides of their mattresses and wailed like babies. One groped to the bathroom, turned on the lights there, left the door wide open, and came back to bed, and they all purred their assent.

When interrogated, the survivors offered only, "Get me another glass of water, would you? There's a dear."

Or, weakly, "I think you'd better take the kids home now. I'm done in."

Journalists jockeyed around in need of a few true things. Human interest angles, first person narratives. But coal miners were a tight-lipped pack, the journalists were discovering. It was hard as heck pulling descriptions out of these crusty guys. "What was it like down there?" the reporters cajoled, jostling around a survivor's hospital bed, offering cigarettes and lighting them.

"Well, sir, I can tell you this: it was dark."

Or, "Nobody got excited. Everybody stayed cool."

Or, "Being trapped gives you an awful feeling. I can't describe it."

Readers loved this story, couldn't buy newspapers and magazines fast enough, and here now, laid out for the reporters like sausages on a buffet table, were actual eyewitness survivors. Under the lights, prodded and poked, they emitted monosyllables.

"I just lay there and I prayed."

Or, "It got hot and the dirt was bad."

One small story making the rounds caught on; for lack of bigger game, it generated interest: According to one of the rescuers, when they broke through to the Group of Seven, Maurice Ruddick had called out, "Give me a drink of water and I'll sing you a song!"

Ruddick told the reporters that he didn't remember saying it, so he couldn't summarize what was behind his bold remark. When they stopped badgering him and he lay back alone on his hospital bed, he enjoyed the waves of sunlight and the high white cracked plaster ceiling. He did recall the instant of rescue: the healthy, booted, headlamped, big-voiced rescuers stepping in and greeting them, and how he and the other ash-mouthed, wraithlike survivors began weeping in gratitude.

Had Ruddick possessed, at that moment, the verve to show off? It was probable that a rescuer, recognizing him as the miner who led songs on the trolleys, said, "Hey, it's Ruddick! Ruddick, why don't you sing us a song?"

And Maurice, weak but obliging, unsure whether the request was said in jest or in earnest, had said with parched throat, "Well...give me a drink of water and I'll sing you a song."

But somehow the reporters found in this vignette just what was required for stories such as "Grace Under Fire," or "Cheerful After Ordeal." They began to question Ruddick's fellow survivors about him, and they wove the monosyllabic replies into headlines like "Hero Keeps Comrades' Spirits Up."

"One came out joking," they wrote. "Maurice Ruddick is known as the singing miner. He kept up spirits of six of the seven men found alive Saturday at Springhill..."

Soon journalists were reporting which songs had been particularly uplifting during the entrapment. Though Ruddick never had thought of himself as anything other than a black man, a Negro, the word "mulatto" was taken up, and began to appear often beside the word "hero."

"He always sang as he worked," a reporter wrote. "His comrades said he had sung plenty in the long hours of darkness, keeping up their spirits."

Continually pressed by reporters for details about the underground, Ruddick managed to come up with a few. "The Old Rugged Cross was the favorite number during the long days and nights. And another piece I sang a lot was a little song I made up as I went along. 'I Come to the Lord in Prayer,' I call it."

One finished account looked like this:

When the draegermen finally broke through the tunnel on the morning of the ninth day, they found Ruddick singing at the top of his lungs. He greeted them with "Give me a drink of water and I'll sing you a song."

The puffery seemed harmless to the press at the time.

ATLANTA

Sam Caldwell got up Monday morning in deep melancholy, showered, dressed, and drove slowly toward his office, certain that he was going to be yelled at, then fired. He couldn't remember how he thought he was going to raise money for this coal-miner boondoggle. Taxpayers would scream if he touched state money. Why had he thought he'd treat these fellows to a vacation?

His secretary stood waiting. "Mr. Caldwell, the governor wants to see you right away."

"Shit."

"Caldwell, come here. Look at this," bellowed Griffin, waving a newspaper at him. It was Sunday's *Toronto Star.* MORE ALIVE, it said in huge black letters. Below the headline was a photograph of a woman holding a newborn baby and a toddler, surrounded by ten other children. "These look like white people to you, Caldwell?"

"I, I don't know, Governor."

"Well, look at them."

"I don't know, I can't tell." The governor waited, exasperated. "That's one of the miner families, right? I guess they're white." Caldwell said, trying to oblige.

"Well, you guess wrong. They're not. It says right here in the paper, 'mulatto.' It's a mulatta family."

"Who are they?"

"Who are they? You're asking *me* who are they? I guess they're friends of yours, Caldwell, since you invited them on a great big vacation."

"They're..."

"They're—let's see—they're 'The Maurice Ruddick family,'" Griffin read aloud. "'Mrs. Ruddick holds her youngest, three-week-old Katrina, while her other eleven children are grouped around her.' Look at that passel of kids. Goddamn, Caldwell, they got nigger coal miners in Canada?"

"I don't know. I didn't think so."

"Hell right, you didn't think. How many niggers did you invite, Caldwell. Here's thirteen of them right here belonging to Mr. Maurice Ruddick." He read again. "'The family waited, hoping, but close to despair for news of the father of twelve. It came today, the electrifying news that he was alive and safe from his ordeal.'"

Without asking permission, Sam Caldwell sat down in an armchair facing the governor's desk.

"Jesus Christ, Caldwell."

Caldwell could think of absolutely nothing to add.

"Of all the monumental blunders, made by all the stupid, inexperienced, impulsive aides, I swear to God, Caldwell, I'm this close to firing you."

"Yes sir."

"I'd have been done firing you if it didn't mean I was going to get stuck with this thing. So, tell me something, smart boy, just where on Jekyll Island are you planning to put *mulatto* coal miners?" He didn't have to tell the desperate aide that the only motel on Jekyll Island was a white-only establishment.

"You had no authority to do this, Caldwell," said Griffin.

"No sir, I didn't." He thought, "There's no hole I can crawl into. I've put Governor Griffin in the position of inviting a black man to a vacation in a segregated state with no facilities to accommodate him."

"I'm a' tell you what, Caldwell," said the governor. "You take a leave of absence and go on down to Brunswick and Jekyll and you work things out. I will not have my motels, buses, restaurants, or beaches integrated, and I won't allow any photographs of them integrated, and I'm not shaking hands with a nigger in public. So you go work it out. Go."

It was even worse than the governor knew, Caldwell thought, swaying disconsolately back toward his office. He'd been contacted already by newspapers and magazines and TV reporters from all over North America, eager to reserve rooms on Jekyll alongside the miners and to cover the story. A few days ago, half a lifetime ago, that had been the plan: the miners were to be set out as bait for the media. But now he knew that the nationwide ridicule and scorn heaped on Governor Griffin during the Sugar Bowl debacle was nothing compared to how it was going to look for Georgia to abuse Canadian coal-mine heroes.

At a press conference that afternoon, the governor told the reporters, "Sam Caldwell invited them. Now he can pay for it."

SPRINGHILL

The search and rescue missions were terminated. By November 5, there were only nine bodies left to be recovered. Sadie Allen had received no news as yet of Fidel, for good or ill. Late on the night of November 6, the last body was brought out, and it was Fidel.

"He was the first one in and the last one out," Sadie said.

The coffin arrived closed and was hoisted onto the dining-room table. Sadie, like all the wives, was strongly warned not to open it, because the sight of her damaged husband would be too upsetting. She waited until the minister busied himself with visitors, then pried open the lid. "All I can see is rocks and stones..." The minister turned, saw what she was up to, stepped briskly to her side, and pushed down the lid.

"All bodies were definitely identified," says Dr. Burden. "There were no coffins of rocks and stones."

But Sadie thought, "I don't think they found Fidel's body." She would never be persuaded otherwise.

The final tally: 174 trapped, 99 rescued, 75 killed.

Part II

38

The Richest, the Most Exclusive, the Most Inaccessible Club in the World

Clean morning light billows over the coast like white sheets on a clothesline. The subtropical barrier islands of Georgia bob half in, half out of the water, like a line of green-and-white buoys. Atlantic tides sizzle up across the beaches, splashing into a network of freshwater creeks. The salt marsh, in golden-green softness and splendor, fills the coastal plain and shimmers toward the horizon in every direction. It buzzes and pops and hisses with life: the razz of cicadas, flap of red-winged blackbirds, gulping of bullfrogs, bellowing of alligators, and ladylike shrieks of blue herons.

On slightly higher ground stand the live oaks, the giant bearded grandfathers of the coast. Gnarled and hairy, draped with Spanish moss, they scatter acorns benevolently upon their roots and shadows, upon which feed jays, quail, whitetail deer, raccoons, and squirrels. In the magnolia trees, thick perfumed blossoms loll open upon glossy leaves.

Tens of thousands of years ago, Creek Indians feasted upon alligators, oysters, wild turkeys, and melons. French explorers and Spanish missionaries blew in on fleets of sailing ships in the sixteenth century and built settlements and missions. The monks cultivated groves of oranges, lemons, pomegranates, olives, and figs. In the mid–eighteenth century, buccaneers and pirates raided ships and preyed upon the coastal settlements. Black-beard is believed to have hidden treasure along the inlets and barrier islands of Georgia, bragging that no one but he and the Devil knew where it was so whichever of the two lived the longest could keep it.

In the eighteenth and nineteenth centuries, the barrier islands were yoked into the Kingdom of Cotton. Sea Islands cotton, cultivated and harvested by brutalized African captives, was the finest in the world, the plantation owners the richest in the Confederacy. In 1818 and 1820, Congress outlawed the four-hundred-year-old trade in human chattel, but profiteers continued to raid Africa and to smuggle their human cargo into America.

On November 29, 1858, the *Wanderer,* America's last illegal slave ship, slid into clandestine harbor at Jekyll Island, then the plantation home of the French aristocratic du Bignon family. Four hundred emaciated teenage boys and a handful of adult men and women abducted from villages along the Congo River had survived the Middle Passage; eighty others had died and been dumped overboard. An hour before sunrise on that late-November day, the young survivors lay wasted and unclothed on the deck, the rest still curled in the slime of the hold, packed infamously "spoon fashion"—the metaphor, no less than the kidnapped boys, the creation and property of a class accustomed to crystal, china, and sterling silver. Businessmen in the upper echelons of New York and Savannah society had bankrolled the *Wanderer*'s criminal expedition; they shared family ties with links to U.S. senators, governors, and Supreme Court justices.

Within a couple of hours of landing, the *Wanderer* was discovered and raided by federal law enforcement agents, but the young Africans were gone, hustled away into the arms of the investors. Some of the boys were kept by the du Bignon family, while others were smuggled to plantations higher up the coast of Georgia and South Carolina. Bedford Forrest's slave-trading company in Memphis offered six "Wanderer Negroes" for sale. Twenty ended up on a Colorado River plantation in Texas. None of the conspirators was arrested.

Some of the young captives failed to recover from the voyage and died; others, too weak to work for many months, lived "at galling expense to their owners." Those who lived and became heads of families told the story of their origins, which survives in coastal folklore. "The thing that set them apart from their fellows," writes Tom Henderson Wells, describing the former *Wanderer* slaves in old age, "was the dimly remembered landing on the lonely beach of Jekyll Island in November 1858."

After the Civil War, without slaves to work them, the Sea Islands plantations were abandoned. The sparkling sunlit islands threw strands of moss, vines, ferns, and wildflowers over the crumbling plantations and slave quarters. The buildings sank under quilts of twittering, knotty, buzzing greenery, just like the remnants of Creek villages, Spanish missions, and English forts before them.

Sam Caldwell spent a long day driving back and forth along the coast, kicking around Jekyll Island, sighting north, squinting south. The new motel was nearly ready. There were stiff new white sheets on the beds, additional colored staff hired out of Brunswick, dry-cleaned uniforms, motel rooms smelling like Lysol, and delivery trucks backing up with crates of soda and beer to the restaurant door.

But where in hell was he supposed to put the Ruddicks? The governor had specified that he didn't want the Negro family within hollering or visiting distance of the white miners and journalists, but Jekyll was a tangled wilderness at its south end. Retired judge A. J. Hartley, the chairman of the Jekyll Island Authority, finally directed Caldwell to a piece of land at the far south end. If he ran a short piece of driveway off the blacktop road, put sand on it, and pushed the woods and underbrush back a few feet from it, Caldwell could just about picture a house trailer installed there. He could cut a footpath through the woods to the sand dunes and beach.

He drove back across the causeway onto the mainland and leased two trailers from a Brunswick lot: one for Ruddick and one for cook and kitchen. With a phone call to Atlanta, he diverted a highway crew and had them assigned to Jekyll to build the short road, and he arranged to have Georgia Power run electrical lines to the settlement.

John Eugene du Bignon, a direct descendant of the plantation owners, bought up the entire island in the late nineteenth century and began publicizing Jekyll as a winter resort for wealthy Northerners; ice is "a rarity," he promised in his brochures, and summers are "rendered . . . quite pleasant by constant refreshing breezes." He and his partner, Newton Finney, founded the Jekyll Island Club, and offered shares to fifty individuals at the crest of Victorian New York society. By 1886, American millionaires including J. P. Morgan, William Rockefeller, Vincent Astor, Joseph Pulitzer, and William K. Vanderbilt began "wintering" in magnificently turreted and ornate "beach cottages" with Tiffany windows, marble showers, skylights of leaded glass, libraries, billiards rooms, indoor tennis courts, and indoor bowling alleys. In 1904, *Munsey's* magazine described the Jekyll Island Club as "the richest, the most exclusive, the most inaccessible" club in the world. Its members enjoyed golf, tennis, cycling, costume balls, sailing, yachting, boar hunting, and driving Ford automobiles onto the beach. They fattened up on ten-course meals in the clubhouse, prepared by a chef imported from New York City's Delmonico's Restaurant. They dressed their children in sailor suits and encouraged them to lead terriers about on leashes. The subtropical paradise of the super-rich lasted until 1942, when, with labor and fuel diverted for the war effort, the Jekyll Island Club closed for the last time. After the Second World War, high society took up elsewhere.

In 1947, Governor M. E. Thompson of Georgia paid $675,000 for Jekyll with the intention of creating a state park. Descendants of the wealthy families withdrew their last personal possessions from their summer mansions, and state convicts began clearing the land for public access.

For Governor Marvin Griffin, Jekyll was the natural weapon with which to duel Florida over the destination of American tourists. He allocated state funds to activate the Jekyll Island Authority. Roads were paved, beachfront developed, picnic areas created, and a restaurant and motel were completed in 1958.

The new motel, for whites only, was named the Wanderer.

SPRINGHILL

Maurice Ruddick was home from the hospital, wrapped in his bathrobe, seated on the sofa like a king among his subjects, the children waiting on him hand and foot, the younger ones crawling all over him, the phone ringing, reporters knocking at the front door, photographers crouching on the living-room rug with their flash equipment. It was a reporter who told them the news: that the family was free to come along to Georgia with the rest, but would be transported, fed, and housed separately.

Norma was frightened. "Where will they put us? We can't stay with everyone else?"

At night in bed, away from reporters and children, she spoke more forcefully. "They hate colored folks down there, Maurice. All the other families from Springhill are going into a motel, and where are we going to stay? They have the Ku Kluxers down there, Maurice. Let's not go. It's not right. You don't need to be treated like that."

But Ruddick, occupied by his recuperation, trying to put back the weight he drastically lost in the pit, gratefully absorbing the attention of the reporters, having been thanked personally in the hospital by some of the miners' wives—"He says he wouldn't have pulled through without you"—felt like he was waking up to a whole new world. He'd been discovered. He felt gratified, justified, satiated for the first time in his life. He always had thought he needed to marshal the musical resources of his family and cartwheel out of town on the road to musical celebrity to win general acceptance and favor back in Springhill. Now it seemed American television was coming to *him*.

"We'll be fine, Norma," he chuckled, and stroked her head on her pillow beside him.

"There are some fellows talking about maybe they won't go to Georgia if you can't be with them. What do you say to that, Maurice?" asked the reporters on Tuesday. Maurice had gotten dressed that day, was regaining his strength; in a double-knit shirt, pressed slacks, and tightly lashed belt, his pencil-line mustache freshly trimmed, he stood in his front door, supporting himself against the doorframe, looking rather pale, and fielded questions from the men standing on his front yard with pads of paper and cameras, wearing hats and shooting off flashbulbs.

"I figure we all need a vacation. I'll agree to go on a segregated basis because I don't want to deprive the rest of the fellows of a holiday. They've got laws down there, I reckon, and I'll obey them. But when I get back, I may have something to say about them. So I say, 'Boys, let's go to Georgia!'"

His brave and generous words were printed in all the newspapers.

"No man stands so high in Springhill today as does Maurice Ruddick, 46, father of 12 children, a Negro known as the 'Singing Miner,'" reported the *Toronto Star*.

The reporters sought quotes from Maurice's fellow survivors. "We all wanted to go together. When I heard of Maurice being separated, I agreed to refuse," said Ted Michniak. "But when Maurice said it was all right with him and insisted we take the holiday regardless, then we figured we'd be showing the Georgia people that we're a little bigger than they are. We'll obey their laws, even though we might not agree with them."

"I'll go if the governor agrees to pay my way down and back, and my expenses while I'm there, and doesn't give Ruddick too much trouble," said Joe McDonald. But privately he complained to his wife, "Doug Jewkes had to go and holler on the news, 'If Maurice don't go, none of us'll go.' Well, they never asked nobody else. Jewkes said that all the boys refused, but he was lying."

With more reporters stepping onto his weedy front yard by the hour, Maurice greased and combed back his hair, brushed his teeth, slapped on aftershave, and notched up his eloquence.

"How you going to cope with the segregation problem, Maurice?" called a journalist. Then he got his pencil ready.

"I'll take Georgia by storm!" He laughed.

"What about you, Mrs. Ruddick?"

"I just want to make sure the children behave on the plane and after we reach Georgia. And I don't know the other families that well anyway. I don't think we'll mind being by ourselves."

"I'll go along according to the rules and regulations," Ruddick announced while the journalists scribbled away in their little notepads. "There is pressure in that part of the world. I wouldn't want to cause an international incident."

He grew philosophical at his afternoon front-yard press conference. "The skin makes no difference, mates, but the heart does." He probably would have been willing to strap on his guitar and improvise a few lyrics and chords about it.

Meanwhile, Frank Hunter resented that they were being told where to go on vacation. "I would like to go and see my married daughter instead of a trip to Georgia. I wish they would give me a check so I could go wherever I like. She has a boy about a year old. It was a blow to me when she left."

Sam Caldwell read the clippings the governor's office forwarded to him, as he sat on a stool in a coffee shop in Brunswick. "Well, goddamn," he said aloud. He looked around him for someone to tell it all to, but it had gotten too complicated. So here he was raising money—two thousand dollars so far from local businessmen—and making arrangements for a fancy vacation for a bunch of types who were already insulting Georgia in the newspaper, and they hadn't even left home yet. "Cause an international incident" indeed!

Meanwhile, a quote from Currie Smith circulated among reporters. Referring to Ruddick and their survival, Smith said: "We were all black down there."

In the evening, lying shoeless on his bed in an ice-cold motel room in Brunswick, feeling sunburned and itchy, Sam Caldwell tried to look at scenes through journalists' eyes: a barren, hot little stretch of road going nowhere, the Ruddicks sitting inside their stuffy little old trailer far from the fun while a colored cook in the other trailer scrambled some eggs for them. It was not going to look good.

He stood up sighing, tucked in his shirt, tied on his shoes, exited and drove down U.S. 17 several hundred yards to a liquor store, bought whiskey and salted mixed nuts, came back to the room, lay down again, and thought some more while his fingers rummaged through the nuts in search of cashews. All right, so he had something like another inspiration, but it was nothing like the first, the billboard-sized one standing in a white blast of sunlight. This was a tacked-on, doing-the-best-you-can sort of thing. He needed to provide some company for the Ruddicks; he needed a celebrity sort of Negro, so it would look like they were all having some fun at their campsite. Well, he couldn't spend any more of the state's money flying someone in, so Sammy Davis, Jr., for example, was probably out of the question. Sidney Poitier, too.

Would somebody come for free to befriend the colored miner family?

To help the state of Georgia preserve and protect segregation, was more like it. No.

He pushed off his shoes with his feet and lay back in a kind of amber, salty haze, letting his mind wander up and down the coast in search of an important but not rabble-rousing Negro, a good citizen, not a "race" man. Someone law-abiding, someone willing to do a good deed, help the governor out. Someone on the governor's payroll . . . And that line of thinking brought him to Savannah State College, a black institution of higher learning with a leafy campus of brick buildings, and to its president, Dr. William K. Payne. Happy again, Caldwell turned on his TV and relaxed.

The next morning, first thing, he ordered a third trailer; second thing was to place an urgent phone call to Savannah State, break in on Payne in a meeting, and explain to the gentleman, in his best bureaucratic voice, interlaced with Southern white civility, that Governor Griffin would count it a personal favor if Dr. and Mrs. Payne could spend a few days relaxing in the pleasant environs of Jekyll Island with their own personal cook and their own personal hero of the mines.

"Dr. W. K. Payne was selected by Governor Marvin Griffin to serve as official host," explained the Savannah State College student newspaper, the *Tiger's Roar*. "Because of Georgia's segregation laws, Mr. Ruddick [will be] unable to remain with his other Nova Scotian comrades during their visit."

39

Sunlight

NOVEMBER 18, 1958

A hundred years to the month after the *Wanderer* glided into secret port with its captives, the Canadian guests and a fleet of journalists arrived at the Jacksonville, Florida, airport on their way to Jekyll Island. Under a hot gray-white November sky, in the windy, roaring air, twelve miners, eleven wives, and twenty-two children came blinking down the steps of the plane from Boston and stood on the asphalt. They wore or dragged the snowsuits and parkas they had worn that snowy morning in Nova Scotia. Two groups of white men in sports jackets and wide ties waited for them at the bottom of the steps, and two buses had drawn up nearby and sat idling with open luggage flaps and open doors. In the gusty gray-particled light, it was a little difficult to pick out the colored people; but no, here they came, and with extended arms and friendly smiles, the aides sent by the Georgia governor's office personally welcomed Maurice and Norma Ruddick and acted thrilled to meet the four children they'd brought with them. With wide-open arms, they steered the family in a different direction from where the rest were being herded. "Excuse me, Maurice? Can you point out your suitcases to me?" In such a civilized and cordial way, everyone smiling, keeping it light, the aides waved over a couple of

Negro airport workers to pull the Ruddick luggage and shove it alone into the first bus's storage compartment. Norma and the children were helped up the steps of their bus—a whole big long bus for two adults and four children (they'd left the eight older children home with relatives)—with a white driver in sunglasses behind the wheel, and off they roared, with a Georgia state patrol car in front of them and one behind. "We'll catch up with you on Jekyll!" called their new friends, the governor's aides, who then turned to assist their colleagues in greeting the white folks and escorting them to the second bus.

A banner was draped across the brand-new causeway to Jekyll Island—WELCOME GUESTS FROM NOVA SCOTIA!—which Norma and Maurice happily pointed out to each other; and other traffic on the road pulled over out of respect to them and the drivers waved. Maurice was relaxed and upbeat, Norma anxious and unhappy. She had a baby on her lap and one beside her—Maurice tended to the other two—and she kept twisting in her seat, trying to see if the other bus was following. It was not. Obviously, with so many more people to get aboard—all the Springhill families and all the journalists, plus all their luggage and camera equipment to load—it would have been a much slower process. Seats would have had to be found for children near their parents, folks scooting over to make room for one more, and there may have been last-minute dashes for the bathroom facilities in the airport, which Norma herself had been interested in; but she was hustled over to her bus so quickly, her hat nearly blew off, and she'd had no time to ask. Now their big empty crate of a bus rattled behind them, rows of empty seats, their fluffy rips patched with electrical tape, and the whole long rusty emptiness of the thing a glaring symbol of the quarantine of the Ruddicks.

———

Gorley Kempt opened the door of his dark motel room the next morning onto a buzzing, twittering scene. The blast of near-equatorial sun was like opening the door of a furnace. Beside the cement balcony and cast-iron railing stood cabbage palm trees rooted in sand, their sharp leaves clattering. Crows and red-winged blackbirds penciled the blue sky. Lawn mowers pushed by black men chewed away at the yellow grass below, and in the spells when the lawn mowers fell silent, fierce metallic grating noises came from jumbo bugs clinging to the trees.

Though they'd never had the chance before (and most never would again) to leave Nova Scotia for a southern holiday, the Canadians took to it right off. "Oh man, oh lovely!" cried the Kempts' teenage children. "Where's my bathing suit? Look, there's a pool. Hot dog!"

Gorley shouted down the cement walkway to Hughie Guthro and Garnet Clarke, who'd emerged in their T-shirts, rubbing their eyes. They banged with their fists on the closed doors of their buddies. "Get up, you layabouts! We're in heaven!" Half-dressed, the miners hobbled down the cool cement steps barefoot and bareback, rolled up their pant legs, danced across the short, prickly grass, and fanned their way through the sand dunes to reach the ocean. Gorley threw himself into the shallow surf, others poked their long, clammy white feet into the water's edge, and others grabbed sand and threw it, all behaving as if they'd never seen an ocean before, for this warm, sparkling, hissing Atlantic was nothing like their steel-gray, ice-cold northern sea.

Released from their black rock prison, the men reveled in light of such abundance as they never knew existed on earth. The buttery sunlight spread over everything: it magnified the sand into tiny gems, ruffled the tops of the cordgrass on the dunes, and warmed the hard brown glaze of the fiddler crabs. Just offshore, dolphins circled, seeming to eye the humans, and pelicans dropped out of the sky to smash into the turf, beak first. The men's underweight, paper-white bodies were blown about by the sunlit wind like kites in the air. They'd climbed out of the earth's deepest pit to frolic on its sunniest island.

In the dark motel rooms from which the men had flown, the wives began tidying. With the hanging brass rods, Margie Kempt slid open the opaque drapes hanging stiffly as cardboard and allowed daylight into the room, a broad enough stripe to cross the bedspreads but not so intense as to kindle a headache. She folded the dry items she'd hand-washed in the bathroom sink the night before. She made up the twin beds as sharp as footlockers, then emitted little noises of dismay, of protest, of embarrassment when a uniformed Negro housekeeper entered and strong-armed the mattresses, wrenching all the covers to the floor. "Oh!" Margie said, and made a movement to help when the housekeeper stepped outside and reentered with a stack of folded white sheets as rectangular as a package of typing paper. But Mr. Caldwell, in his welcome to the visitors the night before on the motel parking lot, had said, "Now, you don't need to be talking to the help. Our colored folks are here to do their jobs and any conversations y'all try to start with them is just going to slow them down." Margie Kempt had harrumphed and lowered her head. When her housekeeper came in, she told her good morning and then asked if she could borrow a can of Ajax, only to be told, in the warm Gullah tones, "Das all right," which seemed to mean, "No." Margie stood about awkwardly for a moment, then offered, "Thank you," as she left, and the housekeeper said indifferently, "Yes'm."

The black women of Georgia were a marvel to the Spring-hill women. Some had brown, round faces, light eyes, and freckles; others were lanky and angular and black-skinned. One felt one began to see, for the first time, the rich variety of Africa (and had to wonder why on earth anyone would think down-to-earth, chatty little Norma Ruddick, as Canadian as a copper penny, belonged among these exotics). The motel maids were calling to one another, back and forth across the walkways and cut grass, in warm slangy syllables of teasing and complaint.

The wives stepped out of the motel rooms in belted dresses and small hats and white gloves, because on their mimeo-graphed schedules it said, "Shopping Spree." The wives tiptoed, in open-toed shoes, over the spiky grass and up onto the sand dunes to call down to the men wallowing about in sand and water, some flapping through the water with earnest swimming strokes, some sunbathing on the sand with bottles of beer in their hands, even at that hour of the morning. "Honey, come on!" a wife would yell, waving the itinerary. "You want to miss the tour?" and here came the men, toweling their hair dry with their own T-shirts. A couple jogged right to the bus and got on, with their lower pant legs wet and sandy, for there were no rules here. They were free men!

They were free men briefly, that is, until their wives ordered them off the bus to go clean themselves up, shake the sand out of their hair, and get their shoes on.

The Ruddicks found themselves camping. A house trailer was theirs to share with the four children; a few yards behind it, the yellow-green maritime forest came to an abrupt halt, still smarting from the machetes that had chopped it back. At the unnaturally precise outer wall of the flora, golden silk spiders shot threads at the air. Crickets rattled in the underbrush all day and all night with a sound like relentlessly shaken maracas.

Norma was placated, somewhat, by the ingenious compression of necessities inside: how the sitting bench became a bed, how the appliances looked like miniatures, how tiny curtains hung from tiny lightweight rods. Maurice was in such jolly spirits that Norma allowed herself to relax. In dungarees, a sleeveless undershirt, and sockless loafers, Maurice sat on his tin stoop in the mornings under a tiny awning and banged on his guitar, yodeling away to his heart's content. In nearby woods and mud sloughs crept terrapins, tree frogs, and chameleons, and the wind rattled the palmetto leaves

In the second house trailer, another, older couple tried to make the best of "roughing it." Dr. William Kenneth Payne, fifty-five years old, president of Savannah State College since 1950 and a member of its faculty since 1937, and his wife, Mattie, a strong-featured woman to whom one would apply the adjective *handsome,* had shown up, as required by the governor, to provide companionship for the colored miner.

If Dr. Payne had been chagrined by the invitation, Mrs. Payne was out-and-out disgusted. He was by nature a gentle and quiet man; robust Mattie with thick, arched eyebrows and heavy, dark lipstick, armored in bead necklaces and bracelets, was the one you wouldn't want to cross swords with. But she loved W.K. and she knew more than anyone that this particular invitation—to soothe the feelings of the recipient of his state's warped hospitality, to disguise the rude insult offered to Canada—unfortunately was within his purview.

Dr. Payne was a well-educated man who had had to cultivate infinite patience and a high threshold for insult. A native of

Alabama and graduate of Morehouse College and Columbus University, he pursued doctoral studies at the University of Minnesota and the University of Chicago, as the South's institutions were closed to him. As college president, he won full accreditation for Savannah State and established curricula in building construction, automotive technology, electrical engineering, and electronic engineering, all outside the humble "traditional" fields for Negro students. He seized upon funding from the state of Georgia to construct a library, a new dormitory, a technical sciences building, and a gym; he knew perfectly well that the state of Georgia's sudden generosity was designed to prove that "separate but equal" was working. Within a few years, Dr. Payne was going to find himself in an even more awkward position: his students would become the foot soldiers of the Savannah chapter of the NAACP in downtown demonstrations and sit-ins, and the Board of Regents of the state university system would order Payne to expel the ringleaders. To preserve all he had built, he would obey the regents; the students would riot, denounce him, and burn him in effigy.

Dr. Payne jauntily appeared each morning at the doorway of his trailer in a business shirt, jacket, and tie. "Good morning, all!" he called to the Ruddicks. Mrs. Payne came banging out, her bead necklaces lying almost horizontally upon her generous bosom as if upon a satin display case. Maurice Ruddick's happiness flowed toward the Paynes, so Dr. and Mrs. Payne crossed the sandy patch—he in his long black business shoes, she in heels and carrying her handbag—seated themselves precariously in folding lawn chairs upon the sand, and made the best of the breezy day and Mr. Ruddick's offbeat, interesting music. The male cook in the third trailer appeared with a tray of coffee. In its way, Dr. Payne thought, extending his legs in a posture of leisure, this was pleasant. He revealed himself as possessing a baritone laugh, Mrs. Payne a soprano one.

The small group was not invited, nor permitted, to visit the Wanderer Motel and beach, nor were they included in the white families' shopping sprees and field trips. Armed Georgia state troopers sat parked at the top of the temporary sand road. To keep troublemakers out or the Negroes in, the Paynes weren't sure which.

Brunswick was a small city at the industrial shore of the water. Shawls of smoke swirled from factory chimneys, as, inside the plants, coastal pine trees were pulverized into paper and turpentine.

"I love the palm trees!" Margie Guthro enthused on the bus to town.

"Yes, well, but the air don't seem as fresh as when you come farther north," said Hughie.

In the middle of Brunswick, a pillared courthouse occupied a green quadrangle, around which live oaks swayed, dangling their long braids of Spanish moss and giving the scene an aqueous tint. Peeking into dime stores, drugstores, and clothing stores, the miners' wives chose their souvenirs thriftily: several postcards; or a tin tray showing the Georgia state flag, bird, and flower; or a pink-and-gold teacup and saucer with a soft scene of fictional Tara. Some shop owners boomed, "Nah, y'all's money's no good here!" and bagged and handed over the stuff for free. Others accepted a few coins and bills of Canadian money as souvenirs.

"You go to buy a pack of cigarettes, you go to that machine, there's somebody behind you to push you out of the way and get them for you," observed Hughie Guthro to his buddies. "When you're treated like that, I'd say you're treated very nice."

The white families were given a tour of a local fish-processing plant and were offered jobs. A shoe store fitted each visitor with a free pair of shoes. At Crews Restaurant, the waiters dressed up like pirates. At Glynco Naval Air Station, the Springhillers sat on folding chairs under the white sky as the U.S. Navy put on a display of jets and blimps. "They're about to kill us with kindness," marveled Doug Jewkes. "My soul, this is terrific."

"Did you notice how the coloreds do in town?" Hughie Guthro said to Margie on the bus back to Jekyll. "I was walking along the sidewalk and here a colored man comes toward me and he steps off the sidewalk into the street to let me pass."

"I don't agree with that," huffed Margie. "I really feel they're as good as I am. We can't help how we're born. One person's as good as another. They have as much right to the sidewalk as we do."

"It doesn't work out that way down here," said Hughie grimly.

At an evening picnic, under a sandy clutch of trees, a few of the wives made their entrance wearing Bermuda shorts, bobby socks, and sunglasses. A band was playing; the kids had a sack race; the miners gamely tried hula-hooping and Gorley proved to have a knack for it. Reporters buzzed around them, darting in for quotes. The white Canadians wearied of being questioned about the Ruddicks. "Nobody minds the segregation," Bowman Maddison snapped at a *Halifax Herald* reporter. "We know it's the law."

On Friday night, the Canadians were bused to a high-school football game. In a salute to them, the maple leaf flag was raised, and Judy Milley, seventeen, and Randall Jewkes, sixteen, paraded in with the Glynn Academy marching band.

In his cinder-block motel rooms, Garnet Clarke, the only bachelor, hung out with Doug Jewkes, made a pyramid out of beer cans, and sat on the edge of his bed and phoned girls in town, shopgirls who'd given out their phone numbers, then looked at each other and gaily laughed. "Is this Missy? This is Garnet Clarke. Garnie. From Canada. Yeah! That's right! So how are you?"

Shyly, murmuring together, moving quietly on flat shoes down the sand road, then drawing apart in occasional outbursts of laughter that scattered the crows from the trees, women from the African-American community of Brunswick came to call. Ambling far behind them, commenting on the weekend football results in the colored high schools, came clean-shaven crew-cut men. All had been recruited by the Negro Chamber of Commerce of Brunswick, or were themselves members, to welcome and host the isolated black miner, the sole survivor of their race from the Canadian mine disaster. Spying Dr. and Mrs. Payne sped them along their way, for many had respectful words of personal greeting for the well-known educator. There beside him, getting up from his lawn chair to greet them, stood the fair-skinned, light-eyed Canadian Negro—the first Canadian Negro any of them had met—with slicked-back hair and a narrow mustache.

"All right, all right," everyone said, crisscrossing handshakes. Here came bright tiny Norma out the tin door, trailing children, and the ladies flew over to pet the babies.

"We'd like to invite you," a matron announced in a deep voice, "to a series of events in your honor."

"Oh my," blushed Norma, pleased.

She and the ladies squeezed the children's fat feet into their little socks and shoes, and Norma took a moment inside to give her hair a fluff and her lips a swipe of color. Maurice reached into the trailer, took his guitar by the neck, and raised it questioningly. "Yeah, bring it, Maurice!" a man called, for they were all on a first-name basis already.

"Norma, bring a sweater, it'll be cool this evening, and something warm for the children," said the women.

"Oh my," said Norma, flushing again, "are we going for the day?" and she, for one, was not sorry to depart the sandy dead end of trailers.

At the top of the sand road, where the visitors had parked their cars, the state troopers leaned against the hoods of their vehicles, arms crossed humorlessly, dark sunglasses neutral under the white sky.

That day the Ruddicks would experience something like a return to Zion. They'd never been surrounded by so many colored folk in their lives: there was an entirely black world of shady neighborhoods on dirt roads, fenced-in sandy yards, small brick and wood houses, corner groceries, churches, bars, pool halls, pawnshops, morticians, beauty parlors, barbershops, and schools. Slash pines flung needles and pinecones everywhere, and their high triangular tops opened out abruptly, like umbrellas.

At a one-floor wooden house, fifty people waiting in the dirt yard raised a cheer when the cars pulled up out front. Inside, the table was crowded with platters of the local specialties— Brunswick stew, buttermilk-fried chicken, biscuits and redeye gravy, salmon patties, hush puppies. There was something they called "shrimp bog," made from bacon, onion, tomatoes, rice, and fresh shrimp; and there was peach cobbler and sweet potato pie waiting on the kitchen stove. "Ooh-wee!" praised Maurice, affecting a down-home accent. He jiggled his loose belt buckle. "I'm going to gain back all my weight in one night."

"Eat up, sugar," urged a turbaned woman from the kitchen doorway.

A tantalizing smoke drew Maurice out the screen door to a long backyard several inches deep in pine needles. Perspiring men in T-shirts poked into an open barbecue pit, where pork ribs roasted, maroon and lacquered. The blue aromatic smoke circled the group. Somewhere farther out in the haze, barefoot children were playing on a swing set. Bottles of soda pop and beer leaned in ice in washtubs and Maurice stooped and withdrew a frosty beer bottle. "How you doing?" he asked the men, and they said, "All right, all right, how you doing?" in low voices. Stepping back inside, Maurice picked up a glass from the kitchen counter. He poured his beer, stepped into the living room, and saw that pleasant, church-reared teenage girls were relieving Norma of the children.

Onto the turntable the host dropped an LP new to Maurice. He was instantly captured by a sound as mysteriously and deliciously alluring as the sweet woodsmoke. He stood still when he heard a waltz—with violins—suddenly explode into swing. He seated himself on the living-room sofa beside the end table on which the record player sat with its hinged lid open. Miles Davis unmistakably was the Pied Piper who was luring the melody from its European origins all the way to Harlem. "Man," said Maurice, shaking his head, "I'm listening but I don't know what I'm listening to."

"You don't know Miles Davis?"

"No, now, I thought that was Miles Davis but, damn, I never heard a song start out like that."

"This the 'Jitterbug Waltz,'" said his host, handing him the album cover.

"Legrand Jazz," Ruddick read aloud, "arrangements by Michel Legrand."

It was, for him, like speed-reading a dictionary, or like thumbing through a road atlas opened out on his steering wheel; he was trying to grasp, in an instant, what had been invented since he last heard a new jazz piece. He closed his eyes, looking almost as if he were in pain, so great and pleasurable was the effort to take it in, to absorb and to memorize.

Outside, the last threads from the wood charcoal spiraled and disappeared from the dirt yard, and the strands of Miles Davis's trumpet twisted around the old-fashioned melody until the thing was turned inside out, modern and hip and smoky. The late-afternoon sun drove horizontally through the smudged side-yard window, brightening to gold tinsel the beer in Maurice's glass on the table beside him.

Families milled in and out throughout the evening. Dinner was heaped upon paper plates, which the men ate in the yard standing, spearing the crisp hunks of meat by yellow porch light; the ladies ate more primly, seated on kitchen chairs and folding chairs in the house. Then, somehow, it was all cleared away, the furniture pulled out, the rug rolled up, and everyone threw off their shoes and began to dance, touching hands and laughing. Fats Domino, Little Richard, the Platters, Elvis Presley, had them all spinning, shaking, and kicking. They slow-danced to Nat King Cole and to Jackie Wilson's "Lonely Teardrops." Norma and Maurice didn't need to speak to signal how flabbergasted they were, how wonderful this was. And then it was night, as cool as promised. The Ruddick children were put to sleep in a back bedroom. Norma, with a sweater over her shoulders, stepped out the kitchen door and found Maurice in the backyard, seated on a kitchen chair with his guitar, strumming and singing to the remaining guests. Much later, the Ruddicks were driven back to Jekyll, back to their trailer. Maurice felt at once a great happiness and a great sadness as he wearily, carrying his shoes, unlocked his trailer: it was nostalgia for what he'd missed, what he'd never had.

Over the next few days, Maurice and Norma Ruddick were guests at more house parties, a beach party, and a church supper. They tasted sweet potato biscuits, "smothered pork chops," "catfish fingers," Brunswick stew, made from squirrel meat, and something called shrimp boil, made out of fresh-caught Georgia shrimp, white pepper, and grits. They were the guests of honor at a special assembly at Savannah State College, during which two selections were rendered by the Savannah State College Choral Society, followed by a catered dinner, served by staff, at the Paynes' elegant home, proof that trailer living was not in the Paynes' true nature. The Ruddicks, like their white counterparts, were given gifts by the Brunswick folks—some nice hand-me-down clothing and sandals for the children, some record albums for Maurice, and some home-canned sweet onion relish and peach jam to take home to Nova Scotia.

"The damn press outnumbers the miners," Caldwell told his wife by a long-distance phone call from his motel room. "All they want is to file stories about is this poor little old lonely Negro family at the far end of the beach deprived of all the modern conveniences."

Maurice Ruddick was being described in all the papers and magazines (by all the reporters availing themselves of Caldwell's hospitality) as the "lone mulatto." The *Halifax Herald,* for example, reported, "The lone mulatto, Maurice Ruddick, went fishing."

SPRINGHILL SURVIVORS ON SEGREGATED SPREE said the *Life* headline, a particular disappointment to Caldwell, who'd earlier exulted at having lured *Life* magazine to Jekyll. "The segregated celebration . . . on Jekyll Island, Georgia, came from an impulsive gesture that wryly backfired on Georgia's Governor Marvin Griffin," the story began. "To house Ruddick . . . Governor Griffin set up in the colored section of Jekyll Island. . . . This little trailer town was especially equipped with electric light poles, septic tanks, beach chairs and sod." The Wanderer Motel was described as being "in the island's white section," and a party there was the "White Main Event." Caldwell leaned back on his motel bed in the evening, leafing through the articles and moaning. He shoved them away, went to the bathroom, wrung out a washcloth in cold water, lay down, and draped it across his closed eyes.

He had reporters to one side of him and the governor to the other. "I will not be photographed shaking hands with a Negro," Griffin had reminded Caldwell. But Caldwell needed to stage an official welcoming media event, a ceremony and photo opportunity starring the governor of Georgia appearing with Canadian coal-mine heroes. Caldwell pictured them in a line under the palmetto trees, squinting in the Georgia sunshine, the governor looking straight ahead at the camera with his black plastic glasses, rumpled business suit, and inscrutable smile. He could picture it printed in the *New York Times,* the *Atlanta Constitution, Life*; he could even picture it on TV. What he couldn't picture was where to put the Ruddicks.

"They're all waiting for their chance to take a picture of Governor Griffin shaking hands with a black man," he thought moodily at the motel bar one afternoon. "They all want to know if the governor is going to visit the south end of the island and greet Maurice Ruddick. It's impossible. No politician in Georgia has ever appeared in a picture with coloreds. Marvin Griffin, the top segregationist in the county, is sure not going to be the first."

"It's a very delicate situation," he whined to his wife later that night. "The governor just can't come to Jekyll and greet the whites and snub the coloreds, it'd be an insult to Canada. But he won't be photographed with niggers."

"Fishing trip!" was announced one morning to the awakening Springhillers at the Wanderer Motel. A bus was waiting on the sandy pine-thatched turf. Kitchen workers were carrying out trays with sack lunches and drinks. "Y'all want to go fishing? Want to go out on shrimp boats?" Sam Caldwell called up to the guests on their cement balcony. He wore khakis, a white polo shirt, and sunglasses.

"You got room for the press?" a reporter called.

"We either got room or you can rent room on one of the boats going along for the ride."

The Canadians got themselves ready quickly and came hurrying along the little walkways. Soon they were bobbing upon the dazzling sea and watching toasty old shrimpers raise the nets, turn the nets, and splash the nets into the deep. Porpoises followed the boats and seagulls looped overhead. "Fresh shrimp for dinner tonight!" laughed the vacationers.

Sam Caldwell had waved them off at the pier, grinning like a fool. "Come on with us, Mr. Caldwell!" a few had called, imagining he liked them.

"Nah, y'all go enjoy!" he'd yelled. The instant their heads turned toward sea and sky, he jogged to his car, squealed west, drove across the marsh back to the mainland of Georgia, headed north, then turned east back across the salt marsh onto St. Simon's Island, where there was a private airstrip. The governor's prop plane had just landed. Griffin stood on the tarmac visiting with the state troopers who'd met his plane. Caldwell ran around to the passenger side and opened his door to await the governor. A lone trooper led the way back, without flashing his lights, to Jekyll Island. The two cars whirred onto the sand road to the trailer camp. The state trooper guarding the road saluted as they drove by. "And not a journalist in sight," Caldwell crowed, but, sliding his eyes sideways, he saw that his glee did not resonate with the infinitely irritated governor, whose thin lips did not waver from their straight line. Caldwell and the governor slammed out of the car and bore down upon the small group in beach chairs.

Dr. Payne sprang up, knocking over his beach chair, said, "Welcome, sir!" and stumbled to his trailer for his jacket and tie. It aggravated him to be caught idle by the governor; it gave such a false impression. Maurice Ruddick didn't know what was up; he stood and waited easily as the white gentlemen came rolling down the sand toward them. "Maurice," said Sam Caldwell, "I want to introduce you to the governor of Georgia. This is Governor Marvin Griffin."

Maurice poked back his fedora with his forefinger, smiled, said, "Good morning, Governor," and stuck out his hand. Griffin took it. There were no photographers around. The only white witnesses to the handshake were Caldwell and the trooper.

The two men constructed the required pleasantries. "This is a fine vacation, Governor Griffin, and my wife and I sure do appreciate it."

"Well, ah'm delighted you're enjoying it. That's all we wanted to do, just give you fellows a break and a chance to relax. You were one of them fellows trapped underground, eh?"

"Yes sir, eight and a half days," said Maurice.

Griffin's eyes snapped over and met Maurice's eyes for the first time, fleetingly. He quickly looked Maurice up and down, taking the measure of the man, and thought, as he later would say to Caldwell, "That's a right light-skinned fella."

"Well, fine, fine," said the governor, "as I say, you folks just relax and enjoy..." Clearly, these sounds meant he was already preparing to back out and be on his way. He knew he'd done enough. When the jeering journalists yelled, "What about Mr. Ruddick?" the governor would be able to holler back, "Ah've already been there. I had a delightful visit with Mr. and Mrs. Ruddick this morning." The reporters would kick themselves for falling for Caldwell's trick of a fishing trip.

But Ruddick, stirred to action by the governor's throat-clearing imminent departure, moved to waylay him.

"Governor, this is my wife, Norma, and here's a few of my young'uns. We left the rest of them home."

To the everlasting astonishment of Sam Caldwell and the state trooper, the governor squatted to say hello to the children and, when he stood up, he had a small colored girl in his arms.

"Governor, may we have a picture with you?" asked Mrs. Ruddick.

Griffin's mouth opened for a long moment before a cough of laughter was forced out. "Well...well, my goodness, that's a nice idea, Mrs. Ruddick, but would you believe we're here without a camera? You got a camera?" he called to Caldwell, who chirped back, "No sir!"

"You?"

"Sir?"

"You got a camera on you?"

"No sir!" said the trooper.

He rounded off his bark of laughter into a more velvety sound of regret, then began backing away again. But Norma said, "We have a camera, Governor! Let me run get it."

A look of hate briefly pulled the governor's face so sharply askew, it was as if his cheek had been grabbed by a great-aunt. The governor did not need a photo of himself making friends with a colored family floating around North America. If the journalists found out about Norma's camera, they'd be waving greenbacks at her and yelling like an auction. He swerved to look at Caldwell with a glare of, "This is your doing, smart fella. You fix this *right* now."

Caldwell hopped to. "I have a great idea!" he yipped. "Whyn't y'all get in the picture together and let me snap it?"

Thus it was that Governor Marvin Griffin of Georgia posed with a black toddler in his arms, two other children clinging to his pant legs, flanked by a beaming Negro couple, and producing a face that was nine-tenths discomfiture and only one-tenth "cheese" for the camera, such a miserable collage of emotion that it was all Caldwell could do not to laugh when he got Griffin in the viewfinder of the Brownie camera.

"Smile, y'all . . . *Smile,* Governor!"

"Just take the damn thing, Caldwell," Griffin said through gritted teeth.

Then it was over and Griffin dispossessed himself of the curly-haired little girl so rapidly, Norma had to spring forward to catch her. "S'long folks!" and off he sprinted for the car.

They scooted into the front seat and Caldwell threw the car into reverse and backed all the way down the sand road. Caldwell, turned backward, thought maybe a moment had arrived for a small bit of joshing. "Why'd you get up in front of that camera with that colored baby in your arms, Governor?"

"You stuck your finger in front of the lens, didn't you?" said Griffin.

"Nope."

"What?" screamed Griffin, his face a thundercloud. "You took that picture?"

"No, no sir, no sir, I was just having a little fun with you. I put it down by my side after I took it and pushed open the shutter and overexposed it."

"Shit, Caldwell," said Griffin, settling back grumpily.

The trooper radioed ahead and a small plane was dispatched to hail the shrimp boats. "Turn back," the pilot called down to the vacationers.

"They're saying to turn back," said Garnet Clarke. "Must be a storm blowing in."

When they reached the pier, the white miners and journalists learned the governor had just landed and was waiting nearby to meet them. "Well, that is just very nice," said Garnet Clarke.

"You're not going to believe me," Norma Ruddick later would tell family and friends in Springhill, "but the governor of Georgia is in that picture with Daddy and the babies and me."

"Yes, Mama."

In the developed photograph, the silhouette of an indistinct group could just be made out through a gray, gritty haze, like figures in a blizzard.

That night, Caldwell escorted Griffin back to the airport after a successful photo opportunity with all the white Canadians. Sure enough, journalists had called, "What about Ruddick, Governor? You going to greet him, too?" and Marvin Griffin had laughed, "Had a nice long visit with Mr. and Mrs. Ruddick and their four children this morning. Nice people! Lovely children!"

"The press knew," said Sam Caldwell later, as he dropped the governor off at the airfield, "that they'd been snookered."

And Griffin finally, for the first time in the whole seamy business, exploded with a joyful cackle.

40

Man of the Year

When the *Toronto Telegram* polled its readers for their choice of "Canada's 1958 Citizen of the Year," out of a field of twenty-one nominees, Maurice Ruddick drew 51 percent of the vote. "Maurice Ruddick, an inspiration to his companions in their nine-day entombment before miraculous rescue came, is the overwhelming choice of *Telegram* readers as No. 1 Canadian in 1958," said the January 22, 1959, announcement of the winner.

The 46-year-old father of 12 children was named by voting thousands not only for his underground bravery; they cited, too, his generous tolerance when he, a Negro, accepted segregation on a subsequent Georgia vacation so that his mates would not miss the trip.... From the Springhill hospital bed, where he and the 18 other rescued miners received the Georgia invitation, he said: "This might be a chance to open some people's eyes. Who knows, maybe it will help to make a better world for some people? I have a small brain, but I think I have enough common sense to see this thing straight."

Straight-seeing Maurice Ruddick received the news of this award with the same nobility of spirit. "I feel very much honored. I feel very good about it. But it's not just for me—it's an honor to all the community of Springhill."

Unlike some fathers, Ruddick was able to rattle off the names and ages of his children without pondering: Colleen, 12, Sylvia, 11, Valerie, 10, Alder, 9, Ellen, 8, Dean, 7, Francis, 6, Revere, 4, Leah, 3, Jesse, 2, Iris, 1, and baby Katrina, born on October 14, just nine days before the 'bump.' "Nothing like a large family," laughed Ruddick. "I wouldn't part with one of them."

Ruddick said both he and his wife are "a little bit less than half Negro." They were born in Joggins, 30 miles from Springhill. His first words to his rescuers were, "Give me a drink of water and I'll give you a song. . . ."

Ruddick returned to Springhill from the awards ceremony in Toronto dazed with happiness. Ontario Premier Leslie M. Frost had spoken of Ruddick's courage and grace in the mine disaster and in segregated America. A big picture of him with bow tie and hat, cigar and cigar holder, and guitar angled across his chest, appeared on the front page of the paper. "The singing miner of Springhill," said the caption, "finds plenty to sing about now."

Home from the ceremony, Ruddick moved through his house with an elegant modesty, patience, and noblesse oblige arising from his having slaked, finally, his inner thirst for notice. Whether he was tending to the children, bringing in the clothes from the line, clearing plates after dinner (for he, like every one of his comrades, was out of work—there was no employment in Springhill after the mine closed), or sitting with the older children while they did their homework at the kitchen table, there was a gentleness and pleasure in his movements.

He was happy. The fame he had dreamed of since childhood, which he'd thought would come through music, had arrived by a slightly different path and was his, "so they tell me!" due to his courage and fortitude in the mine and on Jekyll. Nothing he did had seemed extraordinary at the time, so he meditated about how fame arrives. You can't pursue and lay a trap for it; it shows up on its own terms, like a new neighbor, while you're focused on other things and just trying to do the best you can.

So he continued to focus on other things, and to do the best he could, and he sang a lot around the house, rather conspicuously, with the windows open, and waited for the next installment of fame to arrive. The *Telegram* article even had praised the way he answered the phone when he was notified of his award. "Mr. Ruddick had to go to a Springhill neighbor's phone to take the *Telegram*'s call," the reporter wrote. "The Ruddicks can't afford a phone of their own. 'Anyhow,' Ruddick amiably remarked, 'with all our kids you'd never be able to hear on it.'"

It seemed that at any moment another camera crew would knock on his door, or maybe a committee of town leaders would come to call, to offer congratulations, maybe to sit with him in his front room—chuckling understandingly as Ruddick hastened to pick up the children's toys and jackets draping the sofa and chairs—to talk over some matters of civic importance. The immediate question of employment weighed less heavily on Ruddick than on his former underground comrades. It didn't seem far-fetched to imagine that Premier Frost, who'd made eye contact and smiled at him during the awards ceremony—or even Prime Minister John Diefenbaker, who'd relayed good wishes in a letter—might tap him to be some kind of goodwill ambassador for the mining community, even for all Canada, given his international experience...

Norma, more practical-minded, noted dwindling supplies of flour, oil, frozen fish; she knew which children had outgrown their shoes (the children who pulled off their shoes the moment they hit the front hall after school). Yet she, too, after the roller-coaster half year, felt the future might be unpredictably sweet. She, too, half expected visitors at any moment, though she threw a shorter net than Maurice; she would have been content to open the door to a delegation from the Negro churches in the province. She pictured a Sunday service in one of the churches honoring Maurice, clearly the Nova Scotia black community's most famous son (even if he wasn't a regular churchgoer). She chose a little more selectively than usual from the slim pickings hanging in her closet each morning—not the housedress still missing a button, go with a girdle, low heels rather than house slippers—even though her morning's schedule promised only bread baking and laundry.

For the first few days after their parents returned from Toronto, the children happily reported, "Daddy's famous!" when they ran in from school, or "My teacher saw Daddy in the newspapers." Maurice would smile beneficently and ruffle the child's hair, secretly thinking, "You ain't seen nothing yet, kid." The likelihood that a wider role would be offered soon had grown so real to him that it was all he could do not to share it with the children. "Yep," he said, apropos of nothing, while sitting with the oldest girls in the kitchen one night, "so you're proud of your old man."

"Yes, Daddy," they chimed, looking up from their homework momentarily.

But then one afternoon a child reported, "My friend said it's not fair that Daddy got the prize and not all the miners. That's not right, is it?"

Maurice and Norma both heard him, tried too late to block

the information, to deflect its sharpness. "Sour grapes," laughed Maurice softly as he twiddled the boy's hair, but the information hurt.

A week passed and another week, and the phone didn't ring and no one stopped by. "Guess I'll go to town!" said Maurice one morning, the exaggerated cheeriness a signal to Norma that she'd best not ask, "What for?" He disappeared into the bathroom for a long time and emerged pomaded and combed and splashed with cologne. He wore his sports jacket. "You need me to pick up anything?" he asked almost hopefully.

"Sure do, baby!" she said. "Why don't you get some milk? You got money?"

"Yeah, I got money."

He parked, got out, and walked up the sidewalk along Main Street, his forehead creased, suddenly a bit uncertain of the reception he'd get, though it was sure to be congratulatory. Light on his feet, the old boxer, he felt he could feint in either direction: modest, low-key acceptance of congratulations and praise—"It was really for all of us, all the fellows did great"— or, in a more defensive position—"Yeah, I never claimed half the things they said I did. Funny thing, eh?"

The first man he saw was Currie Smith, with whom he'd been trapped. What luck!

"Currie! How are you, man? How you been?" he cried, beaming, reaching out his arm for a handshake, maybe a manly half hug.

"Hello, Maurice," said Currie dryly. He shook his hand, disengaged, and kept walking.

"Was he down in the same mine as me?" thought Maurice, frozen on the sidewalk.

He found a much warmer welcome, more what he'd had in

mind, from Artie Saffron, who was standing in front of his family's furniture store, enjoying a square of winter sunshine. "Maurice! Our famous citizen. 'Citizen of the Year.'"

"Yep," said Maurice, pleased.

"How are things?"

"Good, good. How are things with you?"

"Slow!" Arthur said. "When the mines aren't running, nobody buys. But you! You've been to the big city, you shook hands with the Premier."

"Yep!" said Maurice again, and the two men stood smiling together.

"How's Norma?"

"Fine."

"The children?"

"Fine, good, everybody's fine."

"So, what can I do for you today?"

"No, not a thing. I'm really just off to pick up a few groceries."

"Well, it was fine seeing you. Take care of yourself. And tell Mrs. Ruddick I said hello!" he called after him.

The Jewish fellow with the wild hair was the high point of his stroll through town, Maurice told Norma later, as he took off his jacket and dress shoes. When he hung up his nice sports jacket in the closet—a jacket he'd bought for the trip to Toronto—he flicked a speck of dust off it and then had a sad feeling of pity and concern for the jacket. Could its tour of duty be over so quickly?

He soaked in the tub a long time, then napped. When the children came in after school and woke him up, he was short with them.

"Timmy's dad says—"

"I don't want to hear it!" Maurice snapped. "You kids are old enough to make up your own minds about things without

'Timmy's dad says this,' 'Tommy's mom says that.'" He made a falsetto voice, meanly mimicking them.

"I was only going to say," said the child, hurt, "that they say a prison might be built in Springhill, to give folks jobs."

"OK," said Maurice, and pulled halfheartedly on the boy's ringlets.

By the end of the month, when no one had stopped by other than their own extended family members, and it was clear there would be no hometown reception whatsoever for Canada's 1958 Citizen of the Year, Norma went back to doing her housework in house slippers and the housedress missing a button, and Maurice got quieter and spent longer and longer hours alone in the basement, and what he banged out now on his guitar, sitting on the old sofa under the hanging lightbulb, was a mournful miner's blues.

He had a hangdog, craven, defensive look about him for the next half year, and if anyone then tried to mention his honor— "How's our Number One citizen?"—Maurice shrugged it off angrily. He'd divined that his great honor meant little or nothing to anybody other than him and Norma and the children—and the children were prepared to discount it, too, depending upon the news borne upon the winds of the playground that day. He understood now that if somebody—a cousin, brother-in-law, or neighbor—mentioned his great honor, the person must be saying it only to humor him, and Maurice refused to be patronized.

"What's eating him?" the visitor would ask after Maurice shoved out of an embrace.

"Oh, you know...," Norma said vaguely. For herself, she was very hurt that the Negro community hadn't pulled together for him—Maurice was the first Negro to be named Citizen of the Year—but she pursed her lips and put it behind her, thinking, "Just wait. They'll see what it's like." What exactly she meant by this was vague, but was something along the lines of, "Wait till one of you has good news. Just try and tell me your daughter's getting married or your son just graduated university, and see who comes knocking at your door with a cake. It won't be me!"

What the Ruddicks miscalculated was what Citizen of the Year meant to their neighbors and townsfolk. The community didn't dismiss or undervalue it, as Maurice surmised in his loneliness. No, they prized it all right, and many were happy for Maurice and proud to have a hometown fellow in the national papers. But others felt baffled, insulted, even disgusted at Ruddick's having been singled out as the hero of a disaster that hurt nearly every family in town. "So Maurice Ruddick gets the prize," Joe McDonald told his wife. "What the hell is he getting it for? He never done nothing. I heard the story on them fellows. Barney Martin was down there; they could have brought him up with them and they didn't. My opinion was they were scared Barney might go crazy and they didn't want him on their hands. So Maurice gets all the glory. He doesn't deserve it, but let him go ahead and have it. He never done nothing."

"That group could have saved Percy Rector," said Ted Michniak, from the Group of Twelve. "He was dying and instead of cutting the pack from around his arm, they sang hymns?"

Why, everyone wondered, was Ruddick the hero? Why was he honored above the scores of brave rescuers who clawed day and night through the rubble to find the living? Why was he especially worthy of gratitude when the entire town was thrown out of work and half the houses were bereft and in mourning?

"Oh, it's all [Prime Minister] Diefenbaker's doing," said Ted

Michniak. "He is looking for the colored vote. Ruddick didn't do very much. Diefenbaker thinks he'll get all the colored votes as a result."

As far as Ruddick having been the "Singing Miner," some from the Group of Seven later said that was nonsense, a fiction invented by journalists who wanted a big story to tell (too bad death and survival in the underground wasn't enough for them). The journalists wanted a hero so they created one. Then Canada wanted to show its superiority to the United States in race relations, so they elevated Ruddick even more.

"The men who were trapped were so glad to get up, the way I look at it, they just added a little more to their stories," said Currie Smith, of the Group of Seven. "That's another thing I don't like; I prefer the truth. All these damn reporters, they are getting everything all mixed up. Of course, it is nothing to me, but it's not right. Why add more to it?"

"Maurice is the same as us," said Herb Pepperdine. "I don't see him any different than us. I guess what they said—that he sang to us—that brought him up in the world, eh? They said he sang and kept our morale up. He must have sang when I was sleeping. Maybe I was asleep or something."

Even Garnet Clarke, who had grabbed and kissed Ruddick in gratitude when the rescuers broke through, later said, "The incorrect newpaper stories bother me a little." Pressed further, he would offer, "I didn't hear no singing. Maybe I was somewheres else when he was singing. But I don't remember any singing."

Doug Jewkes, in the hospital, had said to his wife about Ruddick, "That fellow saved my life." He basically stuck to his story. "He was the old man down there; he kept the morale up. Maurice, he talked and joked, kept the morale up, see; jokes, and he would tell all about his wife, and then he was always singing; Maurice was a great help, always singing, all these boogie-woogie songs, he was always at it, he was really good, Maurice was. I mean he didn't sing much down there in the *bump*; he sang a few songs, I grant you that. He sang a hymn or a couple hymns, but that would be about it. Nobody felt like singing. He used to sing going down in the trolley and coming back up. Yeah, Maurice, he was pretty good company, though."

"Some here don't like it, but I say good luck to him," said Joe Holloway, who'd been in the Group of Twelve. "Old Maurice is pretty popular with everyone here. He deserves it as well as anyone else. There's a lot of differences of opinion. A lot of people don't think he deserved it, but most people like him. Now Gorley got a job helping to lay brick for the new high school. There were a few people sore about that. They picked Gorley out to lay brick on the new Surrette battery factory. There are plenty of other chaps who were already trained, but they didn't get the job. Not that I have anything against Gorley, but it don't seem fair."

"We was all invited over to Maurice's place after we got back from Georgia and the press was going to be there," said Currie. "I said, I guess I'll go. As I was going in, Maurice went out the door and went out by the shed and they was all taking pictures of *him*. And I thought, 'That son of a gun, this is not for us.' Caleb went out the door just a little before I did and we both went home."

"They were supposed to interview all of them, I guess, and then they just did him," said Currie's wife, Mabel Smith. "So, his picture was on television and they left all the others out. Photographers used to be here all the time, but after they interviewed everybody, they just put Maurice Ruddick on television and in the papers and never named the others. Just him."

"I waited and waited and waited," said Currie.

"And they never put their pictures on at all, Caleb or none of them that they interviewed," said Mabel. "So we thought that wasn't very right. Maurice just seemed to want all the praise for himself."

"Sure, there are a few jealous of Maurice," said Gorley Kempt. "But I think he did pretty well."

"We were all used as a marketing gimmick," said Margie Kempt. "A marketing gimmick in Georgia, and a marketing gimmick back in Canada."

If somebody was going to be singled out, maybe there would have been a better choice than Ruddick, some thought.

"I think Joe McDonald should have got the prize," said Larry Leadbetter. "He really done marvelous, he never weakened in any way. He really does deserve a lot of credit because actually he was in pain all the time from his leg and he tried not to show it. He actually took it very good, I would say; he never complained at all."

"For me," said Caleb Rushton, "Gorley Kempt was the man. I couldn't have held up without Gorley. If you have to say there was a *leader,* I'll say it was Gorley."

"Caleb Rushton is the one they ought to be honoring," said Hughie Guthro. "Caleb was the strong one."

"I like Ruddick, but I think he's getting too much praise for being the only man there," said Ted Hunter, also of the Group of Twelve. "He's getting all the praise. You take me for instance, I went through more than Maurice ever thought of going through. He was trapped, that's all; he wasn't injured. I lost out on that trip to Georgia because of my leg. They could have at least sent me a check or something."

"Maurice is a good man, a good father, and a good husband," said Margie Kempt. "But life goes on. Adoration wears a little thin after a while. It's up to a person to get his own life together, to be happy with his own accomplishments, not look to everybody else for praise."

41

"Seems Like a Fellow's Discouraged"

In the months following, Margie Kempt tripped over Gorley constantly as she tried to get her housework done. "What's he doing home?" she asked herself, and then remembered, "He's out of work." But it was more than that. He used to be on the go, popping in and out of everyone's houses—"in everyone's business is more like it," she used to say—and now he was utterly, pathetically, at sea. If she went out at night, she came back to find the house pitch-dark and Gorley sitting alone and small in a chair in the front room. "What you doing, Gor?"

"Nothing."

"Where the kids?"

"Went out."

"You been crying?"

No answer.

He was a smallish man, five foot six, small-boned, with fine hair, but when his liveliness and flirtatious humor had animated him, he'd been like a wiry terrier, able to fill a large house and yard with his mongrelly, aggravating, endearing presence. And he had loved the shore more than anything: catching flounder and visiting the dance hall and playing cards with his best friends while loons bleated on the water. But it was like the mine had sucked all of it out of Gorley when it crashed.

He could barely finish his dinner anymore at home; he chewed and chewed and lowered food by the hydraulics of the throat, but there was no taste to it. The bright, peppy children, Betty, fifteen years old, and Billy, sixteen, fell silent at the sight of their sad Pa and they worked the pulleys of their own throats, trying to get the food down.

He didn't like to leave the house at all anymore. He didn't like Margie to leave it, either. She'd started working for the administration at the hospital in April 1958, grateful for the income with two teenagers in the house. One day she got a message that she was needed in the lobby. There sat Gorley, gray faced, stricken looking, and rail thin as an old man. "What are you doing here?"

"Come to pick you up."

"But...Gorley, my shift's not out for three hours."

"I'll wait then."

"Well, you want to look at a magazine?"

"I'm all right," he said, then turned away so she wouldn't see him starting to cry. Margie was trying to juggle work, the house, little money, Gorley's grief, and their bewildered teenage children. He began showing up regularly and sitting in the waiting room until Margie was ready to go home. He sat hunched over in a chair in the lobby and didn't watch the television and didn't look at a magazine. If she put a magazine in his lap, she'd find it there, opened to the same page, hours later when she clocked out.

So how could he mean it when he said that she, Betty, and Bill ought to go to the cottage without him? Looking like a dog that has been spanked, he stood, ears plastered back, somehow looking up at Margie. He waited by the door as she heaved and grunted and shoved the grocery sacks, cooler, and bedding out to the driveway.

"Think you might give me a hand with this, mate?"

"Sure, Margie."

He drove. Margie asked him to drive, to distract him. But when their old car turned down off the provincial highway, crackled onto the gravel, and slowed down as it passed the row of cottages facing the inlet, some with gardens and pots of bright flowers, Gorley stopped the car, slumped low in his seat, and began to cry.

"Go," Margie ordered the children, and the teenagers escaped. The cabin next door that had belonged to Alfred—their dear friend, lost in the bump—was shuttered; the weeds were waist high around it. Vines had woven a net over the rusted bicycle leaning against a porch post. A high, almost inaudible whine was coming out of Gorley; his fingers were pressed against his eyes. Margie looked at him, then looked ahead. He shook with crying and she sat, looking out at the wavy blue sea through the smeared dashboard.

"Don't give up, Gorley," she said that night after she had fed him and tucked him into bed.

"I wish to God I'd been killed. At least you could file insurance and clothe the kids."

"I think the children are better off with their father than with new clothes. Go to sleep now."

One day back at home she proposed, "Why don't we invite some new friends out? Levi Milley's wife and daughter are keen to go. Shall we try them? How about this: us girls will ride out together and you and Levi come out."

Gorley hung around Levi Milley's driveway and yard for a couple of hours, pacing or sitting on a step, till Levi came home. But Levi had things to put away, things to lock up, hens to feed, wood to stack. Gorley got into Levi's car and waited quietly.

After many hours, it seemed, Levi was ready to go, but the day was spent and they arrived at the cottage in darkness. Holding back tears, Gorley went straight to bed. "Do you want to play cards?" Margie called down the hall, but there was no answer.

"I can't seem to get any new friends," he confided in Margie when they were back in Springhill. "And when we go out to the cottage and I see the widows, well, I'm always on the verge of asking about their husbands—where's Alfred, out on the pier?—and I have to stop myself. I don't think I can bear to see those cottages anymore."

He let go of what had been his life's greatest happiness.

Then other elements of life began to be chipped away, not just his happiness but his essentials. Trying to fall asleep became an awful and precarious task. Having waited till he was in a weakened position, the demons of memory sprang out and replayed bad scenes of men damaged and ripped open by coal. Smashing the pillow over his face, rolling his head, and moaning did not dispel the vivid scenes. He desperately began searching for a shortcut, a way to go from daytime wakefulness straight to sleep, with no twilight. He gave up on bed, and sat up staring at the TV with dry eyes. When the networks went off the air, Gorley sat and stared at the blank gray-white screen, finding in it a small bit of company—maybe on the other end, in Halifax or Toronto, there was an engineer still up and fiddling with wires, or a janitor slowly making damp arcs with a mop on the floor beside the cameras.

Dark circles ringed his eyes like a raccoon's.

"He was strong in the mine, that's what they tell me," Margie told the psychiatrist on staff at the hospital. "But he's gone to the bottom now."

They admitted him for a few days, then discharged him with prescriptions for sleeping pills.

He pulled himself together enough to get work in a new battery factory that opened, and then on a building crew for the new high school, and then in a shallow private coal mine nearby, but the fun had gone out of him for good. In 1967, nine years after the bump, Gorley Kempt died of a heart attack. He was forty-seven.

Margie grieved him long and hard, then turned back to life. Forty years on, *she* was the life of the party, a short, stocky, sun-browned woman with a whirlwind of white curls on her head and a hoarse laugh. She built a modern two-story natural-wood house in the woods to tower over their old cottage; in the cold mornings, even in autumn, she wiggled into a two-piece bathing suit and headed for the inlet. Tilting broadly back and forth, she limped from a bum hip, but she dove into the cold water and emerged with her blue eyes sparkling like the bits of sea glass she sometimes found. She caught and fried fish, slept in a bedroll, made new friends, went back to skating and dancing.

"The bump was a very hard time in our lives," she says. "But we enjoyed our trip to Georgia. We were treated royally; we were flabbergasted at the kindness and generosity of the Georgian people. Of course, had we realized we were being used as a marketing ploy, we never would have accepted. We have pride and we have self-respect.

"It was a pleasure to see the colored community of Georgia take Maurice and his family to their hearts. It relieved a very awkward situation created by racism in Georgia.

"But life has been good. Our kids did well and the grandchildren have grandchildren. What more could I ask for?"

She'd started her adult life as a young miner's wife but had wound up emancipated, opinionated, and full of vigor.

In later years, Sadie Allen—whose children had gasped with surprise and happiness when an emerging survivor said, "Yeah, I think I saw Paul," and turned to see if their mother was also smiling—never overcame her belief that Fidel's body had not been in the coffin under the rocks. She believed his grave was the closed No. 2 mine. In his memory, she maintained a wreath hung on a pole near the original pithead, and every spring for forty years she gave a fresh coat of paint to the five utility poles that seemed to mark the true final resting place of her beloved husband. When urban renewal threatened to raze the unused brick lamp cabin, Sadie Allen rallied other widows to save the property and have it declared an historic heritage site. "That was the last walk our men took and it should be saved." This was done, and the Last Walk is marked out for visitors to see. As each of her children reached adulthood, she ordered him or her to leave Springhill and find a living elsewhere, doing anything in the world besides mining. "What can I say? Losing your husband, half of your life is gone. You're lost, and you stay completely lost for years and years and years."

Joe McDonald felt mostly bitter and alone in later years. "Them fellows I was trapped with, I ain't got too much use for them. Only Michniak. I don't care nothing about the rest of those bastards. I don't care if they ever come around. When a person does a thing to you like that, then you ain't got no use for them. That's just the way I figure. I ain't got no goddamn use for them and they know it and that's why they are staying away. I don't say nothing to them but they know my feelings toward them. I'm cool with them and I don't a bit care to have them around.

"When you go around meeting people and they say, 'What happened to your leg?' and you got to go through that over and over and over. And then when you go home at night, you think about it in bed and you dream about it and you get more night-mares and you just wake up in a cold sweat and you got to turn the lights on and you're scared in the dark then and you got to wait until daylight. It's like my neighbor down the road—it's got him and he can't control it—it's sissy for a man to cry, but it don't mean he's weak.

"In 1960 I got trapped in an elevator while I was visiting my mother in the hospital. I was trapped only for a few minutes. But a queer feeling come over me, a fear that the elevator was going to catch on fire and I wouldn't get out. I had to get out of there quick. I nearly put my crutch up to break down the door."

The only good thing Joe McDonald had to say was, "That was a pretty good trip with our families to Georgia and we'll never get it again."

"I don't make a habit of running to everybody's house," said Ted Michniak. "My crowd is pretty well all broke up now. Some were killed in the '56 Explosion and some were killed in the bump. I have a bench in my yard in the shade; in the summer-time, friends seem to congregate there. It's more or less a liar's bench, you know. The original Liar's Bench is out the west end, but, ah me, the original liars are not there anymore, they're all dead. These are just young fellows and they pretend to be, you know, the so-called liars, but they can't lie like the old fellows. So the old fellows come up here. Somebody will start a conversation and we'll go along with it for a while, and somebody will tell some jokes and one thing and another. We wend the day along."

"What I would like," said Bowman Maddison, after a year had passed, "is to live in a warm climate and to make fifty-five dollars a week; that's about all a man can make without much education. The world is moving faster than a man's brains can keep up with. But I would never work in the mines again after I seen what I did."

"I used to play the accordion," said Herb Pepperdine. "I used to be able to play all kinds of songs. If I heard the tune maybe once or twice, I'd know it. I can't do that now. There's a fellow down there from the States who's a good accordian player and he was trying to learn me the Skater's Waltz the other day. He played it a dozen times and I don't know a bit of it no more than when he came. When he left, I couldn't seem to get it."

"It's altogether different now," said Hughie Guthro, who'd so enjoyed the fellowship of the miners. "Years ago, if you needed a new roof, you had more help than you needed and you'd go and help somebody else. Now I got to put a new roof on here, I got to hire it done."

"It was a big mistake to send Danny away to my neighbor. I realize that now," Bev Reynolds would say many years later. "The last time Danny saw his father, he tied the cart on the back of his tricycle and that was it. Wes was never mentioned again. That was what you did in those days. You didn't want to talk about it. You didn't want to upset him, or that's what I thought. That's what people thought. But that wasn't right. He should have been here for the funeral. He should have known his father was gone and what had happened, but he didn't, and I blame myself for that because he took it very, very hard. He never talks about it, never talks about it, but I don't think he ever got over it. He was angry because he didn't have a father. He would go to clubs and they'd have a father-and-son banquet. I went with him, but it wasn't the same. He blames God. He says he has no desire to go to church because if there really was a god, he wouldn't have taken his father. He's married now, and he has two beautiful children, but he was very, very hurt. Today, when anything like that happens, they have counselors in to talk to the children. There was absolutely nothing like that then. I never talked about Wes. I didn't know that made it worse for Danny."

Eldred Lowther, who'd once been a carefree, easygoing dad, became an enraged one. He couldn't help roaring at his children. "The younger one was just tapping like that on my chair and after a minute I couldn't stand it any longer and I grabbed her book and stuffed it in the stove," he told his doctor. "I say to myself, 'My God, I might never have seen them again, why should I be like that with them? I'm not going to do it again,' and the next thing I know I am hollering, 'Get out of here, get out of there, get out in the kitchen!'"

He'd once been able to work a full vigorous shift, come in at midnight, eat, then pick up his .22 and his flashlight and start on a five-mile hike into the woods to hook up with his friends at their hunting cabin. But now his days were blank, like a flooded lake flat with nothingness, all terrain submerged. One day, another long day of nothing, furious with boredom, he hauled off and punched the window of the car parked in his driveway. He broke his hand.

"You coming to bed, El?" his wife would ask after they'd spent the whole evening watching the television.

"No, you go on up. I'll finish watching." And he'd sit and watch every single thing on the TV till it went off. Then he'd get up, turn it off, and go back and sit. "Better to sit here awake than lie awake in bed. Because I know that's all I'm going to do, look at the bedroom ceiling.

"I want to be alone and yet I don't want to be alone, so I'm mad at my wife when she's here and mad when she's gone.

"Before the bump, I was in A-1 shape; outside of sickness, nothing ever bothered me. I was full of energy. There was not a man in the mine that was scared to work with me. Now I feel rotten all the time. I guess my wife and everybody else is figuring, 'Christ, he's lazy.'"

"There goes the damn television again!" he croaked, sitting in the den with the family. "It's all fluttering up and down and now it's gone over crossways." He got up to fix it, but his wife said, "El, sit down."

That meant, "There's nothing wrong with the TV. It's your eyes. It's your brain."

On another night in front of the TV, he started to cry. "What is it, Eldred?" his wife asked.

"Nothing!" he snapped. "Leave me be."

"I'm going crazy," he thought. "I was never softhearted or anything like that before, but now the little things on the television, little shows, or something will happen . . . oh God Almighty, I sit here and cry over it."

Next time he was overcome by a poignant moment in a commercial or sitcom, he turned his head, took out his handkerchief, blew his nose loudly, then tried quickly to dab his eyes so his wife wouldn't see.

"If I go to try to think of something, it's just like I go blank. I just can't get out of it. There's nothing going through my head. There's just absolutely nothing."

Thunder scared him—he would leap up in panic, eyes wide, heart pounding. A car backfiring had the same effect. His small daughter liked to sneak up on her daddy and surprise him. He grabbed her arm: "Don't! Don't do it no more or I'm likely to hit you."

"Whyn't you go hunting with your friends, Eldred?" his wife asked. "You used to like that."

"I'm scared to go in the woods now," he said forlornly. "I'm too jumpy, too quick on the trigger. I'm afraid I'd shoot somebody."

"I got no smell and no taste since the bump," said Barney Martin. "There's nothing to be done about it. I ate a sandwich a few days ago and didn't even know that there was mustard on it. My nerves are bad; I get to shaking at times. My back hurts, and my dreams and nightmares are awful fantastic and terrible. They generally wake me up about three in the morning, then I go back to sleep, and then back up at four, and then I go back to sleep about five, then on and off until time to get up, about seven or eight. I see Herb Pepperdine and Currie Smith, and I go to the shore at Pugwash in the summer. My mother-in-law has a cottage there. That's the main thing I got to live for. I don't have any ambition anymore. Seems like a fellow's discouraged."

Caleb Rushton aged well, the intelligent forehead and large nose ever more scholarly looking, in a house filled with books, musical instruments, newspapers, and college and wedding pictures of his and Pat's sons. He remained modest and kind, but ever more resembled the teacher or the historian he might have been, if he hadn't been born to the coal mines. On Christmas Eve in later years, Hughie Guthro drove out to Caleb's handsome farmhouse on the hilly outskirts of town and put an anonymous bottle of scotch in the mailbox, just to signal that he hadn't forgotten him.

The chairman of the Jekyll Island Authority, retired judge A. J. Hartley, had picked the sandy spot at the south end of the island as the place for the Ruddicks. Soon after they returned to Nova Scotia, Judge Hartley oversaw the construction of a "colored motel" in that exact spot, as if the Ruddicks and the Paynes had proven that Negro life could be sustained there.

"Total waste of time," said Sam Caldwell years later. "As soon as that motel was built, the other motels were integrated. It ended up being the lone facility on the south end. It's hard to conceive why anyone would have been so shortsighted as to invest in a segregated motel at that time, but I guess the winds of change hadn't created much of a breeze here yet."

In 1966, promising to clean up the patronage and spoils system within the Georgia Department of Labor, Sam Caldwell won statewide election to Labor Commissioner. He would serve seventeen years, longer than any other state department head. His three-thousand-person staff enforced labor laws, distributed millions of dollars worth of government jobs, and oversaw a trust fund for unemployment benefits. He sent "jobmobiles" into Atlanta's poor neighborhoods. He survived 1970 and 1981 investigations into his department's electioneering and kingmaking, but was convicted in 1984 of conspiring to defraud an insurance company by sinking his $95,000 speedboat. He served seventeen months in the Atlanta Federal Penitentiary. Under Caldwell, "the department's reputation as a political machine and network for political fund-raising and campaign electioneering increased, rather than diminished," reported the *Atlanta Constitution*.

In prison, Caldwell wrote an exculpatory autobiography, *The Caldwell Conspiracy*, in which he argued that the FBI created crime. He also revisited his memories of October and November 1958: "Oh how we labored and contrived to maintain those last vestiges of a way of life.... Years later, when we had blacks and whites sharing the same motels and restaurants, swimming together at the beach, dancing together in the ballrooms, it was hard to believe that we had gone to such lengths a few years earlier to prevent one black family from living on the same end of the island with whites. But such were the times, and that was my mission."

"The whites had their hands out all the time they were down here," he recollected privately. "They wanted us to buy them everything. All the miners. I didn't have any trouble out of Ruddick at all. Just that camera episode. But the rest of them expected us to buy their clothes and everything. They asked us to take them shopping."

His final recorded words on the subject: "I wished I'd never heard of Nova Scotia."

Caldwell died of heart failure in 2001 at age seventy-three; "the only state constitutional officer," noted the obituary, "ever convicted of a felony."

Succeeded by moderate Governor Ernest Vandiver in 1959, Marvin Griffin tried to make a comeback in 1962. He ran a backwoods campaign in the old style. "There ain't but one thing to do with agitators," he yelled to his country audience. "And that is to cut down a blackjack sapling and brain 'em and nip 'em in the bud." He stirred up race hatred as he toured in 1962; Klan night-riders suited up in his wake, and two African-American churches were burned to the ground.

Griffin's opponent was a young, urban, telegenic and Kennedyesque racial moderate, state senator Carl E. Sanders, who promised zero tolerance for violence against black people. "The name and reputation Marvin Griffin gave our state during his administration," said Sanders, "made us the laughingstock of the nation and would again if he ever were given the opportunity to do so."

On television Sanders said, "We caught old Marvin in the chicken house once, and we're not going to give him the keys to the smokehouse again."

The electorate agreed. By 1962, the rural population had caught up to the city dwellers in wanting economic development, social services, good schools, and electricity more than they wanted to support the lost cause of preserving segregation forever. "Marvin Griffin manifested the 'old ways,'" writes historian Dubay: "blatant racism, Washington-baiting, violations of human and constitutional rights, and government by cronyism, courthouse clique, backroom deal, and, some said, out-and-out theft."

Griffin lost the election 305,777 to Sanders's 462,065 votes. "Georgians . . . turned down [Griffin's] candidacy," reported *Time* magazine, "by a margin that must have made the state's Ku-Kluxers turn as white as their sheets."

The way to "get up a big crowd," Griffin always said, "was to have a nice barbecue and serve all the fringe benefits that went with a barbecue—pickles and brunswick stew and things of that nature. I think even my good friend Carl Sanders will say that the Griffin crowds were the largest. We checked on

304 • Melissa Fay Greene

him, and frankly his crowds didn't look so large, but they were deceiving. He got the vote and I didn't. I made the mistake. Everybody that ate my barbecue I don't believe voted for me."

He announced that he was retiring from politics for reasons of health: "The voters are sick and tired of me."

"Ed Sullivan had trouble with names," comedian Shecky Green used to say in a routine. "I was on the show about twelve times and he actually forgot my name [impersonating Sullivan]: 'Tonight on our show, from Las Vegas, Riviera Hotel, a young fat, fat young... young... fat...'"

"I go into a Chinese restaurant the following day, and the guy says, "Oh, Mr. Phat Yung, how are you?""

But the Springhill incident put an end to that relationship.

In 1967, Shecky Green was working with Frank Sinatra at the Fontainebleau Hotel in Miami Beach. The two of them stood in the lobby waiting for an elevator. It opened to reveal Ed Sullivan and his wife, Sylvia, inside. Sullivan spotted Shecky Green and yelled, "Sylvia! Close the door! Quick! Close the door!"

As Green hung back in the foyer, watching the elevator doors close, he could hear Sullivan say to his wife, "Sylvia, why do we hate Shecky Green?"

And Sylvia replied, "That thing with the mine."

"Oh yeah," said Sullivan, and they ascended without Shecky.

"Right before he died, we became friends again," says Shecky Green. "At the very end, when his memory was going, he forgot he hated me."

Union benefits and unemployment compensation ran out rapidly for the surviving miners of Springhill. The men trapped underground received no overtime pay for their ordeal. The out-of-work miners tried to juggle odd jobs, but work was hard to find in the newly devastated economy of Springhill. Disbursements from the disaster relief fund were not enough to live on at a maximum of $35 a week for a man with seven or more children.

Elaine Turnbull and her four children moved into her mother-in-law's house soon after she buried Billy. She later felt she had made matters worse for herself, for when she moved back home, she had to face all of his things anew. She couldn't make herself eat and grew so thin the family was alarmed. Billy always had gone to Mass every day. After he was killed, Elaine anguished over the thought that Billy had died in the mine without receiving Last Rites, without making peace with God. Then, one night in the bedroom at her mother-in-law's house, Elaine saw Billy standing at the foot of her bed. "I was wide awake," she always told her children afterward. She moved to embrace him, but he said, "No. It's OK, Elaine. I had time. You'll be fine."

And she *was* fine after that, and began to eat again.

"We were raised to love and honor my father," said Elaine's daughter, Claire Canning, the sponsorship coordinator for Christian Childcare International. She'd been a baby when her father was killed, Springhill's youngest surviving family member. "We went often to the cemetery growing up. When my son was born, of course I named him Billy. A few years ago, when my mother died, Billy was upset that he hadn't had a chance to see his grandma one last time. She appeared to him in his bedroom one night, and told him good-bye."

42

The Miners' Code

Ruddick had thirty years, never moving away from Springhill, in which to puzzle over his brief rise and fall in public favor. In later years he puttered about his yard, trimming the grass with a push mower, taking a paintbrush to the porch railing, and wondering: in wishing for fame, had he wanted the wrong thing?

Once his fame had been the small local matter that he loved to sing. "The Singing Miner." The guys waved him over to hop into the trolley with them going down—the "mulatto" to some, the "nigger" to others—oh, he heard them all right—and a regular guy and respectable worker to most. "Gather together at the river," he'd start, and as they lurched into the darkness, he could hear every man launch into song like a guy singing in the shower, lungs pumping, mouth trumpeting. He'd chuckle to himself.

As a young man, he was content with that, being one of them trudging to and from the underground in husky coveralls, marrying, raising kids. Privately he cultivated a finer and more adventurous taste in music and in fashion. By his mid-thirties, he was seriously striving for grander things than Springhill offered. He, with Norma, founded a dynasty of children. Within their overflowing eight-bedroom house there was love and laughter and wit and music, and he was the king. Fame would choose the Ruddicks for their musical talent, he planned, and airlift the lot of them, "The Singing Miner and the Minerettes," out of town to a freer, richer place.

That didn't happen. But then Maurice had been a steady man in the pit, a decent and kind man when trapped by the bump; and, for his pains, found himself on an isolated beach, segregated due to his race in Georgia; then—whoops, hold on to your hat!—elevated beyond his wildest hopes, the top man in all Canada; then home again to find not acclamation but a cool reception, ranging from indifference to resentment. Folks knew his name, but weren't partial to him.

And there he had come to rest.

As he grew older, and sat to catch his breath on a porch step and wait for a grandchild to come in from school, it was clear to him why he wasn't so popular anymore. Most people never forgave him for winning Citizen of the Year. Even when the Carnegie Hero Fund Commission awarded a gold medal to the rescuers of Springhill, folks weren't mollified.

It seemed that as long as the town grieved the lost men of the bump, it would keep Maurice Ruddick slightly at bay. It was as if he'd taken something from them, tried to snatch something and been caught at it. He knew what they thought: "You allowed yourself to be singled out. You reached for the prize without looking back. You betrayed the memory of the miners and the rescuers who died and you diminished the attention paid to those who lived. *You broke the code.*

He accepted their judgment. He believed in the Miners'

Code, too. It was not the chief thing on his mind, anyway, that he didn't feel so well liked anymore; he went to town less and less often, and then not at all. On his porch, in his yard, in his flower garden, with the growing-up kids tearing up the place, he savored smaller and smaller things. He liked the warm scent of Norma's fresh bread curling down into the garden from the kitchen window; he liked to see a daughter all hopeful and dressed up for a date; he liked to pretend to browbeat her young man when he called; he liked the rumpus of a stick-shift car jerking down the driveway with one of his sons or daughters trying to learn to drive it. He watched it go, and laughed his deep, melodic chuckle. The music he had heard during his week on the Georgia coast gave him enough musical ideas to sustain him in his basement for many years. He figured he had it straight now: he had wanted the wrong thing as a young man. Fame was nothing compared to his wife and his children, to music, to fresh air and sunlight, to a simple glass of tap water.

At the end of the thirty years of internal exile, of making a sweet life with Norma and the children, hidden from public view, working odd jobs, playing his basement music, Maurice lay in bed, waiting to die, surrounded by children and grandchildren. His older daughters, still devoted, made a videotape of him in his last weeks, to get the whole story one last time in his own words. But he wouldn't give them what they wanted: the story of Maurice Ruddick, the hero.

The children were adults now, but they still treasured, like believing in Santa Claus, that Dad had been Canada's Singing Miner. But he knew what he'd known when he accepted the award, saying, "But it's not just for me; it's an honor to all the community of Springhill"—and then thirty-odd years of civic coolness had reminded him—outside of comic books, there isn't a single hero.

"Tell us, Father," said numerous sweet daughters hopefully, running the video camera. Curly-haired, round-faced young women; all had married white men and were raising towheaded youngsters.

"We split up everything evenly," he said in a soft voice, finding it hard to breathe. "Nobody got any more than anyone else."

"You've been called, the Hero of the Bump," Leah said in a professional voice—she worked for a television studio. "What were your feelings about that?"

"We were all heroes as far as that goes," he said. "There was none of us that didn't try to keep spirits up." Then he waved them away and turned a gray face to the wall.

After his death, his family proudly had "The Singing Miner" and "Citizen of the Year" engraved on Maurice's headstone. Then they were bewildered as to why nobody but them ever seemed to visit his grave.

After 1958, Springhill was most famous for its disasters, as if its truest export was not the finest soft bituminous coal in Canada, but rather archetypal images of grief: thin-lipped women in knotted kerchiefs, standing with their bony arms crossed in the rain at the pithead. Springhill was the site, in television's infancy, of "the evening's top story." The fifty yards traversed by the last afternoon shift on their way to the mine is famous in Canadian history as the Last Walk. A few miners stayed alive underground longer than men caught in a mine disaster ever had before; in their honor, Springhill gained the moniker Miracle Town. And one of the coal miners achieved, rightfully or not, the status of hero, "The Lone Mulatto," an "Afro-Canadian hero."

These days, reminders of misfortune are everywhere: the school is Springhill Memorial Elementary and the softball field is Fencebusters Memorial Field. The first Coal Miner's Hall in North America stands at the top of Main Street; memorial monuments crowd and tilt in its side yard. The three famous disasters are commemorated here—the Fire of 1891, which killed 125 men and boys; the Explosion of 1956, which killed 39; and the Bump of 1958, which killed 75—but rows of granite plaques also chronicle the 429 men and boys killed in individual accidents from April 1876 until the closing of the last coal mine in 1971. Since 1876, only three years passed without the death of miners. Available at the public library and corner drugstore are lists of the lost miners: "Stephen Rushton, age 31, left a wife and four children in 1891. Archibald Shipley, age 30, left a wife and six children. Bruce Ryan, age 14, left his mother ..."

"Some people say that 1891, 1956, and 1958 were the great disasters," a local man says as he sidles between the old monuments, "but for me, this was the great disaster." He points to a single name, the only one listed for that year. "That is my father."

A faint cold light reflects off all this rain-washed, wind-dried granite and statuary. The chiseled letters and numbers on the graves and monuments line up to spell the same names and years over and over, as if the monument maker had access to crates full of a few letters and numbers, but was out of stock on the rest. 1891, 1891, 1956, 1956, 1956, 1958, 1958, 1958, 1958. McCormick. MacDonald. MacKinnon. MacLeod. MacNeil. McVey. Murphy. Early death by rockslide, explosion, or poisonous gas ran in families like genetic predispositions, migration to Canada from mining towns in Ireland, Wales, England, Scotland, and other European countries having failed to alter anyone's destiny. 1891. 1891. 1891. 1956. 1956. 1958. 1958. 1958.

These days, old-timers, rock-bitten survivors, amputees, men hacking with black lung, widowers, World War II veterans loiter and chain-smoke and cough and spit and guzzle black coffee from Styrofoam cups in the corner booth of Tim Horton's doughnut shop on Main Street. "There's a hundred thousand tons of coal still down there," says one.

"There's twenty-five, thirty years of coal still under the town, eh?" agrees another.

But Jim Nodwell, a former coal company office worker, who saw more death than he ever planned on seeing, says, "I wish no one had ever discovered coal."

In the cemetery outside of town, the green slopes bristle with headstones as numberless as the sticks in a white picket fence. Uncut grass flattens to silver in the whipping breezes. The men who once shared sandwiches and coffee and newspaper-wrapped slices of cake and complaints about the owners and tall tales about women, far below ground, now share this hillside sleep, in berths closer to the surface than they spent their lives. Six feet of sod is a thin quilt to coal miners who once walked and whistled and played practical jokes five thousand feet underground. Overhead, flat-bottomed clouds cross the sky from horizon to horizon like naval destroyers, in stately fleets.

"I come down to the cemetery periodically and just wander around," says Clyde Murray. "There's a whole section here of my buddies."

"Fathers were a prime commodity back then," said Art Turnbull, whose father died in the bump. "And we didn't have one."

"I had a brother-in-law once," says Herb Pepperdine. "We used to go fishing and hunting. I cried about him for a good long while, him and different fellows. A lot of good fellows was lost. To see them laying around looking like that, it's hard to get out of your mind."

A group of adult children and their mother trek from a parked car up a gravel driveway to a grave. They stand looking down at the slab for Canada's hero, "The Singing Miner," and place a bouquet of flowers across it. Leah leans down to brush cracked acorns and weeds off the granite. She lives out of town; she can't be here every week to tend to things. "I'm sure," she thinks with some bitterness and sorrow, "no one outside the family has been here to pay respects at my father's grave."

Yet the truth of it was that the fellows had liked Maurice Ruddick just fine. If the newspaper and television journalists, and Sam Caldwell and Governor Marvin Griffin, and Premier Frost and the *Toronto Star* hadn't all tried to claim Ruddick for a variety of marketing and political purposes; if the straightforward events had been plainly told, rather than reworked and packaged for public demand, it's likely many an old buddy would have found time, once a year, to step over to Ruddick's graveside during a visit to the cemetery. Hat off, swabbing the eyes with the jacket sleeve, brushing away the nuts, ripping out a few weeds, "Here's old Ruddick," the old survivor would have said. "Always singing. He was a great one for keeping the spirits up, eh?"

For when Maurice Ruddick had led them in song, not in the bump—there hadn't been much singing then—but heading into the hole on the trolleys, as the miners were lowered by chain into the earth like a bucket unwound into a deep well, when they tilted back their heads and howled and yodeled and laughed with him, and occasionally even harmonized, with the whole big sound of it booming off the walls of the tunnel, the voices of the men still living and the echoes and memories of the voices of the men long gone, there had been something thrilling in it. The deeper they were swallowed by the earth, the more valiantly their voices had belted out: "We are alive down here! We are comrades. We are men."

Sources and Acknowledgments

I relied completely for my understanding of the bump and its aftermath upon the words of the people who lived through it: Dr. Arnold Burden recorded his memories in his autobiography, *Fifty Years of Emergencies: The Dramatic Life of a Country Doctor,* the only eyewitness to do so. Dozens of survivors, wives, widows, and townspeople were interviewed in the immediate aftermath of the bump by journalists and researchers; on anniversaries of the bump, reporters traveled to the town to hear about it again, in the stiffening phrases of thrice-told tales. All these stories are preserved on cassette tapes, in transcripts, and in newspaper archives. I interviewed the survivors still living in 1997 when I began my research, as well as wives, widows, and children of miners, other townspeople, surface workers, and rescuers. Old-timers took me down the slope into the depths of a mine on several occasions; though not as deep as No. 2 or No. 4, it gave me a vivid impression of the chambers of coal and the utter absence of light.

Nineteen fifty-eight was the era of the Cold War; in the United States, citizens installed bomb shelters in their backyards or basements. In our cellar in Macon, Georgia, my parents stockpiled canned goods. Sociologists and psychologists, politicians and novelists, were asked to envision how human beings would fare underground.

Two Nova Scotia professors, Dr. Horace D. Beach, associate professor of psychology at Dalhousie University, and Dr. R. A. Lucas, associate professor of sociology at Acadia University, made it their mission to answer that question by analyzing the dynamics and survival strategies of the rescued coal miners of Springhill. The professors and their assistants interviewed the eighteen men immediately upon rescue, then on the first-year anniversary of the bump and on the second.

Their book, *Individual and Group Behavior in a Coal Mine Disaster,* was published in 1960 by the National Academy of Sciences in Washington, D.C. In this long-out-of-print Disaster Study No. 13, Springhill was identified as "Minetown" and the men were identified by numbered code: A6, B6, C6, and so forth; G12 to R12 in the Group of Twelve. It was full of descriptive material, even when framed in these detached terms: "The presence of dead and decomposing bodies was a source of stress for both groups."

Insights about the men were tantalizing: "A senior miner, G12, behaved most adequately right after the bump. While others were dazed and confused, this man helped those who were partially buried."

"E6 became relatively inactive and acknowledged the ascendancy of D6."

"M12 said: 'I tried every trick that I knew and I knew lots of them...I never left a stone unturned...'Boys,' I said, 'keep right close,' and I called one of the other boys up and I said, 'I want you next to me.'"

"J12 said: 'K12, he kept us all from more or less cracking up.... He would say, 'Now listen, boys, now listen,' and he would explain it out to us.... I don't know yet how he done it, but he really done wonders. He kept us pretty well huddled together.'"

The professors discovered fascinating parallels in the passage of time in the two groups. They eventually labeled the first three days the "escape period," observing that leadership at the beginning was provided by G12 and M12, A6 and E6, who were good with tools and hell-bent on getting out. From Day Three until rescue they named the "survival period," during which the escape leaders fell into despair and new leaders arose. K12, N12, and D6 possessed the "endurance, and the intellectual and spiritual resources" to offer solace when hope was in short supply.

It was like an elementary school brainteaser: "The boy eating the blueberry pie is not sitting next to anyone wearing glasses." Or it was like the game of Clue: "Who was at the wall, in the helmet, with the pick?" I spent months absorbing the subtleties of the observations contained in Disaster Study No. 13, months in which I generated color-coded diagrams and flowcharts and sociograms. My copy of Disaster Study No. 13 is full of arrows and exclamation points and algebraic-looking equations like "O12 + P12." Finally, I could see at a glance that G12 was modest about his accomplishments, but highly rated by the group for his efforts during the escape period, while M12 saw himself as indispensable and charismatic, observations not shared by his comrades.

But who was who? One of the two authors of the study, Dr. Lucas, was deceased. I located Dr. Beach in retirement in British Columbia. I enjoyed a lovely correspondence with him; he writes in a fine, spidery hand, on onionskin stationery. But "Ace" did not recall, after so many years, who was who, nor did he keep a codebook.

Well, some were easy. "D6 [had a] keen awareness of his inferior status as a member of the minority Negro community in Minetown," the authors wrote. D6 was Maurice Ruddick, the group-acknowledged leader in the escape period. And there was only one who observed a birthday underground, so B6 was Garnet Clarke. But it took hundreds of hours of my own interviewing and of sifting through my transcripts and diagrams to know who was whiny (M12), who was popular (N12), who displayed flat affect (G12).

It was tricky because the surviving miners did not possess the scientific detachment of the researchers: a psychologist described a man as "having sentence completions which were rather deviant," but that man's brother-in-law saw the fellow as good company when they went hunting. So how could I extrapolate from an interview to find the man with deviant sentence-completions?

I searched for the original cassette tapes and for transcripts of the interviews. They'd last been seen, thirty-some years earlier, in Dr. Lucas's possession. Dr. Lucas's last academic position was at the University of Toronto. Long-distance queries hit gold. Or coal. The original interviews were there. I flew to Toronto and descended to the underground archives of a magnificent library. The archivist wheeled a cart of long-stored boxes to my table and I lifted out the first folder with trembling hands. On the top of the first page of the first transcript was a red-pencilled scribble: "Doug Jewkes. F6."

It turned out that I had cracked the code correctly in sixteen out of eighteen cases. I had thought Currie Smith was A6 and Herb Pepperdine was E6; but I had them reversed.

I photocopied hundreds of pages, brought them home, and spent much of the next couple of years reading and rereading and thinking about them. Ultimately the raw material was of greater value to me than Disaster Study No. 13 because I now had the unfiltered stuff; I could reach my own conclusions about who was cranky, who was cheery, who was panicky, who was calm. I now possessed not only the voices of the still-living survivors forty years after the event; I had in hand the stories of all the men, and in the freshness of their rescue.

This book is nonfiction. I did not make up these words, scenes, or stories. They are events I learned from the voices of survivors, and I have tried my best to retell them using the same words.

I owe special thanks to the Springhillers whose kindness and generosity led them to tell their stories of the bump one more time. I'd like to thank especially Caleb Rushton, Margie Kempt, and Norma Ruddick, who were honest and fair in their handling of painful material, and who have been patient with me. I am grateful to survivors Currie Smith, Garnet Clarke, Herb Pepperdine, and Leon Melanson; to physician and author Arnold Burden; to Kenny Melanson, and Jim Nodwell, and my special friend Arthur Saffron. Valarie Alderson and Claire Canning lost their fathers in the bump and continue to honor their memories. I spent time with the late Ruth Tabor, a sweet woman widowed by the bump, and with the late Hughie Guthro, a survivor of both '56 and '58, a big-hearted man. Pat Rushton and Mabel Smith also offered insights into the world of the miners' wives. For the men and women who lived through these events, I offer this book as tribute to your fortitude, and I apologize for the ways in which it falls short of your expectations or of your recollections of the truth. I have tried as hard as I know how, to get it right.

I interviewed the famous comedian Shecky Green by telephone, and I visited the late Sam Caldwell several times at his house in Atlanta. Both men were surprisingly sheepish about the events of 1958 and reluctant to discuss them. Shecky was still smarting, it seemed, from the wrath of Ed Sullivan, while Mr. Caldwell was still smarting from the fury of Governor Griffin. Shecky was consoled to learn that the Springhillers had never even heard of him and that several had a grand trip to New York as a result of his gaffe. Sam Caldwell was gratified to learn that the Springhill families recalled their trip to Georgia with great fondness; for most of them, it was the only vacation they ever took and a few still display their souvenirs.

I want to honor the work of Marjory Whitelaw, a Nova Scotia–based historian, whose extensive interviews of Springhill citizens in 1993 preserved the voices of many now gone. Dr. H. D. "Ace" Beach has been generous with his own long-ago research. The interviews of 1958, 1959, and 1960, archived by the University of Toronto library, were more than indispensable: without them, I could barely have written the book. The stories and perspectives of *all* the survivors still live in those thick old files and storage boxes.

Joe Cumming gave me a handle on the mood of the Griffin administration. Robert Sullivan, one of my favorite editors, opened the archives of *LIFE* magazine to me. Marty Hagen transcribed the tapes with insight, humor, and affection for the men and women whose voices she came to know. And Georgia state representative Doug Teper told me the story—"Some mine disaster somewhere, and the governor was going to honor the miners, but the last one up was black"—that got me started on the book. Thank you to Jenna Johnson and David Hough at Harcourt whose attention to detail and kindness smoothed the editing and publication process, and to Julian Haynes, whose apprenticeship in the publishing world has been a joy to observe.

Finally my lifelong attachment and gratitude to these: my mother- and father-in-law, Ruth and Howard Samuel, my constant supporters and first readers; my book-loving kids, Molly and Seth Samuel, who have listened and read and critically commented upon drafts of the book, inspiring rewriting; and my son, Lee Samuel, whose constructive feedback consistently has been, "I *hate* that title." To Lily, Helen, and Jesse Samuel, who will, I hope, someday, enjoy my books, or, at least, be assigned them in school. To Garry and Mindy Greene, who have supported this endeavor and who share the particular grief that Rosalyn Greene is not around this time to lug home frighteningly life-size posters of me from book events and to beef up sales single-handedly in Dayton, Ohio. To David Black, of the David Black Literary Agency, who said to me once, "Fasten your seat belt; you're going for a ride," and it's been a marvelous ride and one I couldn't have taken without him. To Jane Isay, my editor and aesthetic soul-mate, with whom it has been, once again, a unique joy and a great honor to work; and to Don Samuel, to whom I've been married for twenty-four years and who is still my most entertaining pal.

Endnotes

1: The Thunder of Baritones

a few of the deepest roads on the planet: The No. 2 Colliery at Springhill, N.S., is described as the deepest coal operation in North America, in a statement by the owners, the Dominion Coal and Steel Company. "Mine One of Deepest," *The New York Times,* October 24, 1958.

"The mines consist of entire mountains of coal": Extracted from a letter from Halifax, *Scots Magazine,* April 1765, quoted in John H. Calder, *Coal in Nova Scotia,* p. 9.

"There was a time when men got coal out of their backyard": Bertha J. Campbell, *Springhill: Our Goodly Heritage,* p. iii.

2: A World without Sun

"Miners are queer people; you do not know them": Ian McKay, *The Realm of Uncertainty: The Experience of Work in the Cumberland Coal Mines, 1873–1927,* p. 3.

"Can nothing be done with these strange men?": Ibid.

"Miners are, when at their work, shut out from the light of day": Ibid.

"They were giants": Ibid.

In fact, the Nova Scotia Mines Minister, E. A. Manson, considered the Springhill mines more dangerous than average: "Hunt for 84 in Pit Is Moving Slowly," *The New York Times,* October 25, 1958.

10: In Black, White, and Silver

"All attempts to mix the races": Marvin Griffin, speech to the Georgia legislature, January 10, 1956. State of Georgia Archives.

16: What on Earth Will I Do without Him?

"Shecky, we don't have time for the whole routine": quoted by Robert B. Weide in his commentary on the 1986 HBO/Cinemax special *But Seriously, Folks* on the website http://www.duckprods.com.

20: "You Know He's Bad People but You Can't Help But Like Him"

"Retreat, hell!": George McMillan, "Talmadge—the Best Southern Governor?", *Harper's Magazine,* December 1954, p. 38.

'My friend, I did not sell any calico here today': "Marvin Griffin Remembers," an interview by Gene-Gabriel Moore, June 1976, for Georgia Public Television, reprinted in Henderson, *Georgia Governors in an Age of Change,* p. 136.

"In spite of its many merits the Griffin regime is fully deserving of its reputation": Robert W. Dubay, "Marvin Griffin and the Politics of the Stump," *Georgia Governors in an Age of Change.* Henderson, Harold P. and Gary L. Roberts, eds. Athens: The University of Georgia Press, 1988, p. 108.

"Never in Georgia history had so many stolen so much": Lester Velie, "The Country Slickers vs. The City Rubes," *Reader's Digest,* April 1960, p. 108–112.

"It is easier to milk a tourist than a cow": Robert W. Dubay, "Marvin Griffin and the Politics of the Stump," *Georgia Governors in an Age of Change*, p. 108.

24: Unnecessary Humiliation

His detractors would point out that there were also scarcely a place: Robert. W. Dubay, "Marvin Griffin and the Politics of the Stump."

"The South stands at Armageddon!": quoted in the *Atlanta Journal*, December 2, 1955.

"I am for segregation": quoted in the *Atlanta Constitution*, December 6, 1955.

"the Sugar Bowl nigger controversy": Robert W. Dubay, "Politics, Pigmentation, and Pigskin: The Georgia Tech Sugar Bowl Controversy of 1955," *Atlanta History, A Journal of Georgia and the South*, Spring 1995, Volume XXXIX, No. 1, p. 28.

Time described Griffin as a "pinhead": "Armageddon To Go," *Time*, December 12, 1955, p. 24.

"but if other people want colored folks sitting in their laps": quoted in the *Atlanta Daily World*, December 6, 1955.

"One of the South's most effective prophets of massive resistance [had] hurtled into the picture": Roy Reed, *Faubus: The Life and Times of an American Prodigal*, Fayetteville: The University of Arkansas Press, 1997, p. 196.

"A roving ambassador of turmoil": Neal Peirce, *The Deep South States of America*, New York: W. W. Norton, 1974, p. 132.

"How can we expect this state to attract anything except ridicule": The *Atlanta Constitution*, December 4, 1955.

29: A Particle of Light

"I never gave up hope! God wouldn't give us Constantine": quoted in "Miners Enjoying Sun in Georgia," *The Halifax Herald,* November 21, 1958.

38: The Richest, the Most Exclusive Club in the World

"at galling expense to their owners": Tom Henderson Wells, "The Slave Ship *Wanderer,"* Atlanta: Emory University, 1961, p. 131. Abstract of a thesis submitted to the faculty of the graduate school of Emory University in partial fulfillment of the requirements for the degree of Master of Arts.

"the richest, the most exclusive, the most inaccessible" club in the world": *Munsey's Magazine,* February 1904, quoted in William Barton McCash and June Hall McCash, *The Jekyll Island Club: Southern Haven for America's Millionaires,* Athens: University of Georgia Press, 1989, p. 1.

"I'll take Georgia by storm!": Mary Casey, "Mine Survivors Off to Sunny Holiday in South," *The Halifax Herald,* November 19, 1958.

"I'll go along according to rules and regulations": "Miner to Accept Segregated Trip," The *New York Times,* November 3, 1958.

"We were all black down there": "Springhill Revisited," *Time* magazine, December 8, 1961.

39: Sunlight

"Oh man, oh lovely. Where's my bathing suit?": "Miners Get Red Carpet Welcome," *The Halifax Herald*, November 20, 1958.

41: "Seems Like a Fellow's Discouraged"

"Oh how we labored and contrived to maintain those last vestiges of a way of life": Sam Caldwell, *The Caldwell Conspiracy,* Lakemont, Ga.: Copple House, 1987, p. 16

"the only state constitutional officer ever convicted of a felony": Tom Bennett, "Sam Caldwell, Ex-State Labor Secretary," *Atlanta Constitution,* March 5, 2001.

"The name and reputation Marvin Griffin gave our state": "Out of the Smoke House," *Time* magazine, September 21, 1962, p. 25.

"Everybody that ate my barbecue I don't believe voted for me": "Marvin Griffin Remembers," an interview by Gene-Gabriel Moore, June 1976, for Georgia Public Television, reprinted in Henderson, *Georgia Governors in an Age of Change,* p. 137.

"Right before he died, we became friends again": Sheky Green in an interview with the author.

42: The Miners' Code

"Fathers were a prime commodity back then": quoted by Barry Moores in "A Test of Mettle," *Atlantic Insight,* October 1988, p. 22–25.

Bibliography

Springhill Mine Disaster: 1958
> Coverage of the 1958 Springhill Mine Disaster. A series of on-the-spot reports principally by Joan Watson, Keith Barry, Jack MacAndrew, Bob Cadman, Ken Homer, and Dave Orr.
> Public Archives of Nova Scotia
> 6016 University Avenue
> Halifax, Nova Scotia
> 83H 1W4
> Production Company: Canadian Broadcasting Corporation
> Release/broadcast date: 23-10-1958
> CBC Radio Collection

Bartley, Numan V. *The Rise of Massive Resistance: Race and Politics in the South During the 1950s.* Baton Rouge: Louisiana State University Press, 1969.

Beach, H. D. *Management of Human Behavior in Disaster.* Canada: Dept. of National Health and Welfare, Emergency Health Services Division, 1967.

——— and R. A. Lucas. *Individual and Group Behavior in Coal Mine Disasters.* Publication 834. Washington, D.C.: National Academy of Sciences–National Research Council, 1960.

———. "Individual and Group Reactions to Disaster and Unemployment: A Follow-Up Study" (unpublished). Minetown Research Team, Acadia University and Dalhousie University, October 1961.

Black, Earl. "Southern Governors and Political Change: Campaign Stances on Racial Segregation and Economic Development, 1950–1969." *The Journal of Politics,* 33 (1971): 703–734.

Blank, Joseph P. "The Big 'Bump' at Springhill," *Reader's Digest.* January 1960.

Brown, James B. *Miracle Town.* Hantsport, NS: Lancelot Press, 1983.

Brown, Roger David. *Blood on the Coal: The Story of the Springhill Mining Disasters.* Hantsport, NS: Lancelot Press, 1994.

Burden, Dr. Arnold, with Andrew Safer. *Fifty Years of Emergencies: The Dramatic Life of a Country Doctor.* Hantsport, NS: Lancelot Press, 1995.

Calder, John H. *Coal in Nova Scotia.* Nova Scotia Dept. of Mines and Energy, 1985.

Caldwell, Sam. *The Caldwell Conspiracy.* Lakemont, Ga.: Copple House, 1987.

Cameron, James M. "Disasters in the Pictou Collieries," *The Nova Scotia Historical Quarterly* 1, no. 1 (March 1971): 27–45.

Campbell, Bertha J., et. al. *Springhill, Our Goodly Heritage.* Springhill Heritage Group, 1989.

Cash, W. J. *The Mind of the South.* New York: Vintage Books, 1991.

Coleman, Kenneth, ed. *A History of Georgia.* Athens: The University of Georgia Press, 1991.

Dubay, Robert W. "Marvin Griffin and the Politics of the Stump," *Georgia Governors in an Age of Change.* Henderson, Harold P. and Gary L. Roberts, eds. Athens: The University of Georgia Press, 1988.

————. "Politics, Pigmentation, and Pigskin: The Georgia Tech Sugar Bowl Controversy of 1955," *Atlanta History, A Journal of Georgia and the South,* 16, no. 1 (Spring 1995).

Fox, Maier B. *United We Stand: The United Mine Workers of America, 1890–1990.* International Union, United Mine Workers of America, 1990.

Harrison, Hope. "The Life and Death of the Cumberland Coal Mines," *Nova Scotia Historical Review* 5, no. 1 (1985): 73–83.

Henderson, Harold P. and Gary L. Roberts, eds. *Georgia Governors in an Age of Change*. Athens: The University of Georgia Press, 1988.

Kytle, Calvin, and James A. Mackay. *Who Runs Georgia?* Athens: The University of Georgia Press, 1998.

Lucas, Rex. A. *Men in Crisis: A Study of a Mine Disaster*. New York: Basic Books, Inc., 1969.

Martin, John Bartlow. "The Deep South Says Never," *Saturday Evening Post*. June 15, 1957.

McCash, William Barton, and June Hall McCash. *The Jekyll Island Club: Southern Haven for America's Millionaires*. Athens: University of Georgia Press, 1989.

McKay, Ian. "The Realm of Uncertainty: The Experience of Work in the Cumberland Coal Mines, 1873–1927," *Acadiensis,* 16, no. 1 (Autumn 1986): 3–57.

———. "Industry, Work and Community in the Cumberland Coalfields, 1848–1927." Thesis submitted for the Degree of Doctor of Philosophy at Dalhousie University, August 1983.

McMillan, George. "Talmadge—the Best Southern Governor?" *Harper's Magazine*. December 1954.

Moores, Barry. "A Test of Mettle, "*Atlantic Insight*. October 1988.

O'Donnell, John C. "Join the Union or You'll Die: Songs Relating to the Labour Union Movement in Canada's Coal Mining Communities." Saint Francis Xavier University, Antigonish, Nova Scotia, Canadian folklore Canadien, 14:2 (1993).

Reed, Roy. *Faubus: The Life and Times of an American Prodigal*. Fayetteville: The University of Arkansas Press, 1997.

Thurston, Harry. *The Atlantic Canada Nature Guide.*Toronto: Key Porter Books, 1998.

Velie, Lester. "The Country Slickers vs. the City Rubes," *Reader's Digest,* April 1960.

Warren, Robert Penn. *Segregation: The Inner Conflict in the South*. Athens: Brown Thrasher Books, The University of Georgia Press, 1994.

Weide, Robert B., "But Seriously, Folks," commentary on the film of the same name, a 1986 HBO/Cinemax special, quoted on the website, WHYADUCK PRODUCTIONS at http://www.duckprods.com.

Wells, Tom Henderson, "The Slave Ship *Wanderer*." An abstract of a thesis submitted to the faculty of the graduate school of Emory University in partial fulfillment of the requirements for the degree of Master of Arts, 1961.

Woodward, C. Vann. *The Burden of Southern History*. New York: Vintage Books, 1960.

———. *The Strange Career of Jim Crow*. New York: Oxford University Press, 1974.

NEWSPAPERS AND MAGAZINES

The Halifax Herald
The New York Times
Time
The Toronto Globe & Mail
The Toronto Telegram

INTERVIEWED BY AUTHOR

Valarie Alderson
Dr. Arnold Burden
Sam Caldwell
Polly and Garnet Clarke
Joe Cumming
Shecky Green
Margie and Hughie Guthro
Margie Kempt
Susan Kingan

Ken and Leon Melanson
Jim Nodwell
Herb Pepperdine
Norma Ruddick
Caleb Rushton
Arthur Saffron
Mabel and Currie Smith
Ruth Tabor
Glenda Shears

INTERVIEWED in 1958, 1959, and 1960 by DR. NOEL MURPHY, psychiatrist; DR. H.D. BEACH, psychologist; DR. R. A. LUCAS, associate professor of Sociology, or their assistants.

Arthur the "reluctant rescuer"
Garnet Clarke
Lloyd Gilroy
Hughie Guthro
Lloyd Henwood
Joe Holloway
Frank Hunter
Bobby Jewkes
Doug Jewkes,
Eldred Lowther
Percy McCormick
Bowman Maddison
Levi Milley
Herb Pepperdine
Maurice Ruddick
Rev. Sinnot
Currie Smith
John Totten

INTERVIEWED BY MARJORY WHITELAW
List of taped interviews with Springhill Miners and their wives
and/or widows. Recorded over a period of time in 1993 by Marjory
Whitelaw, Wallace, NS. BOK 1Y0

Polly and Garnet Clarke
Cecil Colwell
Grace Gilroy
Margie and Hughie Guthro
Bill James (rescuer)
Doug and June Jewkes
Margie Kempt
Ken Melanson
Clyde and Margaret Murray
Herb Pepperdine
Bev Reynolds (widow)
Norma Ruddick
Caleb Rushton
Elaine Turnbull

Index